Transforming the Dream

Transforming the Dream

Ecologism and the Shaping of an Alternative American Vision

Charles Sokol Bednar

State University of New York Press

Published by
State University of New York Press, Albany

© 2003 State University of New York

All rights reserved

Printed in the United States of America

For information, address the State University of New York Press,
90 State Street, Suite 700, Albany, NY 12207

Production by Judith Block
Marketing by Anne Valentine

Library of Congress Cataloging-in-Publication Data

Bednar, Charles.
   Transforming the dream : ecologism and the shaping of an alternative
American vision / Charles Sokol Bednar.
       p. cm.
   Includes bibliographical references and index.
   ISBN 0-7914-5715-X (alk. paper) — ISBN 0-7914-5716-8 (pbk. : alk. paper)
   1. Green movement—United States.   2. Environmental ethics—United States.
3. Environmental economics—United States.   I. Title.

GE197.B43 2003
363.7'0973—dc21   2002070849

10 9 8 7 6 5 4 3 2 1

*To the most important people in my life,
my wife and my parents—
and to all those whose imagination can escape the
gravitational force of the current "reality"*

Contents

Preface   ix

Acknowledgments   xi

Introduction   1

1   Ecological Economics   17

2   Ecological Political Economy   51

3   Ecological Ethics   89

4   Ecological Pedagogy   129

5   Conclusion   167

Notes   183

Bibliography   209

Index   215

Preface

There is a thesis of long standing advanced by such writers as Louis Hartz
and Daniel Bell to the effect that the American society is singularly characterized by a dominant ideology which has its roots in the classical liberalism
of John Locke. According to the thesis, this Lockean liberalism conjoined in
later years with the American constitutional system and later yet with a capitalist economy represents the hegemonic American ideology which has historically marginalized or silenced dissenting viewpoints. For Francis Fukuyama
this dominant American ideology, given the fall of the Soviet Union, may
even represent the culmination of humankind's ideological evolution. The
purported public consensus on American social values and institutions constitutes for these writers an end-of-ideology era in which differences between
the major political parties are based not on fundamentally opposed visions of
the American future but on disagreements over which policies can best achieve
goals on which a consensus already exists.

Yet, within the contemporary American society there exist currents
beneath the surface of the ideological consensus which challenge the status
quo. *Transforming the Dream* draws together the major strands of a contemporary American ecological literature to display the emergence of a cogent
critique of the ideological consensus or what is referred to here as the dominant techno-industrial paradigm. This critique constitutes a new ecological
paradigm that offers a vision of an alternative American future, one very
different from the American Dream and its taken-for-granted assumptions
about economics, political economy, ethics, and pedagogy.

This book represents a more comprehensive and complete treatment of a significant American contemporary ecological literature than I was able to provide in teaching college environmental courses for some fifteen years. In my lectures I attempted to convey both the outlines of a body of ecological thought which could be construed as a new and philosophically sounder way of understanding human relationships with the natural environment and the implications of this new understanding for social, political, and economic institutions. While the students were essential in providing a sounding board for the concepts presented in the lectures, the limited time frame of a one-semester course resulted in something less than a substantial and equal treatment of ecological economics, political economy, ethics, and pedagogy. The book as it is organized provides that needed substantial and equal treatment of these four major areas. The book also answers the plaintive query addressed to me by a student in the last class I taught: "Wherever *do* you get these ideas?"

My own graduate education was in political science and my Ph.D. is in political philosophy. As chairman of a small political science department in a private liberal arts college, I grew intellectually restive in a field which like the other social sciences largely trained students to reproduce the dominant paradigm system rather than to challenge it in terms of the environmental and social instability it created. I found myself increasingly repelled by the way in which the college curriculum reflected the unecological and anthropocentric perspectives of the dominant paradigm. Over the years I had more and more recourse to a literature that had never been mentioned in graduate school, a literature represented in this book and one that deserves to be recognized in all institutions of higher learning if college graduates in the twenty-first century are to become facilitators of, not obstacles to, an American society which is environmentally and socially enlightened. Explicitly or implicitly, the writings that constitute what I have termed the new ecological paradigm are a coherent and compelling rejection of the taken-for-granted assumption that two million years of hominid evolution have found their consummation in a system that thrives on a reckless if not mindless consumerism and aspires to globalize itself while unhinging ecosystems and cloning all of humanity in its image. The new ecological paradigm offers, I am convinced, an opportunity to develop economic and political institutions that permit a sustainable relationship with the environment and offer a socially richer and more fulfilling life for the individual than can the American Dream as promised by the current system.

Acknowledgments

I wish to express my thanks to the writers discussed in the book for the varied ways in which they have provided a pathway out of the narrowly circumscribed boundaries of the still reigning intellectual orthodoxy. Some of them like Herman E. Daly and David W. Orr I met personally. To all I am grateful for making possible a discussion of the American future which is free of the banal rhetoric and sloganeering typical of much of public discourse today. Thanks go also to those colleagues at Muhlenberg College who helped to design the first environmental course ever offered, one that was team taught and interdisciplinary. Dan Wilson of the history department and Carl Oplinger of the biology department were two prominent pioneers in this endeavor.

My deepest appreciation goes to my wife who undertook the entire range of secretarial duties without relinquishing any of her many activities. She not only kept up with my almost daily revisions of the manuscript, but also, when my creative juices occasionally ran dry, she would gently remind me that she had not received any material to type for some time. All of this work was done despite a handicap that limits her to one functioning hand. Without her the book would still be in progress.

I list below sections of this volume where I quote from other sources. I thank these publishers for granting permission to quote from copyrighted material.

Introduction, pp. 1, 5–6, and Chapter 4, pp. 162–64. From *The Dream of the Earth* by Thomas Berry. © 1988 by Thomas Berry. Reprinted with permission of Sierra Club Books.

Introduction

What we seem unwilling or unable to recognize is that our entire modern world is itself inspired not by any rational process, but by a distorted dream experience, perhaps by the most powerful dream that has ever taken possession of human imagination. Our sense of progress, our entire technological society, however rational in its functioning, is a pure dream vision in its origin and its objectives.

—*Thomas Berry,* The Dream of the Earth

Over half a century ago, Aldo Leopold, assessing the growing evidence of generalized environmental degradation, stated:

> One of the penalties of an ecological education is that one lives alone in a world of wounds. Much of the damage inflicted on the land is quite invisible to laymen. An ecologist must either harden his shell and make believe that the consequences of science are none of his business, or he must be the doctor who sees the marks of death in a community that believes itself to be well and does not want to be told otherwise.[1]

The "marks of death" that Leopold alludes to have proliferated since the publication of *A Sand County Almanac* in 1949 and have spread throughout the globe, more evident in some regions than others but no longer absent anywhere.

1

The list of various forms of environmental damage is daunting: depletion of the ozone layer, global warming, species extinction and loss of genetic diversity, acid rain, nuclear waste contamination, deforestation of tropical and temperate forests, destruction of wetlands, soil erosion, flooding caused by deforestation, air and water pollution, paving over of aquifers, pollution of coastal waters and estuaries, destruction of coral reefs, overfishing, oil spills, loss of prime farm land through so-called development, desertification brought on by overpopulation and overgrazing of fragile land, use of landfills to store municipal wastes and leaching of toxic and hazardous wastes into groundwater.[2] These are the physical marks of death on the natural environment caused by an economic and political system which originated in the West and is now globalizing itself. As ominous as this list is, it is matched by signs of decay in the social environment.[3] There is the erosion of democracy as the corporate economic system increasingly determines the political agenda and the growing dependence of Americans on corporate-derived employment undermines the possibility of local autonomy and self-determination. There is the erosion of community with the spread of suburban non-communities which serve as way stations between work days for commuters; the distancing of millions of urbanites from the natural environment that provides the ecological services that make life possible and the land that provides the food for the cities; and the widening income and social gap between the top 10 percent of the population and the remaining 90 percent. There is the stultification of public intelligence with the infiltration of business-oriented values and techniques into the educational system at all levels and the insistence that the way out of environmental and social problems is more economic growth not only in the United States but on a global scale.

That these portentous signs of decay in both the natural and social environments have not caused a profound reexamination of the economic and political system, which is at the root of the problem, can only be explained in terms of outright ignorance, culturally induced denial, and a deeply rooted dominant paradigm whose language and epistemology cannot account for such signs. That the public is generally ignorant about the extent of environmental and social degradation is not surprising given the isolation of most urban and suburban dwellers from the natural environment and the absence from what public discourse there is of serious attention to either the ongoing environmental or social deterioration. The media, reflecting both the cultural preoccupation with economic values and the current political agenda of both major political parties, typically abet this ignorance by marginalizing such issues. While educational institutions at various levels do offer programs dealing with environmental issues, such programs tend to focus on the biological and ecological facets of environmental problems, rather than on the economic and political causes of such problems. Moreover, even in colleges and universities that offer programs in environmental science or environmental studies, the overall academic curriculum is heavily invested in programs that rarely if ever raise questions about the desirability and sustainability of the dominant economic and political system. The pervasive cultural belief in technological fixes for environmental problems is understandable given the prestige of science in contemporary culture and the often spectacular achievements of a technology-oriented science, achievements which normally enter the market in the form of consumer goods. This belief in technological fixes is encouraged by the economic and political establishments since technology sells in the market and the emphasis on technological fixes, whether they work or not, makes it possible to avoid the pivotal question of the need for economic and political transformation.

Denying the existence of a threatening situation occurs on both an individual and social level. Accepting the reality of a threatening situation opens the possibility to a radical reexamination of a hitherto taken-for-granted life-style or taken-for-granted economic and political institutions. Such radical reexamination on a social scale can lead to a new way of making sense of reality and responding with new life-styles and new institutions. The accumulating evidence that the current economic and political institutions and their cultural matrices are moving in a direction which is increasingly inimical to stable natural and social environments, makes urgent a radical reexamination of what we are about as a society and the construction of a new social paradigm, a new way of envisioning our economic and political relations with one another and our relations to the natural environment and the various nonhuman life forms that cohabit the planet with us.

The term "social paradigm" as used throughout the book refers to a body of language usages, beliefs, concepts, and values collectively shared by a society which forms the basis for and provides legitimation of the practices and institutions of that society. All human societies, from preliterate to techno-industrial, embody a common set of beliefs about the way the world works and how humans are to interact with that world and one another. A social paradigm constitutes a particular vision of reality, a story or narrative which makes sense of the human experience at various stages of human development. Preliterate and preindustrial societies are said to rest on social paradigms which are essentially mythic representations of reality. Industrially advanced societies, in contrast, are characterized by a social paradigm largely informed by a science and empiricism which reject mythic accounts of humans and nature. A social paradigm may be viewed as a map which assists individuals in a society to traverse a given natural and social environment. How events are perceived, how things are to be known and described, what is desirable and what is noxious are questions that are answered for the individual within the context of the social paradigm, the taken-for-granted cultural medium in which the individual exists.

The term "dominant social paradigm" refers to that set of language usages, beliefs, concepts, and values that at any given time definitively shapes the practices and institutions of a specific society. The current dominant social paradigm in contemporary American society is described here as the techno-industrial paradigm. It is this paradigm which shapes the economic, political, ethical, and pedagogical beliefs, values, practices, and institutions of American society today. The discrete elements of a social paradigm, specific political, economic, and philosophic beliefs and concepts, need not be fully understood by the majority of the members of a society for the paradigm as a whole to have a powerful shaping influence on the society. While the discrete elements of a paradigm do find expression in a technical literature and are subjected within limits to analysis and critique by professionals in these fields, in the popular culture these elements are more or less uncritically accepted and reinforced by association with catchwords and catchphrases. Within the context of the dominant techno-industrial American paradigm, such linguistic reinforcers are easily recognized: "the American dream," "free market," "individual freedom," "progress," "economic growth." The invocation of these terms serves to explain and justify an individual's behavior as a member of the larger society and thus to act in concert with the practices and institutions that are entailed by the dominant social paradigm. The logic and implied social consequences of the dominant paradigm need not be understood by the popular culture for the paradigm to be dominant as long as its practices and institutions do not become dysfunctional, that is, no longer effectively explain or control events which have a significant effect on the larger society.

The constellation of language usages, beliefs, concepts, and values that constitutes a social paradigm is not, for the most part, amenable to empirical verification. Every social paradigm and the society which is shaped by the paradigm represents only one way, among many, of explaining and ordering the experiences which confront humans. There is no one social paradigm that can claim to be the ultimate representation of all reality, natural and social. Within some obvious constraints, such as responses to a perceived reality which result in the demise of the responders, interpretations of and responses to natural and social realities can vary along a wide spectrum. The natural world can and has been conceptualized by different human societies in different ways. Human societies have similarly been characterized by significantly different governmental, economic, religious, and social structures. Values are embedded in social paradigms and are manifested as preferences for specific social practices, institutions, and ways of relating to nature and other humans. Values may be evaluated for consistency within a context of mutually interacting values, but they are not subject to scientific verification of truth claims. While those elements of a paradigm that make factual claims about natural or social phenomena are, of course, open to verification, a social paradigm as a whole, to repeat, is not to be understood as a body of scientifically grounded propositions that represents an incontrovertible judgment on the nature of social or any other reality. There is, in effect, no final story of the human condition.[4]

In what sense then can it be said that an ecological social paradigm is a "better road map" for American society in the twentieth-first century than the dominant techno-industrial paradigm? Several arguments in support of the ecological social paradigm can be made. First, a number of the explicit claims of the dominant social paradigm can be factually disputed. Economic growth beyond a certain point has not strengthened democracy in America.[5] Current modes of industrial production cannot be made compatible with a living natural environment. Individual freedom understood largely in terms of material accumulation does not promote community or enrich the American culture. Second, the dominant social paradigm was largely in place by the end of the nineteenth century, well before significant changes in human population, economic growth, and technological development began to have an increasingly visible negative impact on natural and social environments. Consequently, the dominant social paradigm cannot recognize the import of these changes and cannot direct the American and similar societies away from their destructive relationship with the natural environment. The social practices and institutions that are needed to support a sustainable and ethical relationship of humans to the natural environment simply cannot be educed out of the dominant social paradigm. Third, the ecological social paradigm and the practices and institutions through which it would express itself offers a more meaningful story or way of understanding the world for Americans and their contemporaries as they confront the twenty-first century.

> It's all a question of story. We are in trouble just now because we do not have a good story. We are in between stories. The old story, the account of how the world came to be and how we fit into it, is no longer effective. . . . A radical reassessment of the human situation is needed, especially concerning those basic values that give to life some satisfactory meaning. . . . We need a story that will educate us, a story that will heal, guide, and discipline us.[6]

That the new ecological social paradigm differs profoundly from the dominant social paradigm in terms of the language usages, beliefs, concepts, and values that should shape economics, political economy, ethics, and pedagogy, and that it is a better guide or story for the American twenty-first century than the currently dominant paradigm, is the argument of the chapters that follow. It must be noted, however, that the new ecological paradigm remains a Western paradigm. It draws on scientific data, especially those derived from ecology. It frequently employs the same analytical reasoning that characterizes a Western science which is itself based on a culture-specific epistemology that treats nature as an object to be manipulated and controlled. Its suggested pedagogical reforms will have to take place in educational institutions where taken-for-granted cultural patterns of language and thought reproduce the assumptions of the dominant paradigm. The language in which it necessarily expresses itself is the very language which carries in its grammar and syntax the encoded meanings the new paradigm seeks to expurgate. Given the ongoing distancing of most individuals from direct and significant contact with nature, the ecological paradigm may never fully develop a "metaphorical language and thought process . . . that is rooted in the natural world [by which] natural phenomena are used as analogs for understanding human relationships . . . as well as human relationships with nature."[7]

However, unlike the dominant social paradigm which rejects all forms of social statis and tradition in favor of constant change and "growth," the ecological paradigm is not incompatible with an appreciation of indigenous cultures that have developed ways of living sustainably with the natural environment. Among other writers, Thomas Berry has emphasized the importance of learning from the culture of indigenous people, in this case the American Indian.

> . . . [T]hey give to the human mode of being a unique expression
> that belongs among the great spiritual traditions of mankind. . . .
> Awareness of a numinous presence throughout the cosmic order
> establishes among these people one of the most integral forms of
> spirituality known to us. . . . This is precisely a mystique that is of
> utmost necessity at the present time to reorient the consciousness
> of the present occupants of the North American continent toward
> a reverence for the earth, so urgent if the bio-systems of the
> continent are to survive.[8]

The new ecological paradigm, therefore, does not reject out of hand the judgment that "wisdom based traditions handed down and renewed over generations" are as important as "critical thought and technological innovation that help carry forward ecologically sustainable cultural patterns."[9] Unlike the dominant techno-industrial paradigm, the ecological social paradigm is not wedded to the notion that change is inherently progressive, that science and technology are the unquestioned agents of progress, that unlimited economic growth as manifested in Western societies is the sine quo non of human development through the globe, and that whatever traditions, values, and cultural patterns impede this economic growth must be swept aside.[10] Indeed, all the elements of an ecologically centered culture, as cited, for example, by Bowers,[11] can be found in the new ecological paradigm.

Whether or not a paradigm shift from the dominant techno-industrial to the ecological social paradigm occurs, short of a collapse of the economic and political systems that institutionalize the dominant paradigm, will depend, however, not on the importation of indigenous cultures but on the ability of the proponents of the new paradigm to connect with those cultural sectors of the American society which still maintain the elements of community and transgenerational communication, of ecologically sensitive technology, of a sense of time that connects the past and future with the present, of a sense of the participation of all life in a universe with moral and sacred dimensions, of a notion of limits to economic growth in a finite globe, and of the need for proper proportion and balance in human endeavors generally. Finding a constituency for the new paradigm means connecting with cultural values that have been marginalized in all existing social institutions, including education, and that represent today a distinctly minority tradition. Transforming this minority tradition into an integral part of a new ecological social paradigm that replaces the dominant techno-industrial paradigm, means, in effect, transforming the current American dream with its emphasis on an egocentric individualism[12] which treats nonhumans, and frequently humans, as objects used for self-gratification, into a vision of an American society whose culture promotes community and a noneconomic notion of individualism, and balances the needs of humans with the needs of nonhumans in a finite earth shared by all life.

To repeat, the paradigm shift in America must occur on American terms. This means that the ecological paradigm will have to be explained and presented initially through the dominant paradigm language forms and its metaphors and within the context of existing American economic, political, and pedagogic institutions. Included in this initial stage must be a sustained focus on educational institutions and their present role in perpetuating an anti-ecologic culture. Beyond the initial stage is the transformation of the dominant economic and political institutions whose present raison d'être is the promotion of a globalized version of unlimited economic growth. Much is at stake. America presently is the chief engine of an economic system which if successfully globalized will virtually destroy all societies and cultures that do not accommodate themselves to that system, irreversibly degrade the natural environment, and further transfer significant decision making from American governments to transnational institutions unaccountable to American citizens.[13] The failure of a paradigm shift from techno-industrial to ecological means that practices and policies inimical to social stability, democratic governance, and environmental sustainability will run their course unimpeded.

When a dominant social paradigm becomes increasingly dysfunctional and its dysfunctions cannot be addressed by minor adjustments in conventional paradigm practices and policies, a "paradigm shift" can occur as the dominant paradigm is fundamentally challenged in its root assumptions and as the elements of a new social paradigm begin to be articulated. The beginnings of such a shift can be found in an American literature which over the past thirty years or so has developed the basis of a new social paradigm that offers a new way of understanding the human relationship with the natural environment and the new social institutions and practices this relationship requires. This literature can be placed in several categories: economics,[14] political economy,[15] ethics,[16] and pedagogy.[17] I have chosen to refer to the new social paradigm that this literature constructs as ecologism. I follow here Andrew Dobson's suggestion to differentiate clearly between environmentalism and ecologism.

> Environmentalism argues for a managerial approach to environmental problems, secure in the belief that they can be solved without fundamental changes in present values or patterns of production and consumption, while ecologism holds that a sustainable and fulfilling existence presupposes radical changes in our relationship with the natural world, and in our mode of social and political life.[18]

Out of these writings emerge the major themes and concepts that constitute the new social paradigm of ecologism: an ethics to guide humans in their relationships with living nature; an economics that focuses on sustainability, efficiency and equitable distribution; a politics that challenges centralization and the reduction of policy to an instrument of economic growth; and a pedagogy directed at advancing ecological literacy. It should be noted that this literature is concerned with the perennial Western philosophic questions raised first by the ancient Greeks about the nature of the good life and its political, economic and social foundations.[19] This linkage, however, should not occlude the new elements and new conditions ecologism faces: general environmental degradation, severe and deadly pressures on nonhuman life, dominant techno-industrial societies which marginalize values not linked to economic growth, and a global human population of some six billion which could double once more in the next twenty-five years and so multiply immeasurably the environmental and socioeconomic consequences of the already enormous energy and material throughputs characteristic of contemporary techno-industrial societies.

Ecologism as represented here does not fit the traditional labels assigned to contemporary political or social or economic ideologies: it is not left or right, socialist or capitalist, progressive or reactionary, liberal or conservative as these terms are used today in any meaningful sense. Ecologism is not the property of any major political party.[20] It can be argued, indeed, that ecologism constitutes the first major ideology that is not rooted in the thoroughly anthropocentric and industrial values that characterize mainstream liberalism, conservatism, socialism, or Marxism. However much these ideologies may differ in their position on the relationship of the individual to society, the status of private property, the functions of the state and the role of the market, there is no disagreement about the use of nature as raw material for production, the indispensability of technological development, and the advancement of what is referred to as the material standard of living. With the demise of Marxism-Leninism in the Soviet Union and the end of even a simulacrum of an economic alternative to Western capitalism's path to technological and material advancement, for the most part even quarrels between the two major political parties in the United States about different means to common goals have now ended in what can be termed the consensus on unlimited economic growth. With the exception of issues such as abortion, school vouchers, and the fiscal integrity of Social Security and Medicare, issues which themselves do not challenge the dominant industrial growth paradigm, elections are at bottom about personalities and the choice of managers to run the economic growth system. The pervasive sense in America that politics is a corrupt and futile business represents a public perception, however inchoate and inarticulate, that current politics and their associated economic policies constitute a treadmill in which forward acceleration only results in more of the same: more environmental destruction; more people seeking more employment; more material consumption (at least in the affluent West) with no end in sight; increasing signs of social anomie; the de-democratization of politics as money becomes the major political lubricant; and the persistent iteration that economic growth solves all problems, including those created by economic growth.

To the extent that ecologism takes seriously the threat to the integrity of the natural environment posed by the endless-growth model and has a sense of the magnitude of environmental and social disruption that awaits the continued operation of this model, to that extent it is a better guide to a decent and sustainable future for humans and nonhumans in the twenty-first century than mainstream ideologies. While the precise lineaments of a decent and sustainable future may escape us, it is not difficult to describe an indecent and unsustainable future: twelve billion people on Earth expected to live at the per capita energy and material consumption of nations like the United States; remaining open spaces developed into new cities and suburbs; the reduction of animal and plant species to a handful maintained for commercial purposes; global cultural diversity replaced by the monotonicity of Western consumer styles; increasing corporate dominance of economic life and the even greater economic dependency of the mass of people on those who control the economy; the subordination of politics to economic priorities as expressed by dominant economic interests; the truncation of significant individual choice and freedom as the spaces and resources for alternative modes of individual and social behavior disappear; the good citizen defined as the consummate consumer of streams of commodities; and the promotion of higher education as the training ground for the skilled workers needed by the technologically based, ever-advancing corporate economy.

While ecologism is far more ecologically grounded, more aware of approaching limits of the growth system and more immune to the infectious promise of ever larger flows of "new and better" commodities than any of the mainstream ideologies, there are major, perhaps insuperable, impediments to its rise in the twenty-first century as the dominant social paradigm. Even with the increase of public concern about the environment and the appearance of various forms of environmental education in public schools and higher education, the influences that shape the daily lives of Americans are profoundly anti-ecologistic. The great majority of Americans participate in an economic system that necessarily violates the premises of ecologism, notwithstanding a plethora of environmental regulations and efforts at recycling and greater energy efficiency. The economic system and its chief delivery mechanism, the market, acknowledges no limits to production or to market shares. It cannot cap its profits, limit its production, or end an environmentally noxious production line of its own volition. Market conditions and competitors may constrict the economic activities of a firm, but the external forces working on the individual firm do not challenge the growth model. Since the vast majority of Americans have neither land nor sufficient capital to be economically independent, they have no choice but to find employment in the prevailing economic system which typically promises that economic growth means more jobs and more good paying jobs if the potential employee has the requisite educational background.

While inequality in the possession of economic resources has always existed in the United States, an earlier, largely agrarian America had a relatively wide distribution of the ownership of land, the chief economic resource in a precapitalist society. The ascension of industrial capital converted land into one factor of production controlled by those with capital. The ability to feed ever-increasing numbers of non-farm labor with a minute farm labor force ended the relationship between land ownership and economic independence, as witness the situation of the small farmer in the United States today. Typically, landowners in rural areas, which today represent the remnants of the earlier agrarian economy, find it necessary to work in the industrial economy to provide more than a subsistence income. This transformation of most

Americans from the self-sufficient farmers of Jefferson's ward republics to, for the most part, employees of the industrial capitalist system is passed over by some critics of the system who urge individual cultural and attitudinal transvaluation but ignore current economic realities and the powerful inertial forces of the dominant socioeconomic system. The jobs that the system provides are not differentiated as environmentally benign or malign. Some jobs are clearly environmentally malign. They strip the land, emit noxious effluents and destroy species habitats. But they also pay wages and thus those who are employed are rarely in a position to recognize the job for what it is and reject it. Other jobs appear to be environmentally benign, such as information processing, but are not as energy or material friendly as they are often made to appear and the information processed may actually support environmentally malign activities.

It is not surprising that even mere hints that the growth economy has its limits and that a new economic system is needed, raise great alarm and renewed reminders that only economic growth can solve environmental and social problems. Compounding the problem is the constant pressure of an increasing population and the millions of new bodies seeking employment in the economy. Strategies to exit the existing economic system are almost impossible to formulate under these pressures which translate into severe political repercussions for the party in power when even a moderate economic downturn occurs. It is as if as a society we have a tiger by the tail. We cannot hold on indefinitely but we cannot let go. An industrial capitalist growth society is the tiger. It is an environmentally and socially dangerous system which we ought to let go of. But if we do let go, then what? Robert L. Heilbroner has referred to this conundrum as the law of the retarding lead, meaning that policies that historically have proved successful in significant ways—economically, socially, militarily—possess a powerful inertial force even when evidence mounts that a continuation of these policies may be disastrous in the future.

It must be noted that the endless-growth economy is not an aberration in an otherwise environmentally friendly American culture. It is a logical outgrowth of the cultural values brought to the American continent by European settlers. As Kirkpatrick Sale has made clear,[21] for Columbus and those who followed what was new about the discovered continent was its vast untapped resource base which offered wealth and power to those who could exploit it. That the new continent was a biological treasure trove populated by indigenous peoples of diverse cultures hardly mattered. As Thomas Berry has observed,[22] the European settlers believed they had nothing to learn from the new continent that they had not already learned in Europe. By the time of Columbus' explorations, there was no European wilderness and its disappearance centuries earlier was regarded as the overcoming of nature—the

Baconian enterprise—by civilization. This same civilizing enterprise was extended to the American continent. That any wilderness remained two hundred years after the first English settlements on the eastern seaboard was a consequence of the size of the continent and the relatively sparse population until the twentieth century. That any residual wilderness remains in the United States as the twentieth century ends has to do with federal and state policies, not with economic self-restraint.[23] America differed from Europe in its history, not because it better protected the environment but because the fruits of environmental exploitation were distributed more widely, at least at the time when land ownership was accessible to so many. The philosophic ideas that characterized European culture in the seventeenth century—the crucial century for English settlements in America—still exert a powerful influence in contemporary American popular, if not wholly in academic, culture. Nature as solely a resource for human production; the sharp dualism between human and nonhuman; the application of mechanistic rather than organic or ecological principles to an understanding of human society and nature; the unqualified confidence in science and technology to solve all problems, even those created by science and technology; the notion that unlike living nature, which can be used at will by humans for their own purposes, humans have an intrinsic, even sacred value—all of these ideas can easily be located in the contemporary culture and constitute the core concepts and values of the dominant techno-industrial paradigm. Rarely, if ever, does American public debate move outside the compass of these ideas.

There is a long history of support for education, public and private, in the United States and there is a prevalent opinion that education is a panacea for social problems: inform the public and needed change will follow.[24] While the education of the public can be a powerful tool for social change, the unqualified belief in the social efficacy of education is both overly rationalistic and sociologically naive. It is overly rationalistic because it assumes that the conveyance of important information automatically triggers behavioral changes. It is sociologically naive both because it assumes that educational institutions are independent centers of learning whose relationship to the larger society is characterized by critical distance and nonpartisanship and because it ignores how education itself is shaped by implicit, taken-for-granted dominant cultural patterns of language and thought. In fact, educational institutions necessarily operate within the existing dominant social paradigm and attempt to educate the new generations to function effectively within the parameters of that paradigm. It would be odd, indeed, to find college and university catalogues promising to educate critics of society, or to train specialists who will challenge the established codes of their professions. While liberal arts colleges do advertise the broader and more interdisciplinary nature of their curriculum, the elements of breath and interdisciplinarity are to be found, if at all, in the college graduation requirements and not in the major programs which infrequently refer to subjects outside of the major discipline. It must be acknowledged that in recent years some colleges and universities have introduced environmentally oriented courses and even major programs in environmental science or environmental studies. A number of such schools have also purchased undeveloped land to augment classroom study with field work. Such efforts should be supported and promoted whenever possible. On the whole, however, even liberal arts colleges, which publicly disdain special-ized education, increasingly attempt to retain or expand their market by promising their potential enrollees and graduates well-paid and professional employment. As tuition and other costs bring annual expenses at many private colleges to $25,000 or more, the need to justify such expenses as an invest-ment which will bring large economic dividends increases. Thus, the goal of college education is, for most, the kind of employment that secures a high material standard of living. No distinction is made, as noted earlier, between employment which is environmentally neutral or benign and employment which is neither. When measured against the status quoism of the standard college curriculum, isolated environmentally related courses and major pro-grams of study have no effect on colleges' role as training grounds for the skilled cadres needed by the growth economy.

Of course, not all institutions of higher learning serve the growth economy equally well. Professional schools of engineering, law, and business are more fully integrated with the structural needs of the growth economy. In liberal arts colleges, not all programs of study play the same service role. English, art, drama, philosophy, languages, and history do not have the same obvious service connections that accounting, business, economics, entrepre-neurial studies, political science and, by and large, the natural sciences have. Yet, even in the former group of disciplines, many faculty, in order to main-tain enrollment, justify their courses in terms of writing and critical thinking skills that will make the students more attractive to potential employers. After all, who hires philosophers or poets as such, other than academic institutions? The end result is, as David W. Orr states,[25] that each spring as thousands of colleges hold their commencements, tens of thousands of bright, ambitious and environmentally illiterate graduates are let loose on the planet. The forms of employment they will find, their personal life-styles, and the social para-digm ideas which they acquired in their respective schools, cannot make those who are concerned about the natural and social environment sanguine about the participation of these graduates in the ecologistic movement of the twenty-first century.

The chapters that follow explicate the major premises and policies of ecological economics, ecological political economy, ecological ethics, and ecological pedagogy. The last chapter provides some perspectives on the status and future of the emerging new ecological social paradigm. The chapters are connected to one another by one ruling assumption, namely, that the American twenty-first century cannot be an extension, on a larger scale, of the American twentieth century if there is to be any meaningful commitment, and any realistic possibility of fulfilling that commitment, to the well-being of humans and nonhumans in the new millennium. The continued destruction of living nature, the drawdown of finite resources, and attempts to universalize American and Western European per capita incomes on a global scale by universalizing the energy and material inputs and outputs which these per capita income levels require, portend, if continued, severe environmental and social dislocation and possible catastrophe.

While the ecologistic social paradigm is not presented here as a system of incontrovertible concepts and values grounded in some equally incontrovertible, value-free science, this is not a neutral text in the sense that for every ecologistic position an opposing view is presented. I am convinced that the other side, call it the "anti-ecologistic side," has the best of it each day in the lives of most Americans. The messages and information conveyed by the media generally reinforce the values of this growth society, as do the shopping malls, suburban developments, television and daily automobile travel. As the natural environment in a growth economy recedes ever further from the consciousness of urban and suburban dwellers, the advocacy of a rapprochement with nature, a recognition of the intrinsic value of its life forms, may strain credulity. As an expanding corporate economy leverages itself against significant government regulation through such arrangements as NAFTA (North American Free Trade Agreement) and GATT (General Agreement on Tariffs and Trade) and increasingly determines the national political agenda, the advocacy of genuine economic and political decentralization may appear utopian. As higher education accommodates its curriculum to the needs of the corporate economy and adopts its marketing techniques, the call for education which trains the critical and philosophic faculties of students sounds exceedingly anachronistic. Yet, given the irrefutable evidence of mounting environmental degradation and the associated threat to social stability and meaningful democracy, the supposed realism of those who brush aside these problems as minor and easily remedied impediments to business as usual, constitutes, in fact, a dangerous naiveté about the foundations of life on Earth and the conditions for a humane and sustainable society.

Existing ecologistic literature is extensive and increasing exponentially. Rather than covering superficially a large number of books and articles, I have concentrated on what I consider to be some key writings in the field, writings which in my judgment make an important contribution to an understanding of the major concepts embodied in ecological economics, ecological political economy, ecological ethics, and ecological pedagogy, and which deserve the attention of a wider readership. My exposition of the ecological paradigm in the following chapters is not meant to suggest that the writers discussed would necessarily agree with all the elements of that paradigm. Ecological economists, for example, might either not concern themselves with ecological ethics or even reject, for reasons internal to their discipline, the principles of a biocentric ecological ethics.[26] Within the field of ecological ethics itself, the concept of the inherent worth of an individual organism will be contested by those whose standard of value is the ecosystem. In what I have referred to as a contemporary ecologistic literature, there are continuing disputes between deep ecologists and social ecologists,[27] and between those who employ Marxist-influenced categories of analysis and those who do not, to name two highly visible areas of contention. I have deliberately avoided elaborating on such disputes and have concentrated on extrapolating from the literature the general features of an ecologistic paradigm which is internally consistent and coherent and can serve as a baseline for a wider-ranging discussion among a larger readership than will be found in a specialized journals where disputes about specific ecological issues tend to obscure the ecological paradigm itself. My concerns with various problematic issues within the ecological paradigm are reflected in endnote commentary. Since the endnotes contain both critical commentary as well serve to elucidate the text, the reader is advised to read the endnotes concurrently with the text.

Chapter 1

Ecological Economics

> *During the question-and-answer time I asked the chief economist [of the World Bank] if . . . he felt that the question of the size of the economic subsystem relative to the total ecosystem was an important one, and whether he thought economists should be asking the question, what is the optimal scale of the macro economy relative to the environment? His reply was immediate and definite: "That's not the right way to look at it."*
>
> —Herman E. Daly, Beyond Growth

Until the 1970s, ecologism had no systematic economic theory to accompany its conservation ethics and its critique of the social and aesthetic shortcomings of the mainstream culture. In his *Sand County Almanac*, Aldo Leopold had stated that the "most serious obstacle impeding the evolution of a land ethics is the fact that our . . . economic system is headed away from, rather than toward, an intense consciousness of land."[1] He urged that the proper use of the land be judged in terms of what was ethically and aesthetically right, rather than in terms of economic expediency. Thus, his classic formulation: "A thing is right when it tends to preserve the integrity, stability, and beauty of the biotic community. It is wrong when it does otherwise."[2] But Leopold, who was trained as a forester and worked for the United States Forest Service, never developed a comprehensive critique of the prevailing economic system which is a "most serious obstacle" to the attainment of the principal goals of contemporary ecologism. The economic implications of ecologism were probably left unarticulated not only because the foremost environmentalists were not economists, but also because a full articulation of these implications necessarily led to a confrontation with the principles and practices of industrial capitalism. Since one obvious alternative to capitalism was socialism (with its perceived association with the Soviet Union), it is understandable why an ecological economic critique of industrial capitalism remained undeveloped for so long.

Reconnecting Economics with the Physical World

In 1977, *Steady-State Economics* by Herman E. Daly was published.[3] Daly, a student of Nicholas Georgescu-Roegen, author of *The Entropy Law and the Economic Process*,[4] reconnected economics with the physical world and its processes. In *Steady-State Economics* and subsequent writings, Daly rejected an economic theory that abstracted economic practice from its real energy and material sources and he reintroduced a concept not unfamiliar to classical economists such as Adam Smith, Thomas Robert Malthus, and David Ricardo but utterly marginalized in neoclassical or mainstream economics—the concept of limits.[5] Daly held economic theory and practice accountable to the second law of thermodynamics (the entropy law) which states that in closed systems, that is, systems receiving no new inputs of energy and matter, useful or low entropy energy and matter are transformed over time into high entropy energy and matter or waste. Translating the entropy law into economic terms, all economic activity necessarily converts potentially useful energy and matter into commodities of one kind or another, commodities which over time are used up or deteriorate and become waste to be disposed of. Thus, all economic commodities represent a kind of halfway house located between the process of extraction and transformation of low entropy resources into commodities and the removal of garbage or high entropy wastes. Since the Earth is not physically growing and receives only solar energy inputs at a rate which cannot be altered, the notion of unlimited economic growth, that is, unlimited inputs of energy and matter into economic production and unlimited outputs of waste into the environment, cannot be seriously upheld. What has given a specious plausibility to the notion of ever-increasing economic growth has been the extravagant use of limited stocks of terrestrial nonrenewable energy sources—fossil fuels. Unlike solar energy which is stock-abundant but flow[6] limited, fossil fuels are stock-limited but flow abundant, since flow from these stocks is determined by human choice and policies although the stocks themselves are nonrenewable. For example, a decision to build more highways and manufacture more automobiles is a decision to use more of the nonrenewable energy stocks such as oil. Since all industry and large-scale agriculture depend on such stock-limited energy sources, it is not difficult to understand why once economic theory and practice are viewed from the perspective of the entropy law, the notion of unlimited economic growth makes no good sense.

If the notion of unlimited economic growth makes no good sense given a planet which is not growing materially, whose only source of unlimited (given estimates of the sun's lifespan) energy is flow-limited and whose terrestrial energy sources are limited and, in the case of fossil fuels, nonrenewable, why then does this notion persist among mainstream economists, government officials, and the general public? In the case of the economics profession one can argue that the nature of the discipline lends itself to the abstraction of theory and practice from its physical and social base in the real world. Standard economics textbooks describe the economic system as a circular flow of national product and income regulated by a perfectly competitive market, driven by individuals maximizing utility (satisfaction) and profit. The schemas that illustrate this economic model give no indication at all of the biophysical basis of all economic activity. Despite accumulating evidence that a healthy[7] economy is not possible in a deteriorating environment, the majority of economists and most economic courses taught still conceptualize economics through the mainstream paradigm which simply cannot accommodate the notion of economic dependency on biophysical factors. The environment in this conventional paradigm remains an "externality," something irrelevant to economic theory and practice. When the second edition of Daly's *Steady-State Economics* appeared in 1991, the author commented that in the years between the first and the second printing "not one economics journal bothered to have *Steady-State Economics* reviewed."[8] Clearly, what cannot be conceptualized within the mainstream economic paradigm goes unnoticed. If the Dow goes up fifty points that is a sign of economic progress. What impact on the environment this fifty point rise has is a question that would puzzle the Wall Street analysts who otherwise speak so knowingly about the intricacies of the stock market. To suggest that the health of the economy is not accurately measured by GNP (Gross National Product), GDP (Gross Domestic Product), Dow, S and P (Standard and Poor), and Nasdaq indices is to bring into question the chief mainstream economic dogma—that unlimited growth is the sine qua non of progressive societies.

Government Promotion of Unlimited Growth

Unlimited economic growth is espoused by government, regardless of the party controlling the branches of government, for several reasons, an obvious one being that the economists who advise government officials all urge economic growth provided such growth does not create unacceptable inflationary pressures. Short-term political interests also dictate that the party in office (and individual office holders regardless of party) encourage economic growth in order to provide employment for the millions of young adults who enter the workplace each year. Since most individuals possess neither land nor capital with which to provide income, jobs have to be created by those who have these assets and it becomes the task of government to support by tax policy, trade agreements, government contracts, subsidies, and infrastructure construction (including schools) the activities of the private sector. Those who argue that the government hinders a free and competitive market overlook the fact that government policy in the main provides encouragement to economic expansion even beyond national borders. This encouragement of economic expansion is dictated not only by the political fallout of economic downturns, but also by campaign contributions from corporate sectors to parties and candidates. Environmental regulations imposed on businesses are not really an exception to the policy of encouraging economic expansion. With some exceptions the major task of the EPA (Environmental Protection Agency) is to regulate end-of-pipe emissions and set emission standards for a limited variety of substances, none of which has a palpable effect on economic production and economic expansion. Moreover, enforcement mechanisms for the existing environmental regulations are hardly draconian,[9] necessary monitoring staff is often not available, fines can be negotiated, and proving a violation in court is a lengthy and costly process. The fact that many if not most metropolitan areas remain out of compliance with EPA-mandated air quality standards, for example, years after the standards were mandated and deadlines set, indicates that the economic activities that cause air pollution (including the manufacture of automobiles, a major source of urban air pollution) are in no danger of being constrained to the point where economic expansion is threatened. Given the present dependence of the industrial production system on fossil-fuel energy, the same energy source which causes much of the pollution problems, it is to be expected that in the present situation economic expansion interests will normally trump stringent and effectively enforced pollution regulations.

The focus on economic growth also avoids serious discussions of policy dealing with distribution of income. It is argued that a rising tide lifts all boats and that economic growth benefits all classes. The argument is staunchly maintained despite data showing an increasingly skewed income distribution pattern in the United States with the top 5 percent of income earners benefiting disproportionately from economic growth while the income of the bottom quintile has decreased in the last twenty years. Data also show that the median income in the United States has stagnated for the last two decades if not actually declined. Economic growth, contrary to standard claims, does not provide significant benefits to all classes; in fact, economic growth given existing tax policies, trade agreements, and subsidies selects for specific groups which occupy strategic positions in the economy.[10]

Advocates of unlimited economic growth also argue that only an expanding economy can provide the surplus funds needed to pay for environmental programs designed to address pollution and other forms of environmental damage. It is said that only more economic growth can correct the environmental damage caused by economic growth. Assuming even that surplus funds generated by economic growth will be directed to environmental protection (a questionable assumption given the customary political maneuvering to capture anticipated federal surpluses), there is no guarantee that the damage done to the environment and to specific ecosystems is reversible. For example, species rendered extinct are not recoverable and eroded soil cannot be retrieved. At this point, the call for unlimited economic growth becomes a mantra uttered whenever various problems appear: unemployment, trade imbalances, crime, decaying urban areas, infrastructure deterioration, environmental damage, destabilization of families, and national security. A more critical analysis of the consequences of policies aimed at unlimited economic growth reveals, instead, that many of the problems which economic growth is supposed to eliminate or ameliorate are directly or indirectly the products of a dogmatic commitment to increase both the inputs of energy and matter and the outputs of the production process with no limits in sight.

The Culture of Unlimited Growth

Thus far, the argument for unlimited economic growth has been connected to the interests of government and economic elites. Given the relatively short-term interests that characterize the activities of elected officials and the discounting[11] of the future by the economic sector, it is understandable why promoting unlimited economic growth is not an irrational policy for these groups to follow. But the public is also attracted to a policy of unlimited economic growth, if for different reasons. There is, first, a fascination (induced by urbanization, industrialization, media advertising, and the pervasive enculturation of consumer values) with the products and services of the growth economy. The symbiotic relationship of scientific research, technology and the production process has resulted in an unending stream of electronic products entering the market; the globalization of trade brings a variety of exotic foods and cheap goods;[12] and credit makes it possible for millions to participate in the market. Increasingly, for many the acquisition of consumer goods and services defines the good life as more and more formerly private forms of production, recreation, and social interaction are transformed into commercial market activities. For most, the workplace offers few opportunities for personal initiative or creative endeavors and the products or services produced and the production processes are outside the control of workers. The purchase of consumer goods and services, therefore, represents the psychic compensation for the hours of work required at the job. "Thank God it's Friday" and "I owe it to myself" are commentaries on both the level of job satisfaction and the justification of self-indulgence as a reward for enduring the job experience. The denaturing of the urban and suburban environment where most industries and businesses are located also contributes to the consumer life-style. The loss of natural amenities such as open space, diverse landscapes, and contact with varied fauna and flora creates an experiential vacuum which is filled, however temporarily and unsatisfactorily, with consumer goods. That today's commodity is replaced by tomorrow's in a sequence for which there is no clear terminal point other than old age and death, would indicate that the consumer behavior involved is obsessive and seeks to fill a need that cannot be satisfied with material goods.

The existing economic system thus operates like a treadmill in that as economic growth accelerates, everything connected with it accelerates without a final goal being reached.[13] Energy and material inputs increase; production outputs of goods and waste increase; consumption of goods and services increases; environmental damage increases; income distribution is further skewed to one end; more jobs are created (if not always in the United States than in other countries, usually developing ones where wages are low). Then more tax revenues are needed to provide social services for the growing population of the poor and aging and to address environmental damage caused by economic growth and social problems such as crime, violence, addiction, all of which are connected to the dominant unlimited growth system. And these revenues can only be produced, under existing political policies, by an expanding economy and so the treadmill again accelerates. However successful the treadmill system is in the short or intermediate term, it operates at the expense of the natural environment, the biosphere, which sustains all life. Like autophagia the system feeds on its own tissues.

Challenging the Dominant Economic Paradigm

Looked at from a critical distance, outside of the mainstream perspective, the prevailing economic system with its assumption of unlimited economic growth appears irrational at the very least. Its major premises and practices run counter to physical laws of matter and energy; its activities undermine the physical basis of life; and its promise of providing the good life can be met only if the good life is defined as the maximum accumulation of material goods, although what "maximum" means when no limits to accumulation are suggested is unclear. Yet, the system has enormous staying power. In the past two hundred years it has managed to place at the disposal of average citizens in developed nations goods and services that even a pharaoh might envy. Its assumptions about economic growth and progress have permeated all existing cultures and, as mentioned, it serves the interests of political and economic elites everywhere. It has been so successful that it illustrates what Robert L. Heilbroner refers to as the "law of the retarding lead,"[14] in that its very success retards efforts to change it even when it is on an unsustainable course.

Despite its enormous inertial force, the existing economic system is creating so many environmental and social perturbations that its emphasis on more growth is being met with increasing skepticism and in the last three decades or so an alternative to the current growth economy has been developed. Called "ecological economics" this alternative has as its core postulate the notion that the Earth has limited capacity for sustainably supporting people and their artifacts over the long run and that this capacity is determined by the interaction of resource limits[15] and ecological service thresholds.[16] What follows is an explication of the fundamental premises and policy recommendations of ecological economies.

Because the dominant economic system is largely immune to substantive criticism, most people in developed countries understand by the term economics such things as stock market reports, unemployment figures, inflation percentages, GNP numbers, corporate earnings reports, median incomes, and so on. But these various economic indices serve to obscure economic activity as human interaction with the biophysical world that supplies the energy and matter that makes economic activity and all life possible. In this most fundamental sense, economics represents the human extraction from the environment of useful (low-entropy) energy and matter which is transformed by historically changing patterns of production into usable goods and services which over time are returned to the environment as waste (high entropy), discarded when considered no longer useful. How the goods and services are distributed depends historically on political decisions which in turn depend on existing power structures. In contemporary market capitalist societies such distribution occurs through market exchanges (goods for money and wages for work) which operate in the context of private ownership of capital with the great majority of individuals working for private employers. Since humans cannot exist without extracting resources and converting them into goods and services, there can be no substitute for economic activity. What is in question here is whether the way the current economic system operates in terms of extraction, production, distribution, and disposal of waste can be continued over the long run without causing irreversible damage to the environment and thus destroying the basis for its existence and the existence of human and nonhuman life.

Economic growth from a thermodynamic perspective represents higher outputs of goods and services which in turn require higher inputs of low-entropy energy and matter, all of which produces more waste and more damage to the natural environment which provides such essential services as photosynthesis, atmospheric gas regulation, pest control, and pollination. Claims that more economic growth nationally and globally is needed to address issues of social instability, economic inequality, and environmental deterioration are credible only if it is assumed that for the foreseeable future there is no danger of overstressing environmental limits or that capital can be indefinitely substituted for natural resources, or that technology will somehow evade the energy and resource constraints that presently exist. If, as ecological economics postulates, the economy is an open (in the sense that it receives inputs of energy and matter) subsystem of the biophysical environment (which is semiopen in that it receives a solar flow of energy but no material inputs) and is utterly dependent on the latter both as a source of low-entropy energy and as a sink for high-entropy wastes, then the argument for an ever-accelerating economic growth is not credible and the problems such growth claims to address will only be further aggravated by increasing levels of throughput. Social instability in the United States in terms of crime, violence, divorce, family disintegration, and addiction has risen in past decades and continued economic growth has not prevented habitat loss, suburban sprawl, soil erosion, air and water pollution, and increased use of nonrenewable fossil fuels. Continued economic growth therefore begins to appear as a cure worse than the disease it claims to remedy.

The Complementarity of Natural and Man-Made Capital

The conventional argument for continued economic growth made more sense when the economy operated in an empty world scenario, when the scale of the economy was small compared to the planetary environment as yet unaffected by economic activity. In a full world scenario, when the scale of the economy is such that it affects almost the entire planetary environment, unending economic growth combined with exponentially increasing human populations creates patterns of production and consumption which are not sustainable over the long run. The 1987 Brundtland Report, *Our Common Future*, sponsored by the United Nations, defined sustainable development (not growth)[17] as development which meets the needs of the present without undermining the ability of future generations to meet their needs. Daly has refined this definition and made it especially applicable to the developed nations of the North: ". . . [A] level of resource use that is both sufficient for a good life for its population and within the carrying capacity of the environment if generalized to the whole world."[18] Thus, sustainable development is defined as population and production levels that do not breach the capacity of the environment to provide renewable resources and absorb wastes. A sustainable economic system is one that stops physically growing once environmental limits have been reached. At this point, as Daly states, production of goods and reproduction of humans is for replacement only. Physical growth ceases while qualitative improvement continues in the use of a given scale of throughput, for example, achieving greater natural resource productivity, utilizing "wastes" as resources elsewhere in the production cycle, reducing energy inputs through greater energy efficiency and conservation, producing more durable and repairable goods, recycling materials, regenerating and maintaining natural capital, and providing local, regional, and national land use policies that not only prevent wasteful use of natural resources and spaces, but also reduce the present transportation costs reflected in inefficient energy use, air pollution, accidents, and traffic jams.

The existing economic system is like a spendthrift, living off its capital, natural capital,[19] rather than off its interest, the services provided by a natural capital which is either renewable or nonrenewable and naturally occurring or cultivated. Capital, be it natural or man-made, is defined as stock which produces a flow of valuable goods or services. Renewable natural capital or stock can be maintained indefinitely but its flow of goods and services is limited by biological reproduction rates. Trees are renewable and provide goods and services as long as such stock exists but they cannot be cut down faster than their natural reproductive patterns. Nonrenewable natural stock is obviously a limited stock and the volume of its flow of goods and services is determined by economic demand and to some extent by government policy which allows access to nonrenewable natural capital on public lands. Neoclassical or mainstream economics still maintains the concept of the infinite substitutability of man-made capital for natural capital and entertains the notion of increasing production accompanied by a reduced stream of natural capital or resources.[20] Ecological economics, on the other hand, maintains that man-made capital and natural capital as factors of production are not substitutable for one another but must be seen as complementary. "The complementary nature of natural and man-made capital is made obvious by asking: what good is a sawmill without a forest? A refinery without petroleum deposits? A fishing boat without populations of fish?"[21] Thus, the limiting factor of production when using renewable resources is not the number of fishing boats but the reproductive rates of fish; not the number of sawmills but the remaining forests. One kind of natural capital can be substituted for another and man-made capital can reduce the amount of natural capital used in production either by more efficient use of natural capital or by changing the mix of natural and man-made capital in production. But man-made capital cannot be a substitute for natural capital. Machines are made of natural capital and can no more replace natural capital than a hammer can replace iron ore. If natural capital is the limiting factor of production in a full world scenario, it makes no sense economically to use up the scarcest resource first.

In a sustainable economy, renewable resources would not be harvested beyond their reproductive capacity, wastes exported into the environment would not exceed the assimilative capacity of the environment and the depletion of nonrenewable natural capital would be offset by investments in renewable natural capital, for example, fossil fuels replaced by solar and wind energy. An economy based on sustainable development would understand income as defined by J. R. Hicks:[22] the amount that could be spent by an individual in a period of, say, one week without jeopardizing one's well-being at the end of that time. No economy can be better off if its income is derived from the liquidation of natural capital any more than it can be better off from the liquidation of man-made capital. Individuals who draw their income from their savings rather than the interest from the savings are not better off when the savings are spent. National economies that count as income the liquidation of natural capital cannot be better off when the natural capital is exhausted. The individual or business or nation whose income depends on interest from man-made capital investment assumes that the depletion of natural capital can be more than matched by the increase of man-made capital, for example, $5NK+5MMK=1NK+9MMK$[23] or what is defined as weak sustainability. For ecological economics, strong sustainability or the increase of natural capital along with a constant or increasing man-made capital is essential. The Hicksian definition of income applies, therefore, to income based on strong sustainability with renewable natural capital utilized in such a way as not to destroy its reproductive base and with some of the income from nonrenewable natural capital used to invest in renewable natural capital substitutes (El Serafy's rule).[24] Weakly sustainable income is possible in the developed world only if some nations and regions export their natural capital to the developed centers. Some nations can escape the constraints imposed by the carrying capacity of their environment and its natural capital only if other nations stay below the carrying capacity of their environment so as to be able to export their natural capital. "In other words, the apparent escape from scale constraints enjoyed by some countries via trade depends on other countries' willingness and ability to adopt the very discipline of limiting scale that the importing country is seeking to avoid."[25] The unsustainability of an economy which liquidates its natural capital is thus hidden, in the short run, by importation of natural capital from other regions and by the liquidation of domestic natural capital stocks when the flow of resources from the existing natural capital stock is no longer sufficient to serve the input needs of accumulating man-made capital. This unsustainability is also hidden to some extent by cultivating natural capital, for example, by developing plantation forests and providing a constant flow of timber. But plantation forests are developed to provide wood, not habitats for a diverse plant and animal population. A more ethically complete definition of a sustainable economy is one, therefore, that meets the needs of the present without compromising the ability of future generations of humans and nonhumans to meet their needs. Including consideration for the well-being of future generations of nonhumans further limits the optimal scale of economic development and makes more urgent the preservation of natural capital stocks, the biological basis for all life on Earth, human and nonhuman.

Economic Man and the Fallacy of Misplaced Concreteness

Mainstream economic theory has no place for ethical judgments or more precisely it has room only for the ethics of individual self-interest at a given point in time stripped of biophysical reality. Since the point in time is the immediate present, it can be said that economic markets are the meeting places of producers and consumers separated from history, social context, and biophysical reality. Market exchanges are seen as the means by which scarce resources are efficiently allocated among alternative uses. Consumers in mainstream economic theory are individuals who prefer more goods to fewer; who prefer a mix of goods to goods of only one kind; who are interested in maximizing their own utility (satisfaction) and are willing, in principle, to trade any good for any other good (more automobiles for less clean air) in order to achieve that end. In mainstream economic theory it is assumed that if individuals are allowed to pursue their self-interests, that is, if economic transactions take place in a free market, such competition among individuals each striving to maximize self-interest will lead to the greatest social welfare. In the jargon of neoclassical economics, a free and competitive market will tend toward Pareto optimality[26] in consumption, a situation when no further market exchanges can make one person better off without making someone else less well off. The production theory of neoclassical economics includes conceptual elements similar to those of its consumer theory. More output is preferred to less. All outputs (as all consumer preferences) are on the same footing in that they cannot be judged as better or worse within the market framework. Resources have value only if they generate economic benefit. In production theory, a free and competitive market achieves Pareto optimality when no further trading of inputs can increase the production of one good without decreasing the production of another good. In this neoclassical economic paradigm, the market is the decisive mechanism through which free consumers and free producers engage in exchanges which maximize their respective utilities. Through its price structure, the market permits individuals and firms to precisely determine their respective preferences and achieve the desired mix of consumption and production goods. As the economy expands, the tendency to devalue non-market transactions and decisions strengthens. To be taken seriously, issues outside of the market must be brought within the market, assigned appropriate prices and subjected to market forces.[27]

The neoclassical economic set of assumptions about individual maximizing behavior, the assumed positive consequences for society of such behavior, and the centrality of the free market in the life of society constitute what Herman E. Daly and John B. Cobb Jr. have described as the fallacy of misplaced concreteness in economics,[28] the application to concrete events of the high-level abstractions of a deductive science. In its assumptions about human behavior, the neoclassical model creates an artificial Homo economicus or economic man whose goal is to maximize utility by engaging in market transactions to obtain goods and services that satisfy. If human existence were indeed centered on having things, Homo economicus would not be so much a caricature of Homo sapiens. But human existence involves the experience of more than possessing, of having something. Humans are not only consumers. They are family members, community members, citizens, activists, friends, lovers. They not only experience having but also creating, being, relating, doing. They seek not only economic goods and services, but also affection, understanding, friendship, participation, leisure, identity, and freedom. The goods and services the market provides are essential for meeting subsistence and security needs but all human needs cannot be collapsed into those of subsistence and material security. In the neoclassical economic paradigm consumers are assumed to be knowledgeable about the goods and services they seek in the market (indifference curves and Edgeworth Box diagrams displayed in standard economics textbooks depend for their validity on this assumption) and to be consistent in their market choices (if A is preferred to B and B is preferred to C then the consumer should prefer A to C).[29] But in the real world of market transactions, consumers can be quite ignorant of how commodities work and how well they will supply the service (utility) expected. Most car owners cannot repair their car engines and cannot identify the engine parts and their functions. Foods, pharmaceuticals, vitamins are ingested without any real understanding of their chemical composition and their effects on internal organs. Many items purchased have only the value ascribed by advertising which often does not correspond to the intrinsic composition of the item. There are consumers who have expert knowledge about specific products, usually because they are professionals in their field, or because they have formal education in specific areas, or because they have made a special effort (as in the case of individuals with illnesses that require a long-term regimen of pharmaceuticals) to be knowledgeable. But the very presence of daily pervasive advertising, much of which is aimed at persuasion rather than at providing information, is evidence that the market does not depend on expert consumers to purchase goods and services but instead persuades consumers to purchase commodities that they did not know they wanted until advertising told them or purchases by others persuaded them they did. As there are clothing fashions, so there are fashions in toys, VCRs, computers, and cellular phones. Such purchases are as much in response to what are currently considered fashionable items as they are to real or perceived needs. The current popularity of SUVs cannot be attributed to changed road conditions, the disappearance of local shopping centers, significantly expanded one-time grocery shopping, better gas mileage or other circumstances that would provide a rational warrant for owning such a vehicle. Moreover, given the plethora of goods available in the market, it is increasingly beyond the competence of the typical consumer to understand the environmental and social impacts of all such commodities and as the market becomes increasingly global, the environmental and social impact of commodities produced outside of national borders is entirely outside the consumer's range of understanding. The Homo economicus view of human behavior serves to obscure the many noneconomic variables that shape human life. It also serves to obscure how the market fails to serve individual and social needs outside the narrow realm of individualized, self-interested, utility-maximizing behavior, a form of behavior which is as much manipulated as self-directed.

Understanding the Appropriate Role of the Market

The free market serves to allocate resources and commodities to producers and consumers efficiently, that is, it allocates to those firms and individuals that have effective market demand (cash or credit) those resources, goods, or services sought. The market is far more sensitive to demands of potential customers than a centralized command economy such as existed in the former Soviet Union. Ecological economics accepts the market as a necessary device to provide efficient allocation of goods and services but it recognizes the need to provide an extra-market framework within which such allocation takes place and which insures that two other goals of ecological economics are met:

fair distribution of goods and services and the maintenance of a scale of
throughput that is sustainable and that does not undermine the carrying capacity
of the environment.

Appropriate scale is a function of population, throughput, per capita
consumption, and specific bioregional characteristics that differ geographi-
cally. The setting of appropriate scale for a modern industrial society is a
contentious problem and suggests policies that will be discussed in a later
section. Appropriate scale requires a concept of limits, particularly to economic growth or throughput and as such is not a relevant concern within the
neoclassical economic paradigm. Similarly, the concept of an equitable distribution of goods and services stands outside the neoclassical paradigm. If
sellers and buyers meet freely in the market, the resulting distribution
of goods and services, as determined by the market must, by definition, be
appropriate. Pareto optimality in consumption and production will be the
direction in which market forces necessarily trend. The exclusion of both the
notion of appropriate scale and of fair distribution from the neoclassical
paradigm is another example of the fallacy of misplaced concreteness or the
application of high-level abstractions to the real world of humans. Excluding
appropriate scale means, as pointed out earlier, the disconnection of economic activity from operating biological and physical laws. Excluding fair
distribution means ignoring the existing disparities in the ownership of land
and capital and the effect of these disparities on the distribution of goods and
services in the market. With each different pattern of income distribution
there will be a different Pareto optimality in consumption, the point at which
additional transactions cannot occur without someone being worse off.

The market allocates resources, goods, and services to those who have
effective demand (unlike, for example, the Soviet economy which often did
not supply goods to consumers who wanted them and could pay for them)
and because those who want these and can pay for them can secure them, the
market is said to allocate efficiently. "Efficient" in this context does not mean
the same as the operation of an automobile that delivers twice the mileage
compared to other models. "Efficient" in the market context means delivery
of desired resources, goods, and services to those who want them and can pay
for them. Whatever the existing distribution of income and wealth, the market
will allocate efficiently as long as it is free to deliver to buyers what they
want and what they can pay for. In this context, allocative efficiency does not
ensure distributional efficiency in the sense that those whose needs are the
greatest will have these needs satisfied. Those with the economic means can
own several cars. Others without the same economic means may have to be
without a car or may purchase one on credit and thus pay in the long run
more than the sticker price. Since an individual cannot drive more than one
car at any given time, multiple car ownership represents an inefficient use of

that particular commodity, because the natural capital consumed in the production of relatively infrequently used cars (or any other consumer durables) could have been better utilized in the production of commodities whose use value is more fully maximized. Moreover, efficient allocation in the market sense can result in the breaching of environmental limits. For example, as fish catches exceed the reproductive capacity of the fish, the market will operate to accelerate the fish catch and thus further damage the fish stock. Given an existing demand for fish and dwindling catches, fishermen will be motivated to send out more boats and use larger and heavier nets to harvest as many fish as possible as market prices for fish go up.

Following the scenario in Garrett Hardin's "Tragedy of the Commons,"[30] individual fishermen who attempt to reduce their catch in order to counteract the decimation of the fish stock will simply allow others to catch even more fish to supply a market willing to pay high prices. The logic of the market is not sensitive to environmental limits. The market also typically discounts the future, in that it sees the present value of a benefit as greater than its future value. If current interest rates are higher than the reproductive rates at which different forms of natural capital, for example, trees, increase, then market logic calls for selling off the natural capital, clear-cutting trees, and investing the returns at the higher interest rates offered by the market. Given the priority of the present over the future, the monetary value of a future project calculated in present terms can be quite small particularly if current interest rates are high. The discounted present value of a future project is the amount of money that would have been invested today at prevailing interest rates to generate the monetary value of a project, say, twenty years from today. A relatively small investment at 10 percent compounded over a twenty-year period can generate a substantial amount so that the present value of a future multimillion dollar benefit, for example, forest preservation, is small. Thus, the logic of the market ignores the long-term future as it ignores environmental limits. It is a logic entirely in keeping with the assumptions of the neoclassical paradigm, among these, as discussed earlier, that more goods are preferred to fewer and that consumers maximize their own utility and will trade any good for any other good to achieve that end. From an ecological economic perspective, the market serves only the needs of the present generation of buyers and sellers. The needs of future generations of humans and nonhumans are discounted and the present-oriented needs of firms and individuals with effective demand are satisfied. In an empty-world scenario market logic can prevail without severe environmental repercussions. In the full-world scenario, the world of today, market logic as it globalizes itself can be environmentally and socially disastrous.

In addition to its failure to maintain sustainable development and provide fair distribution, the market has been cited for other failures:[31] not maintaining competition, not enforcing ethical business practices, not providing public goods, and not internalizing externalities (failing to operate with full-cost pricing). The tendency of firms to protect themselves against competition has been countered at the state and federal levels by antitrust legislation, however variably enforced since the last decade of the nineteenth century. Unethical business practices such as fraudulent advertising, insider trading in the stock market, and sale of defective products have been countered by government regulation such as the Pure Food and Drug Act and the Securities Exchange Act. State and federal public lands, public education and interstate highways are examples of public goods provided by government and not the market. The failure of the market to internalize costs through prices represents, along with the failure to maintain competition, a major violation, even in neoclassical economics, of the conditions that enable the market to allocate goods and services efficiently. In Adam Smith's market theory, the existence of a large number of small entrepreneurs, competition, and cost internalization by each entrepreneur ensure that all market competitors will strive to lower costs, to use the factors of production as efficiently as possible so as to provide competitive prices in the market. Externalizing costs of production by draining effluents into public waters, releasing emissions into public air, dumping wastes into landfills without proper safeguards against leaking into private and public wells, surface mining without even a minimal attempt to restore the original topography, all represent a shift of the costs of production to the public whose taxes must finance any government programs aimed at air and water pollution control, remediation of toxic waste sites, and other forms of environmental regulation. Thus, cost externalization shifts costs from the producer and the individual as consumer to the individual as citizen and taxpayer. Externalized costs represent in Smithian market theory unearned profit. Environmental regulations as they operate currently inhibit but do not eliminate unearned profit at the expense of the environment (and citizens who are adversely affected by environmental degradation) just as the Fair Labor Standards Act, Wagner-Connery Act, Social Security Act, and more recently the Occupational Safety and Health Act inhibit unearned profit at the expense of wage earners.[32]

The Ecological Meaning of Efficiency

While ecological economics recognizes the importance of policies aimed at cost internalization and therefore greater market efficiency in the use of the factors of production, it expands the notion of efficiency well beyond the conventional cost benefit calculations.

For ecological economics, efficiency is a measure of the ratio of the benefit from services received from man-made capital and the cost of the loss of natural capital services or

$$\frac{\text{MMK services gained}^{33}}{\text{NK services lost}}$$

where MMK is man-made capital and NK is natural capital. The ultimate benefit received from economic activity is the services provided by the stock of man-made capital. The ultimate cost of economic activity is the loss of natural capital and the ecological services it provides. Since man-made capital can only be produced from natural capital, efficiency from the ecological economic perspective requires that services from man-made capital be maximized and natural capital stock and ecological services losses be minimized. Daly represents this concept as a four-part identity

$$\frac{\text{MMK services gained}}{\text{NK services sacrificed}} = \frac{\text{MMK services gained}}{\text{MMK stock}} \times \frac{\text{MMK stock}}{\text{thruput}} \times \frac{\text{thruput}}{\text{NK stock}} \times \frac{\text{NK stock}}{\text{NK services sacrificed}}$$

The first ratio on the right represents service efficiency and requires that products are efficiently designed, that resources are allocated to different products according to market preferences, and that the stock (commodities) is distributed efficiently among individuals. The second ratio represents maintenance efficiency or durability of man-made stock and requires that the stock is repairable, recyclable and durable, thereby reducing thruput. The third ratio represents the growth efficiency of natural capital in providing inputs into thruput. The faster growing the natural capital, the more efficient its use in the sense that its biological growth rate provides more without additional inputs of fertilizer, pesticides, and similar man-made capital. The fourth ratio represents ecoservice efficiency or the minimization of losses of ecosystem services as natural stock is taken as raw material for thruput. The point of the four-part identity is to stress that the ultimate cost of all economic activity is the loss of natural stock and the ecosystem services that flow from it. The ultimate cost in thermodynamic terms is the increasing disorder in the ecosystem. If life, an open system in temporary equilibrium, exists at the cost of increasing disorder in the surrounding environment then economics, which is the metabolic organization of human life, operates at the cost of increasing disorder in the planetary environment. A growth economy accelerates the disorder. Ecological economics aims at decelerating the disorder so that more generations of life, human, and nonhuman, can come into being, but cannot eliminate entropy.

Measuring Economic Welfare

If economic activity subject as it is to the second law of thermodynamics necessarily creates high entropy, then it is possible to speak of uneconomic growth or growth which creates more costs to the natural and social environment than benefits. Ecological economists like Daly have developed indices designed to measure the level of welfare accompanying economic growth as measured by the GNP. The ISEW[34] or index of sustainable economic welfare when plotted over several decades in conjunction with the GNP shows that in recent years while GNP continues to rise the ISEW has lagged behind the GNP. Since the GNP measures the domestic money flow of goods and services as well as exports, it is essentially a measure of throughput or the volume of energy and matter that is processed within the economy. All market exchanges are counted equally with money spent on housing construction or environmental remediation or HIV research or additional police or traffic accidents all added to the total GNP. To the extent that more economic growth, for example, more automobiles, creates more pollution and traffic congestion and accidents, paves over more open land, cuts through neighborhoods, requires higher automobile insurance premiums and purchases of antitheft equipment, consumes at an accelerating rate nonrenewable fossil fuels, and undermines a more energy-efficient public transportation system, to that extent more economic growth reduces welfare. Accordingly, several subtractions have to be made from the GNP in order to arrive at a more accurate measure of welfare. Since man-made capital depreciation is already subtracted from the GNP in the national accounts, subtractions are made from the net national product. The subtractions include the depreciation of natural capital, defensive expenditures such as automobile anti-theft devices (defined as intermediate costs of production rather than final consumer goods), expenditures on national advertising, costs of commuting, costs of urbanization, costs of air and water pollution, among others. Counted as contributing to welfare are non-market household services such as caring for aging parents and public expenditures on health, education, streets, and highways. An index of distributional equality measuring the degree of difference between each of the four lowest income quintiles and the highest income quintile is also included in the ISEW. In 1950, the per capita ISEW was 2,496 and per capita GNP was 3,512; in 1990 the per capita ISEW was 3,253 and the per capita GNP was 7,755.[35] The conclusion drawn is that economic growth increases welfare until a threshold is reached where costs of additional growth exceed welfare benefits.

While indices such as the ISEW serve to reveal the uneconomic elements of contemporary economic growth and the increasing disparity between per capita GNP and per capita ISEW, such indices, nevertheless, do measure as contributing to welfare the largest element in the GNP, private consumption. Unless dangerous and deleterious forms of consumption are identified and subtracted from the GNP, private consumption will be included without qualification in indices such as the ISEW as a contribution to welfare, and increases in the GNP, to the extent they are tied to increases in private consumption, will always be reflected in some increase in welfare indices. Sorting out beneficial from injurious consumption requires judgment that may not be supported by empirical evidence. Just how much tobacco and alcohol consumption is acceptable before becoming deleterious to one's health? Since the purpose of economic activity is to provide goods and services to satisfy consumers' wants, welfare, on the face of it, is better served by more goods and services. Consequently, indices such as the ISEW subtract from the GNP not consumer expenditures as such but the external costs of production and distribution in an expanding economy. Traffic congestion, air and water pollution, defensive expenditures, depletion of natural capital, and the loss of ecoservices are not calculated in mainstream economics as costs to be subtracted from income. In the ISEW, these items are monetized and subtracted from the GNP as the unintended but real costs associated with the provision of goods and services for private consumption. But private consumption as such remains the major form of human welfare in the ISEW and similar welfare indices.

The Ethical and Social Limitations of an Unlimited Growth Society

Since there is no assumption of limits to economic growth in neoclassical economics, the provision of goods and services for private consumption can continue indefinitely, constantly changing the forms and characteristics of goods and services with ever more rapid cycles of change induced by technologically driven production. The nearest boundary in sight, if such can be called a boundary, is the creation of a global economy which will provide all members of the global community with a material standard of living equivalent to that presently enjoyed by citizens of developed nations such as the United States. The rejection by ecological economics of this mainstream scenario as an "impossibility theorem"[36] requires that human welfare not be linked exclusively or even predominantly to the consumption of physical goods and services which require substantial inputs of energy and matter. Private consumption of goods and services represents only partial human welfare. Total human welfare involves the satisfaction of existential needs (having, being, doing, relating) and axiological or value-laden needs (subsistence, protection, affection, understanding, participation, leisure, creation, identity, freedom).[37]

Humans have need of one another; they are as Aristotle noted, political and social animals. They seek to express themselves through the arts and literature. They are curious about the physical world which surrounds them and they develop sophisticated sciences to explain and control physical phenomena. They can find satisfaction and even pleasure in working with their hands and creating artifacts. The languages they speak are meant to be heard and responded to by other humans. The neoclassical economic view of the self-interested, utility-maximizing solipsist or Homo economicus who calculates which bundle of goods best serves his/her interests is a dreary reductionist abstraction from the richness and complexity of human life. When ecological economics speaks of uneconomic growth, that is, growth which subtracts rather than adds to human welfare, it is referring not only to the unsustainability of current physical throughputs needed to expand production and consumption, but also to the chilling effect such ultimately unsustainable economic growth has on the development of human emotional, intellectual, and social capacities which do not depend, in the main, on the consumption of goods and services. Given the assumption in mainstream economics that the consumption of goods and services defines the good life (or is, at the very least, the central feature of the good life), it is not surprising that the elements needed to satisfy non-consumption activities (stable communities, open spaces, participatory workplaces, education for self-enlightenment rather than for work skills required by businesses, an authentic politics of public discourse) are, intentionally or not, effectively undermined.

For ecological economics, economic activity is not an end in itself; it is a means to ends defined by individuals and society in private and public discourse. In the hierarchy of human activities and within the reality of the physical world, economics, as Daly has pointed out,[38] represents a set of intermediate means (labor power, physical capital created by human and natural technology). These intermediate means are dependent on the ultimate means of low-entropy energy and matter and serve or should serve such intermediate ends as health, comfort, and education which are part of the existential and axiological needs noted above. Beyond the intermediate ends is an ultimate end, the subject matter of religion and philosophy. This placement of economics clearly subordinates it to a democratic politics in which individual and social ends are defined in a public discourse which is translated into individual preference and public policy.

The notion that economic activity should be subject to the constraints of socially constituted values (religious, political, cultural) was commonplace until some two hundred years ago when the Industrial Revolution began to provide the technological infrastructure for a rapid acceleration of economic production. If at one time economics was a subset of society, it may be said that today's society, in the sense that its politics and cultural values are largely shaped by economics, is a subset of economics. For reasons already explained—expanding populations without land or capital dependent on business-generated jobs, the technological feasibility of global markets, the control of politics by economic interests, a consumption-addictive culture nourished by advertising and education—for many, if not for most, citizens of developed nations such as the United States, life without the constant purchase of goods and services is difficult to envision. To imagine a day without any activity related to the consumption of goods and services or to the maintenance of acquired goods, would be, in most cases, to imagine a void. Given the breakdown of genuine communities, shopping becomes a form of social interaction. Given the breakdown in public discourse, language becomes a market-related conversation in which the participants exchange tidbits of information about places to shop, bargains to be had. Given urban decay and suburban sprawl, shopping malls with their fountains, their air-conditioned walkways, and their cornucopia of goods, serve as shelters from the weather and as cultural centers for many. At an early age, children, wittingly or not, are socialized into the culture of consumption even as their recreation is increasingly formed around goods purchased in the market. While children of several generations ago could devise various forms of recreation not dependent on market goods, the progressive disappearance of open fields and natural areas and the decay of publicly provided recreational areas has resulted in the commodification of leisure and recreational activities by the economic system. While the full potential of a system which increasingly commodifies activities heretofore carried on privately and which marginalizes non-economic activities generally may never be realized because of its unsustainability on a global level, the logic of the current economic system is unambiguous and daunting. The system drives toward a world order in which wild nature will be preserved only for genetic research and potential commercial value. Western technologies of production will become the standard global model. The great majority of humankind will work in the service of economic growth, rewarded in varying degrees with the means to participate in the consumption of the goods and services they themselves produce but do not own. Those in control of the economic system will play a dominant role in politics and in the shaping of cultural values and social institutions such as education. Along with the disappearance of biodiversity, differences in national and regional cultures, technologies and life-styles will be dissolved in the homogeneity of a global consumer culture. People in such a new world order may still speak different languages, but their personal images will be those of a globalized Homo economicus and their freedom to shape their own lives will be largely confined to their roles as consumers, choosing the bundle of goods that best satisfies their personal tastes as these tastes have been shaped by a global unlimited growth system. Thus, the failings of mainstream economics are not solely failures of sustainability and distribution. They are failings which have significant political and cultural consequences. Politically, an economics of unlimited growth destroys authentic democracy, because it silences or limits public discourse to a discussion of the means, not the ends, of economic growth. Culturally, the economics of unlimited growth creates a one-dimensional society[39] in which non-economic values are either marginalized or converted into market commodities.

Moving Toward an Ecological Economics

Shifting the dominant economic growth system from its present unsustainable track to a sustainable one is a Herculean task for several obvious reasons. First, the growth system assumptions (e.g., perpetual economic growth solves all problems, individuals find fulfillment through material acquisition) are part of the dominant techno-industrial paradigm culture. Second, both major political parties and, indeed, most third-party movements support the growth economy. This support is assured by the money contributed to candidates and parties by business and by the cultural baggage which most elected and appointed government officials bring with them. Third, shifting from an unsustainable to a sustainable economy requires a long-range plan that provides for the gradual phasing out of fossil fuels, the implementation of renewable fuel technologies, the provision of government assistance to sectors of the present economy which will be most adversely affected by the new policies (employment in fossil-fueled industries will be severely affected, for instance), new patterns of international trade, new educational programs designed to provide the cultural values and the work skills suitable for a sustainable economy, and policies designed to stabilize the population so as to reduce the pressure for increased employment and the human impact on the remaining natural habitats. One can assume that the transition to a mature sustainable economy may take a half century or more and that the transition over such a period of time can take place only if both major parties or, if such be the case, major and minor parties move forward the policies needed for the transition, regardless of which party sits in the White House, the Congress, and the state legislatures. Given the short-term focus of political campaigns, the presence of corporate influence at all levels of government, the reduction of contemporary political discourse to issues which have no relevance to the goals of a sustainable economy (although they are relevant to the winning of an election), and the abstention of half of the electorate from the political process, there is no realistic expectation that the existing political structure can produce a long-range plan for a transition to a sustainable economy in the twenty-first century. Moreover, the very notion of long-range planning is anathema to most Americans since it smacks of state socialism and the dominance of government in private life. Market decisions are the culturally accepted form of "planning" in that market decisions represent arrangements that producers and consumers have ostensibly freely agreed to. If the market provides energy efficient bulbs then this is what producers and consumers want. If the efficient light bulbs do not sell well because the prices are too high, then all indications are that consumers can maximize their utilities better with bundles of goods that do not include the energy-efficient light bulbs. It is in this context—structural and cultural resistances to long-range planning and the faith in a market that in reality by itself cannot move producers and consumers to a sustainable economic mode—that ecological economists make policy recommendations to address the endemic problems of the contemporary growth system.

Monetizing Environmental Stocks and Services

Before describing the major policy recommendations of ecological economists, it is essential to note that these policies require that monetary values be assigned to environmental stocks and services. Is biodiversity important? If so, can this importance be assigned a monetary value? Are grizzly bears important in Yellowstone National Park? If so, what is the monetary value of grizzly bears? Is natural capital important to the national economy? If so, then what is the monetary value of the nation's natural resources? Robert Costanza[40] in 1997 calculated that the current economic value of the entire biosphere was $16 to 54 trillion per year with an average value of some $33 trillion per year. By comparison, the GNP of the United States is approximately $18 trillion per year. Four major techniques have been devised to determine the monetary value of environmental goods and services. First, there is the conventional market approach which uses market prices for the environmental services that are affected. Take the case of the degradation of forests in developing countries. The decrease of wood for use as fuel leads to the use of dried dung as fuel. The use of dung as fuel instead of fertilizer requires that farmers buy chemical fertilizers for the land. The price of chemical fertilizers thus represents the monetary value of the environmental services provided previously by the now degraded forests. Second, the household production function method examines expenditures on commodities that are substitutes or complements for the environmental good or service that is involved. An example of this method is the calculation of the travel costs of visitors to a national park, for instance, using these costs as a measure of the recreational value of the park to visitors. A third method is hedonic pricing which imputes a price to an environmental good by examining the effect its presence or absence has on market-priced goods. The difference in price between a house located in a pollution-free environment and a similar house in a polluted environment represents the monetary value of clean air or an unpolluted beach. The fourth method involves the use of contingent valuation in which individuals express their preferences for specific environmental goods and services by stating how much they would be willing to pay to ensure the preservation of a nonmarket environmental good and service or how much they would have to be paid to accept the loss of a nonmarket environmental good or service. Thus, individuals may be asked how much they would be willing to pay to maintain grizzly bears in Yellowstone National Park or how much they would have to be paid to accept additional air pollution in their neighborhood. These several methods of monetizing environmental stocks and services have been criticized on both methodological grounds (complex decisions with important environmental impacts cannot be based on a single scale of values) and ethical grounds (how can one assign a dollar value to any life?).[41] Nevertheless, the commitment of ecological economists to the market as the most efficient allocator of goods and services requires that policies affecting the environment be subject to a monetized cost-benefit analysis even if, admittedly, the valorization of environmental goods and services cannot in most cases be tied to existing market prices and represents what economists refer to as "shadow prices."

Related to the monetization of environmental goods and services is the attempt to provide for the full cost pricing of the goods and services produced by the economic sector. The market price of wood does not reflect the loss of biodiversity when trees are removed or the silting of rivers and the concomitant degradation of the spawning grounds of salmon, for example. The price of tomatoes shipped from Mexico does not reflect the wear and tear on the interstate highways and state roads which carry the trucks that deliver the tomatoes to east coast cities. Nor do tomato prices reflect the air pollution caused by trucks which contributes to global warming and adversely affects human health. Until very recently, the prices of tobacco products did not reflect the medical costs borne by individuals and state and federal governments as a result of the severe health problems associated with long-term smoking. Until the federal government enacted regulations such as the Resource Conservation and Recovery Act, the cost of handling and disposing of wastes created by various production processes was often passed on to individuals and communities. In short, without full cost pricing of the facets of economic activity—extraction, processing, manufacture, distribution, disposal—the market treats as externalities some very real costs that are passed on to those who were not involved in the market transactions that created the costs in the first place. It has been understood at least since the writings of Adam Smith that full cost pricing is a prerequisite for market efficiency. Competing firms that must calculate the full cost of utilizing the factors of production will, of necessity, take steps to reduce costs which will otherwise be reflected in the market prices of their goods. When a company under federal and state law is responsible for the cost of disposing of waste there is a very real incentive to reduce the volume of waste or even to turn what was once regarded as waste to commercial use. All actions which shift some of the costs of production to sectors of the public, whether because of a lack of government regulation or from deliberate government policy as in the case of subsidies to business, undercut economic motivations for efficient operation, regardless of justifications such as protecting American businesses abroad, providing employment at home by stimulating economic growth in a depressed region, and creating economic opportunities for minority groups.[42]

Assigning monetary values to environmental goods and services in cost-benefit analysis expands what are called the "asset and production boundaries"[43] in that the natural environment is recognized as having recreational and aesthetic value and as providing environmental services essential to production, for example, waste absorption or water for industrial uses. Given the dominant economic impetus to growth and development, the failure to assign some monetary value to the environment means that in standard cost-benefit calculations the environment will be treated as an externality and development will trump environmental considerations. If, on the other hand, the environment is treated as natural capital essential to all economic activity and therefore having value greater than zero, cost-benefit analysis of projects having an impact on the environment will have to internalize, to some extent, the environmental costs of projects proposed. However imprecise and one-dimensional the assignment of monetary values to environmental stocks and services may be, the calculation of environmental costs in the cost-benefit analysis of various projects that affect the environment is unlikely to be taken seriously unless some price is attached to the environment. Typically, for example, in the cost-benefit analysis connected with the proposal to build a shopping mall the benefits are not difficult to calculate. The creation of jobs, tax revenues for the local government, and profits for businesses are listed as benefits. Non-environmental costs are also obvious: construction costs, architect's and engineer's fees, permits to be obtained. In the conventional cost-benefit analysis, paved over open spaces that adversely affect aquifers, rising air pollution as traffic volume increases, alteration of stream flow, degradation of animal and plant habitats represent externalities which are not relevant to conventional cost-benefit analysis. Assigning some monetary value to the water aquifers provide and to clean air allows for the calculation of at least some environmental costs associated with the building of a mall. It may well be that a full cost pricing in this case, including environmental costs and costs to the public (local government, in many instances, subsidizes a project by building access roads, regulating traffic, providing sewage facilities, and tax relief) will indicate that the total costs outweigh the total benefits.

Along with calculations of total costs and benefits, it is essential that distributional and equity issues also be raised: which groups receive the benefit and which groups bear the cost. Recent environmental justice studies show that it has been and continues to be commonplace for developments of one kind or another to provide disproportionate benefits to some and disproportionate costs to others, usually poor communities of ethnic groups without political clout and representation. Accordingly, it has been suggested that "economists should recognize that cost-benefit analysis [with monetary valuation of the environment] is only part of the decision-making process and that it lies at the same level as other considerations."[44] These other considerations include ethical, political, and historical issues which when markets fail to provide a solution can only be addressed through a "transparent decision-making process, not old-style cost-benefit analyses."[45] Thinking like the market and assigning prices to all entities under consideration cannot substitute for public discourse and political debate about values and the kind of society we wish to live in.

The Policy Recommendations of Ecological Economics

Ecological economics addresses the issue of sustainability with several major policy recommendations.[46] First, a broadly based natural capital depletion tax to assure that the impact on the environment from resource extraction is sustainable and to provide incentives for the development of new technologies and processes to reduce resource extraction. Second, application of the precautionary polluter pays principle to assure that the full costs of outputs from the economy are charged to the polluter in a way that adequately deals with the true uncertainty surrounding the environmental impact of pollution. This precautionary principle states that rather than await certainty, regulators should act to anticipate environmental harm in order to prevent it. The instrument to allow regulators to anticipate environmental harm and prepare for a response is a flexible environmental assurance bonding system in which the size of the bond is large enough to cover the worst-case damages. Refunds are provided if the worst-case scenario does not occur or if the damage is less than expected. Companies unable to post the bond would not be licensed to do the work. The precautionary principle assumes that reasonably precise assessment can be made of the worst-case scenario for environmental damage. Third, the imposition of ecological tariffs to make possible the application of natural capital depletion taxes and the precautionary principle without placing the nation at a trading disadvantage relative to countries where such policies are not in effect. Ecological tariffs in conjunction with the other two policies would protect the domestic and global environments from private polluters and nonsustainable resource users.[47]

The three policies discussed above address issues of efficiency and scale in the use of natural capital and the environmental impact of economic activity. Addressing the issue of fair distribution is a recommended shifting of taxes over time from such social goods as jobs and incomes to environmental bads such as industrial pollution. To address the issue of fairness in taxation, zero taxes for low-income groups and a progressive tax aimed at the wealthy are recommended. Daly and Cobb in their *For the Common Good* have argued for an end to corporation taxes on the grounds that corporations often make decisions based on evading the tax, decisions which may undermine both efficiency and environmental considerations. Rather than a tax on corporations, individual stockholders would be taxed. In his earlier *Steady-State Economics*, Daly made the case for placing a cap on maximum income and a floor on minimum income. Maximum income would be set at fifteen times the minimum. The focus on changing current tax policy to achieve greater distributional equity is based on the rejection of the mainstream position that more economic growth will promote distributional equity by allowing all individuals and groups to share in the ensuing prosperity of a constant-growth economy. Data on current trends in the distribution of income and wealth do not support this contention and, at an rate, if there are physical limits to economic growth the issue of distributional equity will have to be addressed by tax policies and related legislation. This is to say that distributional equity issues will have to be addressed politically and not by operations of the market.

Contrary to what one might expect, there are no recent major policy recommendations to address the question of the increase, in some cases the geometric increase, of the human population. In his *Steady-State Economics*, Daly proposed that both throughput of matter and energy and the human population be maintained at a steady state, a constant stock of physical and human capital. To keep the population at a determined number, Daly suggested that each female infant at birth be given a birth license, expressed in deci-units.[48] Presumably, the number of deci-units in birth licenses would depend on an assessment of how many people, consuming at a given rate, could exist without destroying the environmental resources needed to maintain the economy in a steady state. Thus, initial birth licenses might be issued with twelve deci-units or 1.2 which would mean that the holder (a female) could have one child and either sell the remaining two deci-units or buy another eight deci-units (or more) on the market. Deci-units would trade at prices reflecting the desire of women to have children. In a strongly pronatal society the units would sell at high prices. Conversely, in a society where having children competed with other desiderata, the price of a unit would be lower. In this system, a woman could choose to sell all her units or continue buying additional units to have as many children as she could afford. The total number of births would be controlled, providing macrostability of the population while allowing microvariability on the individual level. In subsequent writings, Daly did not return to this scheme and the standard position of ecological economics is that population is only one factor, albeit an important one, in assessing environmental impacts: I=PAT or environmental impact is a function of population, affluence or per capita consumption, and technology in use. While the United States population is small compared to that of India, per capita consumption in the United States may be a hundred times that in India. Thus, in the United States, affluence is a more significant determinant of environmental impact than the absolute size of the population. Given the low per capita consumption and the comparatively primitive technology in use, the absolute size of the Indian population is the more significant determinant of environmental impact in India. But cultural factors and geographic features also affect environmental impact. A relatively small population living in a fragile ecosystem can have a significant environmental impact. A relatively large number of people living in a more robust ecosystem or influenced by cultural norms of respect for the environment may have comparatively less impact on the environment. While it is thus clear that a large population in a given area may not do more damage to the environment than a smaller population in another area, it seems equally clear that a global population of six billion must have more of an impact on the environment than three billion. With the exception of Daly's birth license proposal, ecological economics offers no unique perspective on the population problem, supporting instead the education and economic empowerment of women, especially in the developing nations, birth control technologies, raising the general standard of living and similar policies supported by groups with no special interest in ecological economic issues. Perhaps it is assumed that once limits to economic growth are generally recognized by the public, individuals will limit their own reproductive activity in a post-growth society.

Also suggested is a system of graded ecozoning within which the economy would operate,[49] the ramifications of which go well beyond taxes on environmental bads since it would require local, state, regional and national land use planning. Briefly, a system of graded ecozoning would provide for three zones: a property rights zone identified as an area where current economic activity is causing no measurable environmental damage and the productivity of natural capital is not impaired; an incentive zone where pollution emissions and concentrations have measurably damaged the environment and threaten the productivity of natural capital; a regulatory zone where pollution emissions and concentrations threaten to reach the point where ecological criteria indicate the real possibility or actual occurrence of irreversible and unsustainable damage to the ecosystem and its natural capital. In the property rights zone there are no emission or other environmental regulations and such remains the case unless further economic activity begins to stress the environment. In the incentive zone, emissions are taxed providing an incentive to reduce emissions by more efficient production processes. A system of tradable emission permits could operate achieving the desired emission levels without the expense involved in command-and-control regulation. In the regulatory zone, characterized by actual or potential irreversible and unsustainable damage to the environment, drastic regulatory and punitive measures would be justified, including the banning of further economic activity in this zone.

It is pointed out that the most important decisions made at the local level concern land use and that market processes by themselves do not necessarily result in land use consistent with local carrying capacity, that is, land use which does not seriously impair or destroy the local ecosystem.[50] Current land use policies reflect the lobbying of developers in state legislatures and their cost benefit analyses focus on private benefits and costs, not total social benefits and costs, including environmental costs. Moreover, many local governments compete with one another to attract developers, in the process lowering standards which developers must meet. The economic benefits of a development are readily discernible in the form of jobs and tax revenues for the local government. Protecting the environment usually involves future benefits and costs which in the conventional cost benefit analysis cannot be calculated. Accordingly, the following criteria are advanced for improving the quality of local land use and land use planning: assigning priority to net social welfare gains over net private gains; providing for the scientific evaluation, protection and management of local ecological resources to promote sustainable use; open participation in land use decision processes by all parties affected; oversight and review at higher levels of government to prevent interregional competition for economic growth from degenerating into the sacrifice of natural capital and critical ecological areas; full cost pricing of all local government services offered to developers; full cost pricing of the environmental impact of development, including waste disposal, runoff from nonpoint sources, and air pollution. All local projects should be subjected to a full environmental impact assessment and relevant information along the lines of the Toxic Release Inventory (required of all chemical manufacturers in the United States) mandated by the Superfund Amendment and Reauthorization Act of 1986, provided to the public when firms plan to locate in an area.

Other policies recommended are ecological labeling to indicate inputs of energy amounts for recycled materials, outputs of pollutants, and use of nonrenewable resources in the manufacture of a product.[51] Ecological labeling assumes that consumer environmental intelligence is such that purchase decisions will be made on the basis of technical data, in the same way that weight-conscious individuals examine data on the caloric content of a particular food item. The state and federal governments are seen playing a potentially significant role as purchasers of environmentally benign products and environmentally advanced technologies such as the electric car, providing market incentives for further production and development. The federal government can also advance environmental priorities by subsidizing research for renewable energy sources and eliminating subsidies for economic activities which damage the environment. In the latter case this would mean ending the underpricing of sales of public timber and public land sold for mining, as well as ending subsidies for fossil fuel use in the form of tax deductions, for example, for the cost of fuel in the trucking industry.

The recommended policies discussed above are seen as interacting with and supporting general ecological values. Thus, natural capital depletion taxes and ecological tariffs promote the value of knowing our ecological place. Internalizing all costs helps to promote nonlinear understanding of the way things are connected. Taxing throughput (natural capital extraction and processing) underscores the value of scaling back life-styles and reducing energy and material consumption. A market adjusted to reflect the real costs of the commodities we consume assists us in taking a realistic measure of the way we live and in beginning to confront the current dominant cultural beliefs which are at the root of our environmental and social problems. These beliefs, as already indicated, include the notion that humans are fulfilled through material acquisition; that unceasing economic growth solves all problems; that other species and natural capital in the ecosystem exist for human appropriation (particularly private rather than public appropriation); and that technology makes it possible to avoid moral choices about wealth, poverty, and appropriate population levels. All of these dominant paradigm cultural beliefs weaken community and closer links to place and locality because they stress the private aspects of an individuals' life: consuming, acquiring, moving from one job or locality, and giving priority to private benefits over public welfare. But it is precisely at the local level that efforts can be most effective in linking economic activities to their environmental impact and applying the needed regulations. At the translocal, let alone at the transnational, level the circuits of economic activity are difficult to trace. Who can follow the path of all the parts that make up a computer and catalogue the environmental and social damage done in the production, transportation, and assembling of the computer parts?[52] The weakening of community and local relationships, accelerated by the globalization of the economy, which treats localities as fungible economic factors, results in individuals progressively losing any significant citizen functions as closely linked government and corporate bureaucracies shape a global market system which is not accountable to the general public and increasingly eludes accountability to national government.

Ecological Economics: Recapitulation

Ecological economics is, as stated earlier, critical of the efficiency, sustainability, and distributional equity of the current mainstream growth economy. It makes a convincing case for limits to industrial growth based on the carrying capacity of the Earth, that is, on the ability of the Earth's living and inorganic environment to sustain contemporary economic activity without the collapse of the Earth's ecosystems and the natural capital which they contain. Thus, ecological economics connects the economic system with the natural environment in which it functions and with the laws of thermodynamics which govern the energy transformations that occur in the extractive, productive and disposal processes of the economic system. Ecological economics emphasizes the need to protect and expand natural capital and to invest in renewable natural capital substitutes for depleted nonrenewable natural capital. It accepts the market as the best instrument for the allocation of goods and services but recognizes that left to its own devices the market cannot provide for the appropriate scale and sustainability of economic activity, efficiency through full cost pricing, and distributional equity.[53] Just as ecological economics connects economics with the physical world in which it operates, so it connects economics with the ethical and political dimensions of human life. For ecological economics, economics is an instrumentality for the provision of the goods and services that are deemed by the members of a society to be the desired material foundation of a good life and good society. A foundation is not desired for its own sake but as a base for an edifice to be built on it. The contemporary endless growth economic system makes the foundation itself the rationale for economic activity. Thus, the so-called foundation becomes simply an enlarging accumulation of artifacts which may serve private needs but cannot provide for the ethical, civic, aesthetic, political, and spiritual aspects of human nature which a stable, humane, and democratic society must provide. Unlike mainstream economics, ecological economics recognizes ethical obligations that existing generations have to future generations. Economic policies that deprive future generations of the use of natural resources consumed in the present may be justified in the short-term calculus of the existing economic system but such policies are ethically reprehensible. Thus, unlike its mainstream counterpart, ecological economics does not pretend to be a value-free discipline. The maintenance of viable ecosystems is valuable; the existence of nonhuman species is valuable; human communities in control of their economic and social destinies are valuable; the concern of present generations for the welfare of future generations is valuable, a trade among nations in which all pay decent wages, enforce environmental laws, protect workers is valuable; open public discourse about social and economic goals is valuable.[54] In this respect, ecological economics is far closer to classical economics in its engagement with philosophical and ethical issues than mainstream economics whose analytic models are elegantly mathematical but frequently so abstract that their attempted applications to significant social issues exemplify the fallacy of misplaced concreteness.

The end of the cold war provided an opportunity to reexamine existing policies that impede the possibility of shifting from unsustainable economic growth to sustainable development. Instead, policies that promote economic growth which in the long run is unsustainable remain in place and the globalization of free trade policies threatens to undermine what national legislation exists or could be enacted to protect the environment.[55] The dominant culture of consumer materialism in the industrialized nations and the understandable aspiration of developing nations to achieve the material affluence of the former group also militate against serious opposition to pro-growth policies. Ecological economics underscores the conditions that will have to be met if the present generation is to avoid "continuing on into disaster and social chaos."[56] First, a consensus must be reached, utilizing educational and democratic institutions, on a set of policies that reflect the emerging science of complex (nonlinear) systems, achieve true economic efficiency, and acknowledge nature as a partner in the program of sustainable development. Second, the current appetite for material consumption and possession must not be allowed to cloud the moral intelligence needed to recognize what will be required to achieve sustainable development. Third, and related to the second, personal failures in choosing current life-styles and consumption patterns must be confronted, for it is these personal choices when cumulated that determine the quality of the social and natural environments. Ecological economists urge a broad public discourse on the policies they propose to move toward a sustainable economic system.

> Democracy is not merely the process of voting. The two are far from the same thing. Voting, without broad-based discussion, information exchange, and, most importantly, agreement on shared goals and visions for the future, is merely the facade of democracy. We have a long way to go to actually achieve the kind of participatory, "living democracy" which . . . many others advocate. It is within this context of living, participatory democracy that the policies and instruments we describe . . . need to be evaluated.[57]

The participatory, living democracy referred to above is the subject of the next chapter, "Ecological Political Economy." That chapter explicates what several authors understand to be the essential elements of such a democracy and its relationship to the principles of ecological economics.

Chapter 2

Ecological Political Economy

A community centered economics [and politics] challenges the fundamental assumptions of an industrial political economy. It not only challenges the industrial dogma that the economic realm can be separated from the political realm, and that political democracy can exist without economic democracy; it also argues that the human needs of the majority must not be kept subservient to the economic needs of the minority.

—*Roy Morrison*, Ecological Democracy

The Early American Political Economy

Ecological economics has reintroduced the concept of limits into economic theory and practice and reconnected economics with the natural environment in which it operates. The ecological critique of politics,[1] spurred by the contemporary disempowerment of most citizens, reintroduces the political economy concept that politics as a discipline cannot be separated from the social and economic order and that operations of the latter two significantly affect the workings of the political system. Since Aristotle's *Politics,*[2] it was understood that various forms of government required a specific social and economic order for their successful functioning. An aristocracy could not flourish in a society with a reasonably widespread distribution of property, an economy with a vigorous foreign trade and a large commercial class. A democracy

51

could not flourish in a society where landed property was concentrated in the hands of a few. A stable democracy would not be possible in a society characterized by polarization between the many very poor and the few very rich and with an enfeebled middle class.

This relationship between the polity and the social and economic order was also well understood in the early years of the American Republic and was at the center of the conflict between Thomas Jefferson and Alexander Hamilton. Both Jefferson and Hamilton were aware that different social and economic arrangements in America would produce the conditions for very different forms of government. When Jefferson argued for a primarily agrarian economy serviced by a domestic manufacturing system, he was arguing for a social and economic order capable of sustaining and nurturing a republican citizenry, that is, a citizenry with the moral capacity to function as active citizens, willing and able to maintain an accountable republican form of government. For Jefferson and his followers, Hamilton's plans to develop an industrial system in America which would rival that in England meant that the same social conditions that existed in England would be reproduced in America. In England, a large landless population worked in the manufactories for masters and was characterized by poverty, dependence, and misery. Ignorant and dependent laborers, however, could not be the social foundation for a republic. For Jefferson, America could hope to avoid the English pattern of an ever-widening gap between the mass of people and the few rich and the resulting political oligarchy only if it provided for widespread land ownership accompanied by small-scale industry based on independent owners of shops who would produce the tools needed by an agrarian society. How much wealth and luxury a society could accumulate before the republican values of citizens were eroded was a question frequently asked. If the economy became primarily industrial-commercial how long would it be before the citizens of the republic became consumed with the pursuit of their private fortunes rather than concerned for the welfare of the Republic? Moreover, if large-scale manufacturing with its increasing emphasis on division of labor replaced an agrarian economy, then the same physical and mental degradation of the worker as commented on by Adam Smith could be expected,[3] as could Smith's conclusion that such a class of laborers was not fit for citizenship.

For Jefferson (and Madison), if America was to avoid, at least for several generations, the social and political conditions in England and Europe generally, then westward expansion to provide more land as the population increased and international free trade to allow American farm surplus access to all foreign ports had to be key national policies. A fifty-acre conveyance in fee simple to all adult white males, universal manhood suffrage, and the development of ward (township) government with all officials elected for short terms, with the ward as the primary agency of public education and political discourse, were key state and local policies.[4] Such national, state, and local policies would allow for a broad distribution of land ownership, enfranchise all white men, provide numerous opportunities to engage in politics and hold office at the local level, and provide public education for the citizenry.[5] Taken together, these policies would establish the social and economic conditions necessary, even with an increasing population,[6] to maintain a citizenry imbued with republican virtues, that is, citizens capable of meeting their private needs without losing sight of the welfare of the Republic. This ability to balance private and public interests was according to Jefferson best promoted through the life-style of the independent farmer who was the keystone of an agrarian economy and who could in association with his farm neighbors understand and work through politically the problems of an agrarian society. The laborer in a manufactory, given the English and European experience with a manufacturing economy, could not understand, let alone address politically, the problems of such an economy. The result in England and Europe was that, as Jefferson said, every man was either an anvil or a hammer. Neither situation could provide the social and economic prerequisites for stable and accountable republican government.

Hamilton's unqualified endorsement of a commercial and manufacturing society assumed that a republic as Jefferson understood it was irrelevant to the American future. As population increased relative to accessible land, manufacturing would be needed to absorb the available surplus labor, including women and children.[7] Hamilton supported a system of pecuniary bounties to promote American manufactures and to make American exports competitive with subsidized European exports. He assisted in the establishment in Patterson, N.J. of a capitalized enterprise, the Society for Establishing Useful Manufactures, financed by federal bonds and shares of the Bank of the United States, an enterprise whose workers were exempt from military service and taxes and the corporation exempt from property taxes for ten years. These policies prefigured an American society characterized by a propertyless citizenry, dependent workers, and political control by the rich. His program also foreshadowed a government acting as a partner to business interests, ready to support the needs of a rapidly developing industrial society modeled after England. Such a government would create an environment conducive to investments from abroad and provide financial instruments such as the national bank to facilitate investment and development. The incentive for investment would be the prospect of enrichment in an expanding market. Like many of his contemporaries in America and Europe, Hamilton accepted the argument that commerce and manufacturing advanced civilization, that status and enrichment were spurs to progress, and that the opulence of the rich provided employment for the poor. In short, private vices would lead to public benefit, a position expressed by both Bernard de Mandeville and Adam Smith.[8]

Hamilton ignored the Jeffersonian perspective on the social impact of an aggressively expanding commercial and manufacturing society, namely, that such a society would undermine the initial benefits of fostering habits of industry, frugality, and punctuality among its citizens with the result that "in any commercial society, notwithstanding the pretension to equal rights, the exaltation of the few must depress the many."[9] Hamilton's view of the nature of citizenship is quite contemporary. To be a citizen meant the opportunity to engage in the economy, seek wealth and status and influence the government to promote policies advantageous to one's economic interests. Given the absence of an hereditary aristocracy and an already entrenched economic elite in the American society, economic opportunities would be available to more citizens than in England or Europe. The American government, correspondingly, would be subject to multiple economic interests, thus becoming a more broadly based oligarchy or, in Aristotle's terms,[10] a moderate oligarchy. In Hamilton's vision of the American future the major elements of the contemporary political economy are already present. There are the expanding economy and the government's active role in its promotion; citizenship understood largely as participation in the economy (for most, employment in the economy); and political participation by the mass of citizens confined mostly to voting. There are the majority of Americans with no significant economic property (land or capital), dependent on private employers for jobs; the increasing disparity of wealth between the rich and the poor; and a void outside the culture of personal aggrandizement. Hamilton's policies did not bear immediate fruit. The largely agrarian economy, particularly in the South,[11] impeded the full development of an industrial society but by the end of the Civil War that impediment was eliminated and at the start of the twentieth century the Hamiltonian elements in American society were clearly recognizable.

The State of Contemporary American Democracy

The ecological political economy position confronts several related and increasingly suspect propositions advanced by the current economic and political system: that economic growth is without limits and that its globalization offers the promise of economic security for all; that democracy in America depends on unlimited economic growth; and that democracy elsewhere depends on a global free trade market. The ecological economic critique of limitless growth and its promise of generalizing American per capita income on a global scale has already been discussed. The ecological political economy perspective provides a critique of the claim that American democracy depends on unlimited economic growth and that it can be globalized through the widespread adoption of the structures and instrumentalities of the contemporary American economy.

This ecological perspective also rejects the analytic separation of politics and economics, a separation typically maintained in colleges and universities where politics and economics are taught in different departments. This separation of economics and politics is not countered by media accounts of the amount of money, hard and soft,[12] spent by and on candidates seeking office and by proposals to reform current campaign spending practices. Such accounts and proposals do not expose the deep penetration of economic values and motivations into politics and government policies. Even if legislation were passed to curtail significantly private contributions and personal spending and expand the public funding of political campaigns, the political agenda would still continue to be shaped primarily by the dominant economic interests that constantly push for more production and more consumption on both the national and global levels and in so doing largely shape the social practices and institutions of American society. A more level playing field for the funding of political campaigns, while desirable, will not ensure that the current subordination of politics to economics will be eliminated and that fundamentally different economic and political alternatives to the present system will be presented to the American public. If open political debate on serious national issues and alternative solutions is a criterion of a robust democracy, then absent such debate the condition of democracy in America is anemic. Universal suffrage is a necessary but not sufficient criterion for democracy. The right to vote abstracted from the economic dependency of most voters is not by itself an accurate measure of the condition of democracy in a society. To the extent that in the American society the deep structure of the economic system determines which policies will or will not be enacted, the exercise of the right to vote is more an exercise in a plebiscitary politics than an expression of democracy.

Criticism of the anemic state of American democracy is also forthcoming from writers whose point of reference is not ecological political economy. One such analyst is W. E. Hudson whose book, *American Democracy in Peril*[13] discusses seven challenges to a viable democratic future. Among these are the trivialization of politics, declining political participation by citizens, the overweening influence of business, and the national security state. All of these share one common feature not mentioned by Hudson: they are the result of the ideological dominance of an economic growth culture. Politics is trivialized because a national agenda has been set which is not open to serious debate.[14] Voting by the qualified electorate is barely 50 percent at the national presidential election, less in all other national elections and at the state and local level, and is causally connected to the trivialization of politics. The overweening influence of business on government policies and the election of candidates to office is a major factor in closing off debate on alternative visions for the American society and contributes in turn to the trivialization of politics and thus dampens interest in voting and participation in politics generally. The national security state is heavily invested in the technology of war, and military spending and procurement are a considerable boon to the corporate economy. The secrecy and unaccountability of the national security state, features which are inimical to a democracy, stem from the desire to minimize information about military spending and the small group of corporations which are its major beneficiaries and, more significant still, from the need to shield from public discussion the economic interests advanced by America's status as a military super power. The closing off of debate on issues characterized as dealing with national security once again trivializes politics and reduces political motivation among the general public.

Conventional responses to the need to resuscitate a flagging democracy have included amending the Constitution to allow for proportional representation in Congress, changing present state requirements for third parties to secure access to the ballot, campaign expenditure reform, automatic voter registration as in Europe, more televised debates with participation of third-party candidates, a national holiday during national elections, assured transportation for the elderly and disabled to the polls, and public school programs to acquaint students with the actual practices of American politics and government. All such suggestions, however desirable, address only the mechanics of the political process. From an ecological political economy perspective, they ignore the deep economic structure which remains unaffected by such reforms, even if millions of new voters were to be added to the voting lists and third parties were to secure representation in Congress.[15]

The following sections examine several writings which exemplify the key concepts of ecological political economy. Whatever their different emphases and nuances, these writings share a common judgment that existing political and economic institutions are progressively less accountable to a democratic public and that their continued existence implicitly legitimates the de facto dependence of most Americans on decisions made by political and economic elites. The popular interpretation of the dominant techno-industrial paradigm in the form of the American Dream significantly contains no promise of a democratic reawakening and renewed control by citizens of their destinies. Rather, the dream is replete with the cornucopia images of the consumer culture and the promise of unending material acquisition and consumption. Images of self-determination, empowerment, and community are not what the American dream is currently about. Accordingly, these same images developed as major themes in ecological political economy will be literally interpreted within the context of the dominant social paradigm as utopian or "no place." That ideas of democratic governance, self-determination of communities, and the political and economic empowerment of citizens should no longer resonate within the American popular culture is an indication of how thoroughly the taken-for-granted values and assumptions of the unending growth paradigm have permeated American society.

Morrison: Associative Democracy

Representative of the ecologic political economy approach to the current condition of American democracy is Roy Morrison's book, *Ecological Democracy*.[16] Emphasizing a theme frequently voiced in the ecological perspective on politics:

> Democracy is not engendered by reform from above, but by insistent action from below. An ecological democracy arises from popular ferment, aspiration for a better life, intolerance of the abuse of power, and collective and personal determination to build a just and enduring community. *It is the product of civil society, that realm of community and self-assertion that lies outside domains of ruling power.*[17]

Morrison describes ecological democracy as "decentralist, flexible and devolutionary"[18] and based on the empowerment of democratic, community-based associations. Such associations can be involved in all social and economic activities, including human-resource activities, and can serve to protect the community from potential polluters, for example, by nonviolent direct action. Associations can take many forms, from social clubs to nonprofit corporations, to local government organizations. Whatever their organizational form or content, they represent the basic instrumentality for moving power away from state and corporate bureaucracies.

> In broad compass, then, associative democracy is an attempt to redirect the capitalist industrial state toward a democratic cooperative commonwealth with power largely, but not entirely, shifted to civil society. Associative democracy aims to move from domination by large firms and government bureaucracies to a much more convivial, local, cooperative, and responsive social and economic order.[19]

Morrison describes three basic strategies for community empowerment. First, using tax support (providing start-up budgets from public revenues) to help establish democratic (one-member-one vote) community associations which would evolve to perform such social welfare functions as schooling, health care, and housing.[20] Second, assisting in the "parallel and interrelated growth of community-based and community-controlled democratic economic institutions: co-ops, nonprofit corporations, municipal corporations . . . and small businesses of all kinds (including banking, production, retail, and service businesses and institutions)."[21] Community economic development would be supported by providing start-up and working capital from public revenues and by recycling and reinvesting community income and savings within the community.[22] "Typically, in poor communities, consumer spending and social welfare transfer payments do not go to community-based, community-owned, or community-controlled businesses or institutions, and are not reinvested in the community."[23] Government funding for community economic development would not mean a bail-out in case of failure. Funding would be aimed at providing resources (training, technical assistance) community groups need if they are to have a realistic chance of achieving plans for which they are held accountable. Third, accepting the social wage (also referred to as guaranteed annual income or basic income) as a basic transitional principle "necessary in the long run to respond to changing economic and social realities."[24] These new economic and social realities include the production capacity of new technology which reduces the use of labor and makes full employment problematic, the widening gap between most Americans and the very rich, and the increasing unsustainability of an endless growth economy which promises employment for a growing population through ever accelerating production and consumption. Thus, Morrison states: "Reduction of the work week, job sharing and the social wage must be part of our long-term vision."[25]

The development of economic cooperatives represents for Morrison the crucial instrumentality for making a living independently of the employment offered by the corporate economy. The economic cooperative is the modern analogue (in a vastly different social and economic setting) of Jefferson's ward republics where independent farmers in control of their economic destiny related to one another through a network of community associations and a political system characterized by democratic participation and relative equality of economic resources. A contemporary version of Jefferson's ward republic economics and politics requires that members of a community be able to address their economic needs through community cooperative efforts, thus maintaining control and accountability over the economic policies that are vital to their security and well-being. The economic cooperative uncouples livelihood from the corporate sector and transforms politics at the level of the cooperative at least, into a politics of authentic democratic dialogue and decision. A crucial difference between the Jeffersonian ward republic and the modern economic cooperative, however, is that the first was based on the existing ownership of land by independent farmers. The latter does not begin with substantial economic resources, either capital or land, and must rely for start-up funds from membership fees or from subsidies from government, the same government which Morrison describes as socializing "the costs of providing terrain and attitudes sympathetic to industry"[26] and supporting through NAFTA and GATT the globalization of an economic system which places maximization of returns to corporate shareholders above the interest of communities and environments.

Morrison describes three existing cooperatives which could serve as models for efforts to uncouple livelihood from the corporate sector: Mondragon Cooperative in Spain, Seikatsu Consumer Cooperative Club in Japan, and Co-op Atlantic in Canada. Established in the 1940s, Mondragon has some 26,000 workers, 150 cooperative businesses including heavy industry and department stores with $3.1 billion in 1993 sales, a bank with billions of dollars in assets, a research center, a social insurance and health system, housing and an educational system from preschool to postgraduate technical education.[27] Each co-op is the basic unit of democratic decision making on the one-member-one vote principle. There is open enrollment with each member paying a one-time membership entrance fee. A Co-op Congress makes policy that affects all the co-ops but such policy must generally be voted on by each co-op. Morrison considers Mondragon "as a model of successful response to the forces transforming industrial civilization; a success that is not only economic but based on the conscious pursuit of both freedom and community."[28] The Seikatsu Consumer Cooperative Club was founded in 1965 in Tokyo for families to buy milk at affordable prices. It has since evolved into building alternative production, consumption, and social welfare units as well as an activist network involved in peace and ecological issues. In 1992, Seikatsu had 225,000 participating families, total sales of $700 million and some 161 worker collectives with 4,200 owner-workers.[29] The worker collectives are composed mainly of women and the largest collectives are now in home care for the ill and disabled. Morrison notes that since funding is not available from conventional banking sources, the worker collectives depend on membership to raise funds with some assistance from Seikatsu. Co-op Atlantic was established in 1927 and now includes 161 retail, producer, agricultural, housing and fishing cooperatives. It operates Atlantic People Housing, Ltd., a subsidiary that manages and contracts for co-op housing. Unlike Mondragon, Co-op Atlantic consumer co-ops are owned by members, not by the workers who are employees in the member-owned retail co-ops. Twenty-nine of the retail co-ops open only to co-op members use a direct charge system which requires a $30 initial investment, weekly contributions until the total reaches $600–$800 and weekly payments of $3 to cover operating costs. Members are entitled to substantial discounts on food, gasoline, and appliance purchases.[30] Currently, Co-op Atlantic is encouraging consumer co-ops to invest part of their surplus in community producer co-ops and members of producer co-ops to become more fully integrated in the cooperative system by becoming members of consumer co-ops.

These examples of existing cooperative efforts in different parts of the globe all have in common elements which define ecological democracy. Each allows its members to meet their economic needs through voluntary, collective effort. Each allows its members to participate directly in the decisions the cooperative must make. Each teaches the lesson of the importance of solidarity with other members in the cooperative. Each offers an alternative to employment and investment in the corporate economy.

The importance of cooperative social systems is not merely their economic success, but their significance as creative and amelioratory responses to industrial reality. Association, cooperation and confederation [multiple alliances of co-ops at different spatial and functional levels] in action are not means to better accomplish industrial ends; they are the counterweight to the consequences of industrial activity. . . . *Ecological democracy means the conscious melding of the political and social with the economic.*[31]

For Morrison, the "conscious melding of the political and social with the economic" means that market and planning mechanisms are seen as rooted in political choices and social values. In ecological democracy the effects of economic activity, not simply the prices, are considered. Pollution, resource depletion, species extinction, constraints on future generations created by the dominant economic system are not issues which can be decided by the market and the price system. "The focus of an ecologic economic system is on effectiveness and value, not on production and consumption."[32] Ecological democracy will produce and protect an ecological commons, a space or realm of activity where the rights and responsibilities of individuals are balanced with the rights and responsibilities of the community of individuals that uses the commons.[33] Morrison asserts that an ecological commons is sustainable because "the community has democratically chosen limits to its use"[34] and because in ecological democracy the concept of private property conventionally defined as the right to exclusive use of something even to its detriment (as clear-cutting of privately owned forest) is redefined and all property is "seen as having attributes of both personal and social or community property, protected by both individual and community."[35] The social and economic sustainability of an ecological commons in which a community economy replaces absentee ownership and managerial government with direct ownership and participatory democracy is possible, because the real costs and effects of economic activity are very quickly visible and cannot be externalized into the affected community. Economic activity in such an ecological commons is "not limited to protecting financial well-being, but must consider what is produced, how it is produced, why it is produced."[36] The what, how, and why are questions which must be resolved by the community to which they apply. To resolve such questions it is necessary, according to Morrison, to develop an industrial ecology which regulates production and consumption within an ecological commons. The three principles of ecologically sustainable industrial activity are the elimination of products and production methods that are toxic; a focus on efficiency in resource and energy use; and development of production and consumption based on reuse and recycling and the reclaiming of so-called waste as inputs for other production processes, for example, cogeneration in which waste heat is used to heat homes or businesses.

Along with an industrial ecology, Morrison might have suggested an agricultural ecology for the ecological commons, one found in organic farming today. "Organic farming began with a vision of ecological sustainability and a commitment to rebuilding community."[37] In the United States currently, CSA (community-supported agriculture) and subscription organic farms exist in many states and are, as the statement above indicates, committed to the same ecological sustainability and social community that Morrison describes as a hallmark of ecological democracy. A CSA is a group of food consumers who agree to support a farm by buying stock (or paying scheduled fees) in the farm, helping with the farm work, and dividing the produce among themselves. A subscription farm, as the CSA, requires pay-in-advance from members but unlike the CSA does not involve working on the farm or visiting the farm to pick up the produce. The CSA allows the members to physically experience the farm—"the soil, the smells, the animals, the look and feel of the countryside, the taste of food before it is processed, and the rhythms of the season"[38]—an experience missing in modern urban life and one which assists in understanding the elements of ecological sustainability, including limits, biodiversity, and interrelationships between humans and the natural environment. Ecological sustainability and community values are reflected in both CSA and subscription farms:

> Since CSA members recognize the farm as the source of quality produce, and feel connected to it, they are more committed to its survival and more willing to help out. Even subscription farms with minimal member participation educate consumers in organic values, while giving them a stake in political issues affecting sustainable agriculture such as ensuring the integrity of organic certification standards.[39]

The optimum size of a CSA in governance terms is determined by the presence or absence of effective member participation.

> If the volume of products becomes so large that multiple packing facilities need to be built and multiple shifts employed, then the

> CSA is getting too big to maintain the social relations of coop-
> erative face-to-face work groups and a sense of member partici-
> pation. . . . Do CSA members know the names of the delivering
> staff? Does the CSA coordinator recognize most members? Are
> resources allocated on the basis of status competition among
> managers? If an optimally sized CSA cannot meet consumer
> demand in its area, then it spins off another CSA, independently
> owned and operated.[40]

While the goal of the CSA is to achieve optimal size and maintain it, the goal
of large-scale industrial farming is to transform farming into an industrial
model with farm products becoming resource inputs which are then processed
and distributed to supermarkets. Farm machinery, chemicals, fertilizer, and
seeds are sold in an oligopolistic market in which four companies, for example, control 69 percent of the global pesticide market. The processing of
grain and beef, turkey, chicken, pork, and seafood is also dominated by a very
small number of corporations.[41] As the food chain becomes increasingly
controlled by vertically integrated (controlling the entire food process from
farm to supermarket) international corporations, ecological sustainability and
community are dispensed with. The corporations involved are in a position
because of their size to dictate commodity prices (buy cheap) and retail prices
(sell dear). To simplify processing and marketing operations, the corporations
standardize crops (genetic modification) and products. The focus is on brand
consistency, ingredient uniformity and high volume—the higher the volume
the lower the commodity prices. As commodity prices fall, producers react by
increasing volume still more by applying chemical fertilizers, increasing the
use and size of machinery, thereby necessitating increasing the amount of
land involved. Under the economic arrangements of the agribusiness oli-
gopoly, sustainable farming practices are not possible, farm communities
disintegrate, small farmers sell out and the cosmetic appearance insured by
the application of pesticides replaces the taste and quality of the produce. The
percentage of the consumer's food dollar that goes into input of machinery,
agrochemicals and seed, and the marketing activities of processing, shipping,
brokerage, advertising, and retailing has skyrocketed since 1910 when the
farmer's share of the consumer dollar was forty cents. "The typical U.S.
wheat farmer . . . gets just 6 cents of the dollar spent on a loaf of bread—so
when you buy the loaf, you're paying about as much for the wrapper as for
the bread."[42] In the CSA and subscription farms in contrast:

> The farmer benefits too. The connection channel [CSA and sub-
> scription farms] bypasses the middleman, giving farmers profit
> margins more comparable to the farmers market. The farmer can

retain a higher portion of the final selling price while bringing the cost to the consumer more in line with conventional agricultural products, thereby reaching more people. Advance ordering and knowledge of member preferences fine-tunes the planting process, reducing the farmer's risk of spoilage, surplus production, storage costs, and missed sales. With a pay-in-advance policy, the farmer gets the capital needed for planting and improvements.[43]

Robertson: Protecting Communities in a Global Economy

James Robertson in his article "The Economics of Local Recovery"[44] makes another argument for economic decentralization on the grounds that a globalizing economy seeking cheap labor makes full employment of the industrial labor force problematic and shows little evidence of improving the economic status of the masses of people in the less industrially developed nations.

> By the middle of the 20th century local economies throughout the industrial world had become largely dependent on outside employers to organize their work, outside suppliers to supply their needs (for food, energy, clothing, shelter, entertainment . . .) and outside agencies to provide for their health and welfare.[45]

Given the increased dependency of local economies on external sources, local communities have engaged in competitive bidding to attract outside employers. The result has frequently been that municipalities have subsidized such employers with the standard justification of increased employment and an enhanced tax base. Subsidies have taken the form of road building, police protection, tax relief, construction of water and sewer lines, donation of land for an industrial site, and informal exemption from environmental regulations.[46] Such inducements, however, do not guarantee the permanent stay of a new employer who may withdraw after reaping maximum benefits, nor do they guarantee that the best jobs will actually go to local workers or that subcontractors from the local area will be used. A full cost accounting of such subsidies may actually reveal that overall benefits are less than the overall costs. Moreover, the attempt to provide a stable economic base for a local community by relying on outside sources only makes the local economy more vulnerable to decisions made far outside the local community, decisions which in most cases are driven by profit-maximizing, not community-enhancing, motivations.

Local employment initiatives (LEIs) are efforts to "encourage the creation of genuinely local initiatives to organize local work to meet local needs with local resources."[47] Some local municipalities have developed programs aimed at the encouragement and support of LEIs. The focus on creating a stable economic base that can provide local employment with lessened vulnerability to shocks from the outside is apparent in a statement by the mayor of St. Paul, Minnesota, describing the goals of the Homegrown Economy Project:

> . . . [J]ob creation remains an important goal, but the project broadens the focus by emphasizing the most efficient managements of all local resources. Its goal is to extract the maximum value from the community's human, natural and technological resources. Its aggregate results will be significant increases in local wealth, added employment, a more diverse and resilient economic base, *increased citizen efficacy, and a self-reliant orientation among St. Paul's institutions.*[48]

Robertson describes some expected changes in consumer and production modes that will accompany the shift to greater local economic self-reliance: more people growing and cooking their own food, more purchases from local shops rather than supermarkets, local shops stocking more goods produced locally, improved opportunities for small local farmers and other small local producers to sell locally. The elimination of restrictive planning regulations which inhibit the siting of local enterprises and of subsidies to outside employers which create a bias against local enterprise will help to strengthen such tendencies. Robertson expects similar changes to more self-reliant behavior in the use and supply of energy. Decentralized solar energy technologies combined with conservation make it possible for a local community to reduce its dependence on external energy sources and to some extent cushion the local economy from the energy price fluctuations of the global market.

LEIs are distinguished from the economics of the private and public sectors by two distinct characteristics: their localness and their mixture of economic and noneconomic objectives, the latter referring to investment for purposes other than profit, such as, for example, investment in housing, health, and education.

> Encouragement from public authorities, local or national, for the setting up of community enterprises . . . will be an important form of social investment—investment in enabling local people to meet a greater proportion of their own needs for work and income, as well as for goods and services. This type of social investment of public funds in local self-reliance, in place of

expenditure programmes that perpetuate and even increase dependence on publicly provided social services, is likely to play an increasingly significant part in housing, health, education and other social services. . . .[49]

Robertson distinguishes four different sources of funds for investment in local economic development: national financial institutions (banks, insurance companies, pension funds), local financial institutions, large nonprofit organizations, and individual savers and investors, particularly local residents who wish to see their money invested in projects that reflect their purposes and values. Presently, the first and third sources cannot be expected to invest in local economic development that offers little assurance of a profit return comparable to that of investments in national and global markets. The second source of private sector social investment, local financial institutions, can play an important role in funding LEIs since the prosperity of local banks, local insurance companies, and other local financial institutions depends on the prosperity of the local economy. The trend toward the centralization of the financial system and the outflow of local funds into national and international money markets, however, can weaken even the commitment of local financial institutions to local communities. Robertson provides several examples of local financial initiatives for local economic development in both developed and developing countries. In Chicago there is the South Shore Bank that serves as a revolving loan fund for the Institute for Community Economics which allows private foundations and corporations (including local banks and churches) to invest in local enterprises. In Oregon the Association for Regional Agriculture Building the Local Economy (ARABLE) enables local people in rural areas to invest in small-scale projects that increase local self-reliance. In India the Self-Employed Women's Association (SEWA), a trade union representing poor women working in the unorganized sector as vegetable and fruit sellers, seamstresses, and similar occupations, set up its own bank to provide savings and deposit facilities to enable women to keep their cash safely, credit to support income-generating activities, technical and management assistance, loans against jewelry to avoid pawnbrokers, and deposit-linked insurance.[50] Such grassroots banking initiatives can provide similar financial assistance to deprived communities in the industrialized nations. In Massachusetts, the Self-Help Association for a Regional Economy (SHARE) is a community land trust which finances local development, raising the money needed to purchase land to be held collectively by using the value of the land itself as security. In local communities where the standard currency is scarce or unavailable, the Local Employment and Trade System (LETS) allows economic activity to take place through a local exchange arrangement such as one on the west coast of Canada whose members issue and manage the money used within it in the form of claims on themselves. Every member has an account, as in a banking system. Every account starts at zero and then records the member's net credit or debit balance with other members of the system. The system as a whole is exactly balanced, the total debit of the members in debt being exactly equal to the total credits of those in credit.[51]

In connection with SHARE in Massachusetts, the local currency called Berkshares is indexed against the United States dollar according to the going local dollar price of cordwood, a basic local commodity. A local bank handles exchanges between Berkshares and dollars as deposits into and withdrawals from accounts opened by SHARE.

Robertson's focus on strengthening the economies of local communities derives from his conviction that the "present course of national and international development in the economic and financial sphere may not be sustainable for more than a few years longer,"[52] and that policies aimed at encouraging self-reliant local economies which can buffer to some extent the negative impacts of faltering national and international markets, represent "prudent contingency planning"[53] and a "Sane Ecological vision of the future."[54]

Bookchin: Libertarian Municipalism

For Murray Bookchin in his *Remaking Society,*[55] the chief impetus to decentralization is not the need to provide employment in local economies now destabilized by national and international markets (in itself a desirable goal), but the need to combat hierarchy and domination in the human community, a hierarchy and domination which set the stage for the domination and destruction of nature.

> . . . [A]ll our notions of dominating nature stem from the very real domination of human by human. . . . [T]he domination of human by human *preceded* the notion of dominating nature. Indeed, human domination of human gave rise to the very *idea* of dominating nature.[56]

Bookchin maintains that most contemporary social ideologies have assumed, wrongly, that to free humans from the domination of nature it has been necessary historically and to the present day to "harness human beings . . . in the form of slaves, serfs and workers"[57] in order to harness nature for human use.

It is the task of a social ecology, according to Bookchin, to search out all systems of command, coercion, and obedience that preceded and can coexist with forms of domination associated with the emergence of economic classes, systems that are not economically motivated but represent cultural forms of domination

> that exist in the family, between generations and sexes, among ethnic groups, in institutions of political, economic and social management, and very significantly, in the way we experience reality as a whole, including nature and nonhuman life-forms.[58]

Bookchin argues that early preliterate societies were marked by supportive and community-oriented values such as the principle of the irreducible minimum which entitled all individuals to the means of life regardless of the individual's productive contribution to the community.[59] A substantive rather than formal[60] equality existed in these early societies, along with respect for the individual,[61] a usufruct[62] principle toward things and a non-exploitive view of nature. Such societies were also characterized by complementary roles of women and men.

> Indeed, it is doubtful that an early human community could have survived if gender-oriented cultures initially tried to exercise any commanding position, much less an antagonistic one, over the other. . . . We easily forget that early human communities were really domestic societies structured mainly around the work of women, and were often strongly oriented in reality, as well as mythology, toward women's world.[63]

Bookchin describes the purported causes and associated events that brought about the emergence of hierarchies and classes. Age was the original source of hierarchy. The old, the most vulnerable members of the community, were also the living repositories of the traditions and collective experience of the community, especially so in the absence of a written language. Vulnerable as they were, the old "may have been more disposed to enhance their status, to surround it with a quasi-religious aura and social power, as it were, that rendered them more secure with the loss of their physical power."[64] A male-female hierarchy was engendered by male biological characteristics that made possible the physical domination of women. As communities were caught up in intercommunal conflict engendered by expanding populations, the domestic sphere of women was subordinated to the civil sphere where systematic warfare and institutionalized violence required material resources drawn from women's domain.

Out of the skin of the most able hunter emerged a new kind of
creature: the "big man" who was also a "great warrior." Shortly,
every domain of preliterate society was reoriented toward maintaining his heightened "civil" functions. The blood oath, based on
kinship loyalties, was gradually replaced by oaths of fealty by his
soldierly "companions" who were drawn from clans other than
his own. . . .[65]

Hierarchy which first appeared in gerontocracy, the rule of the old, gradually
expanded its ambit

as "big men" began to dominate "small men," when warriors and
their "companions" began to gradually dominate their followers,
when chiefs began to dominate the community, and finally, when
nobles began to dominate peasants and serfs.[66]

Following the logic of the parable of the tribes,[67] once a hierarchical
and oppressive society appears, it forces other societies to reshape themselves
along similar lines if they are to survive. The state appeared in history, says
Bookchin, as the institutionalized apex of a patriarchal civilization. Rejecting
the Marxist definition of the state, Bookchin maintains that the state historically does not necessarily represent an institutionalized system of violence
which defends the interests of a specific ruling class.[68] Ancient empires such
as the Egyptian were seen as the ruler's household and the people as his
servants. Fully developed states, those entities that practice statecraft and are
rooted in class interest,[69] appeared first in modern Europe.

The nation-state, as we know it today, finally divests politics[70] of
all its seemingly traditional features: direct democracy, citizen's
participation in the affairs of governmental life, and sensitive
responsiveness to the communal welfare. The word "democracy"
itself undergoes degradation. It becomes "representative" rather
than face-to-face; highly centralized rather than fully confederal
between relatively independent communities, and divested of its
grassroots institutions. Educated, knowledgeable citizens become
reduced to mere taxpayers who exchange money for "services"
and education surrenders its civic orientation to a curriculum
designed to train the young for financially rewarding skills.[71]

Developing a theme reminiscent of Jean-Jacques Rousseau's *Discourse
on Inequality*, Bookchin states that there were certain turning points in history

which led to priestly, monarchical and other statist institutions and away from matricentric and nonhierarchical communities. One of those turning points was the rise of the city, a territorial arena in which the individual was identified by place of residence and economic interests, rather than by ancestral connections based on consanguinity. In the city, communal ownership of land and resources was replaced by private property; classes emerged based on the ownership and management of land and resources. While the city accepted the "outsider" in a way that tribal societies based on blood ties never did and thus adumbrated the notion of a common humanity, its class structures and its privatization of property resulted in the loss of such earlier values as usufruct, the complementary social roles of women and men, and the principle of the irreducible minimum.[72] Again echoing Rousseau, Bookchin states that "all of humanity's extraordinary gains under civilization have always been tainted by the 'evil' of hierarchy."[73]

Europe in the Middle Ages was at a turning point with its mixed economy of serfs, tenant farmers, yeoman,[74] and craftsman all of whom coexisted with capitalists who were mostly engaged in commerce rather than industry. There were periods in the Middle Ages when there existed a balance between town and country, crafts and agriculture, city dwellers and food cultivators, and technological innovation and cultural constraints on such innovation. In the sixteenth century, Europe, according to Bookchin, vacillated between the alternatives of a confederation of cities and the nation-state. Neither the nation-state nor capitalism was an historical necessity. As regards the latter, European culture in the sixteenth and seventeenth centuries did not fully embrace capitalist values of competition and accumulation. The classic principle of moderation or the golden mean, the rejection of competition as the core of human relationships, and the tendency of the early bourgeoisie to emulate the values of the landed gentry were all impediments to the efflorescence of a fully developed capitalist culture. The ascendance of capitalism in England and its displacement of precapitalist culture on the European continent gradually eliminated these impediments.

> The upsurge of English capitalism in the eighteenth century, and its global outreach in the nineteenth century, altered such prospects [of balance between town and country, crafts and agriculture, etc.] radically. For the first time, competition was seen to be "healthy"; trade as "free"; accumulation, as evidence of "parsimony"; and egoism, as evidence of a self-interest that worked like a "hidden hand" in the service of the public good. . . . No human values and communities were warped any less than the ecosystems of plants and animals that were despoiled in the original

forests of Africa and South America. . . . Capitalism divided the human species against itself as sharply and brutally as it divided society against nature.[75]

For Bookchin, capitalism is at odds with evolutionary processes. The evolution of nature and human society toward greater differentiation and the development, on a planetary level, of greater subjectivity and consciousness are negated by capitalism[76] which disregards limits and "embodies every social disease— from patriarchal values, class exploitation, and statism to avarice, militarism, and now, growth for the sake of growth. . . ."[77] Thus, capitalism represents the culmination of a social development which was not inevitable but which combined such historically contingent events as the English economy and state in the seventeenth century that opened the way for the rise of a capitalist class and exacerbated such inveterate characteristics of human society as hierarchy and status. Capitalism makes authentic freedom impossible. Demands for justice in a capitalist system are at best only demands for corrective alterations in a society that is basically unfree and should not be confused with attempts to achieve a free society. To achieve a free society, there must exist the will to move beyond hierarchy and statism and toward a fundamental reconstruction of the existing social system. To be free for Bookchin means to be free to function as an ethical being, as one who makes reasoned choices of alternative values and actions. The individual as a market egoist, the capitalist version of freedom, or as the instrument of historical forces, the totalitarian version of freedom, is not free. Bookchin points to Marx's own failure to define the task of reconstructing society in truly libertarian terms. Marx accepted capitalist industrial concentration, large-scale technology and the centralized state as preconditions for a proletarian revolution. Workers were seen primarily as economic beings rather than as individuals with a wide range of interests outside of economics.

> . . . [T]he Marxian revolutionary project reinforced the very degradation, deculturalization, and depersonalization of the workers produced by the factory system. The worker was at his best as a good trade unionist or a devoted party functionary, not as a culturally sophisticated being with wide human and moral concerns.[78]

Classic Marxism[79] thus celebrated economic and political centralization and industrial nationalization aimed at maximum production and consumption. Reason was identified with the instrumental engineering of control over nature and people, and nature was viewed as an ensemble of objects useful for economic purposes.

In the 1960s, the New Left went beyond Marx and redefined the task of reconstructing society on the premise that technology offered the promise of affluence and leisure for all.[80] Work was no longer an historical necessity and sexual repression was no longer required to channel libidinal energies into work.[81] The realm of necessity could now be supplanted by the realm of freedom, and participatory democracy or transparent social relations in which the subjects involved would determine their destinies, would replace elite control. While Marxism offered a theory of the material conditions for freedom (in which the full development of capitalism was a necessary precondition for the proletarian revolution) the New Left sounded the anti-hierarchical, decentralizing, communal and sensuous values that had been the hallmark of the pre-Marxian utopian writings of William Morris and Charles Fourier.[82] As the New Left waned after the end of the Vietnam War, the American environmental movement began to wax. Bookchin believes that American environmentalism has always been linked to a mystical passion for wilderness which provides a sense of freedom from the routinized urban-business life, demonstrates the fecundity of life, encourages a love of nonhuman life forms and aids in the development of a richer aesthetic outlook and appreciation of the natural world. This same passion for the wilderness can and does lead, in some instances, to a misanthropy, which sees humans as the cause of environmental degradation and fails to make the connection which social ecology makes between hierarchy, the domination of humans, and the domination of nature. Unlike the wilderness movement with its often simplistic condemnation of the human race for its destruction of the natural environment, social ecology distinguishes between those who control the economic decisions that denature the environment and those who must live with these decisions. Social ecology, therefore, requires that the currently centralized political and economic institutions be replaced by nonhierarchical and decentralized communities that promote eco-technologies like solar power, organic agriculture, humanly scaled industries, face-to-face democratic forms of governance and are compatible with the ecosystems in which they are located.[83]

Bookchin's political principles, which he labels libertarian municipalism,[84] rest on the premise that "every normal human being is *competent* to manage the affairs of society and more specifically, the community in which he or she is a member."[85] For Bookchin, no substantive or authentic democracy is possible unless people, as in classical Athens, can meet in face-to-face assemblies to decide on policies which affect the community. Members of the community cannot delegate decision-making power to representatives without losing their democratic rights. The administration of popularly decided policies, however, can be delegated to accountable others. "Popular assemblies are the minds of a free society; the administration of their policies are the hands."[86] Bookchin assumes that no population can be so large or the number of popular assemblies so numerous that coordination cannot maintain the integrity of face-to-face policymaking. "Delegates to town, city, and regional bodies, can be regarded simply as the walking mandates of the local assemblies."[87] Bookchin regards the city, despite its historical association with classes and hierarchy, as the space where citizens meet to decide the future. The city as a terrain for reflective citizenship is not today's megalopolis but a human-scale city which fits the Aristotelian description of a city large enough to meet the material needs of its inhabitants but small enough to allow face-to-face relationships among inhabitants.

> Although [popular] assemblies can function as networks on a
> block, neighborhood, or town level, they fulfill traditional ideals
> of civic democracy when the cities in which they are located are
> decentralized. The anarchic vision of decentralized communities,
> united in free confederations or networks for coordinating the
> communities of a region, reflects the traditional ideals of a par-
> ticipatory democracy in a modern radical context.[88]

Current "citizens" are constituents of the state who live in urbanized areas, not true cities, and are the objects of statecraft, not the subjects of politics. The ethical content of city life as an arena for the practice of civic virtue, democracy, and social responsibility is replaced in the megalopolis by such economic concerns as income, taxes, growth, and employment. Bookchin emphasizes that libertarian municipalism is about a movement (not about isolated instances in which the people in one community assume democratic control and restructure the municipality on the basis of neighborhood assemblies), that "alters one community after another and establishes a system of confederal relationships between municipalities, one that will form a regional power in its own right."[89] Such a movement is, for Bookchin, an ecological imperative given the data now available on the environmental impact of a globalizing industrial capitalism. The very real threat to the material and natural basis of human life on the planet calls for decentralization, a balance with nature and the harmonization of social relations.

> Decentralization of large cities into humanly scaled communities
> is neither a romantic mystification of a nature-loving soloist nor
> is it a remote anarchic ideal. It has become indispensable to an
> ecologically sound society. What is now at stake in these seem-
> ingly "utopian" demands is a choice between a rapidly degrading
> environment and a society that will live in balance with nature in
> a viable and on a sustainable basis.[90]

Libertarian municipalism offers perspectives on technology and private property in line with its call for a balance with nature. No one can have a moral, social or ecologically based right to own property on which the lives of others depend; nor does anyone have a right to design, employ, or impose privately owned technology on society that damages human health and the health of the planet. Technology when divested of any moral constraints becomes demonic.

To advance the ideas of libertarian municipalism, a new politics must be structured around the problems of the individual's immediate environment, such as housing, neighborhood problems, transportation facilities, economic conditions, pollution issues, and workplace conditions, with political power steadily shifted to neighborhoods and municipalities in the form of community centers, cooperatives, occupational centers, and, finally, citizen assemblies. An ecological community would municipalize its economy (land, factories, workshops, and distribution centers) which would be controlled by popular assemblies of citizens. An ecological community would be characterized by the use of soft energy, bicycle transportation, niches for wildlife, wilderness areas, organic farming, industrial installations based on small, multipurpose machines, production of durable quality goods and minimal expenditure of energy as such. Work would be rotated between town and county and between everyday tasks.[91] Bookchin states that every revolutionary project is an educational one, complemented by objective reality, and that every such project must make contact with the popular longings of the people "and find ways to rework them into the contemporary [libertarian municipalism] ideals of freedom."[92]

> Perhaps the greatest single failing of movements for social reconstruction . . . is their lack of a politics that will carry people beyond the limits established by the status quo. Politics today means duels between top-down bureaucratic parties for electoral office that offer vacuous programs for "social justice" to attract a nondescript "electorate." . . . To the modern political imagination, "politics" is precisely a body of techniques for holding power in representative bodies—notably the legislative and executive arenas—not a moral calling based on rationality, community and freedom. . . . [Libertarian municipalism] . . . is an effort to work from latent or incipient democratic possibilities toward a radically new configuration of society itself—a communitarian society oriented toward meeting human needs, responding to ecological imperatives and developing a new sensibility based on sharing and cooperation.[93]

Sale: The Bioregional Project

The social ecology of Bookchin represents an important contribution to eco-logical political economy. Another major contribution, based on a bioregional vision, rather than on an analysis of the history of the roots of hierarchy in human society and its linkage to the domination of nature, is Kirkpatrick Sale's *Dwellers in the Land*.[94] A bioregion is defined as any part of the earth's surface whose boundaries are determined by such natural characteristics as fauna, flora, climate, landforms, and soil. Bioregions include human settle-ments and the cultures that have developed within and been influenced by the features of the bioregion. The largest bioregion is the ecoregion of which there are some forty that can be identified in the United States. An example of an ecoregion is the Ozark Plateau. Smaller than an ecoregion is a georegion of which the White River watershed in the Ozark Plateau is an example. Smaller yet is a morphoregion characterized by human settlements adapted to the landscape, and it is at this scale that it is possible to speak of the existence of an effective response to ecological problems.

> For if there is any scale at which ecological consciousness can be developed, at which citizens can see themselves as being the *cause* for the environmental *effect*, it is at the regional level; there all ecological questions are taken out of the realm of the philo-sophical and the moral and are dealt with as immediate and per-sonal. People do not, other things being equal, pollute and damage those natural systems on which they depend for life and liveli-hood if they see directly what is happening. . . .[95]

From an evolutionary perspective, all life is organized into communities which are self-sufficient collections of different species that have adapted to the conditions of their material surroundings. Communities of species interact with one another and maintain a flexible balance in their interactions with populations of communities fluctuating (more rabbits, more foxes; then fewer rabbits and fewer foxes) within a more or less constant range. Humans, too, live in communities both in the human and in the surrounding communities of nonhuman life. Sale maintains that for most of their existence humans lived in "clusters of 500 to 1,000 people for the basic village or intimate settlement and 5,000 to 10,000 for the larger tribal associations or extended community."[96] Modern industrial cities of even half a million inhabitants act as colonizers of the surrounding area extracting resources from an ever-widening area—the region, the nation and, in the global economy, the world—and returning its wastes to these areas. "The contemporary high-rise city, in short, is an ecological parasite as it extracts its life-load from elsewhere and an ecological pathogen as it sends back its wastes."[97] Sale maintains that the small community has always had a better developed sense of place and has exercised an ecological wisdom made possible by the feedback systems and information loops that can operate effectively on a scale where people can come to know the maximum number of other people with some degree of intimacy and can retain a sense of self within a community. Developing the potential of a local or regional place requires liberating the self from distant markets, corporations, and governments, and from ignorance of practical ways to utilize resources and opportunities available in the locality.

> It will take some time before people recognize that the project of understanding place is neither nostalgic nor utopian but rather the realistic sort of occupation anyone can participate in every day that has an immediate and practical chance of curbing our present waste and recklessness. . . . [I]t is not the bioregional task that is irrelevant but precisely the business-as-usual politics of *all* the major parties of *all* the major industrial nations, not one of which has made ecological salvation a significant priority, not one of which is prepared to abandon or even curtail the industrial economy that is imperiling us.[98]

The bioregional perspective on an appropriate economy stresses conservation, stability, self-sufficiency,[99] and cooperation. What Sale describes as the industrial-scientific paradigm stresses exploitation, change defined synonymously with progress, a world economy, and competition. For bioregionalism, an appropriate economy depends on a minimum number of goods and a minimum amount of environmental disruption, along with a maximum use of renewable resources and human labor and ingenuity. Energy sources would be solar and renewable; transportation would be electric and human-powered; agriculture would be organic with markets adapted to seasonal and regional foods, supplemented by greenhouse products; industry would utilize local artisans and crafts people and emphasize nonpolluting production processes and quality and durability of goods. Sale maintains that a community of ten thousand people can provide the agricultural, industrial, and service functions necessary for a decent life, with some one thousand individuals providing the labor needed to sustain the industrial base.[100] Overall, an appropriate bioregional economy would reduce the throughput of matter and energy, minimize production, encourage recycling and conservation, and hold population and stocks, industrial and agricultural, at fairly constant levels. Such an economy would aim at sustainability, living within the limits of bioregional resources, rather than at growth. Bioregional economics would be less vulnerable to outside disruptive economic influences. Various bioregions would need to practice import substitution to eliminate or substantially reduce dependence on imported foods and materials. Bioregions without indigenous wood supplies would look to local building materials such as adobe or brick. Bioregions that are presently major meat exporters and produce importers would have to set aside land for farming. Bioregional currencies like the Local Employment and Trade System (LETS) would provide freedom from currency fluctuations and could be confined to the region to avoid capital flight. Since no bioregion could be completely self-sufficient, a flow of economic information among bioregions would be expedited by use of the internet, as in the case of a bioregional group in Austin, Texas, the Center for Maximum Potential Building Systems, which discovered practical uses for the mesquite trees growing abundantly in their area but regarded as a weed by contacting two bioregions in Argentina and Uruguay.[101]

> Self-sufficiency . . . is not the same thing as isolation, nor does it preclude all kinds of trade at all times. It does not *require* connections with the outside, but within strict limits—the connections must be nondependent, nonmonetary, and noninjurious—it allows them. And, in one area, it encourages them. . . . Indeed, it may be the self-sufficient society that most needs information from without—about new techniques and inventions, new materials and designs, and innovations scientific, cultural, technical, political and otherwise.[102]

The bioregions would be characterized by communal ownership modeled after the community land trust (CLT) which is a nonprofit corporation open to all members of a local community that purchases a tract of land to be held in trust in perpetuity and rents parcels of the land to individual members on long-term, low-cost leases which are renewable and inheritable. The use of the parcels is regulated by the original agreements made by the trust concerning ecological practices, types of buildings permitted and related matters. Sale states that "people should not be allowed to *own* the land, or its ores, or its trees, any more than they can own the sky and its clouds. . . ."[103] Fields, factories, workshops, and stores should be owned by the community with individuals and families given usufruct rights to land and goods.

The politics of a bioregion would necessarily reflect bioregional economic structures and values. Bioregional politics would emphasize decentralization, interdependence of human and nonhuman communities, and diversity with different bioregions developing political forms suitable to their culture and values. Some of the political forms might not be compatible with the political systems of other bioregions and might even harbor social tendencies that are at variance with general norms of social behavior. Sale argues that aberrant behavior would be marginalized and contained in any bioregion by strong community bonds forged by the economic security and stability of the bioregion, and by the widespread consensus on communal and ecological principles created by the active participation of citizens in the life of each bioregion. Even the most virulent antisocial behavior of a bioregion would be less likely to affect other bioregions given the decentralization of economic and political institutions than would similar behavior in centralized and increasingly globalized societies. Thus, diversity is as important to healthy human societies as it is in nature where it contributes to ecosystem stability and resiliency when environmental disruptions occur.

> Diversity has its own special values, its own nurturant complexities; and it is to be welcomed even though at times it may give rise to the unwanted novelty, the unpleasant mutant, and even though in human systems it may allow those practices that stem from the baser rather than the nobler motives.[104]

Bioregional politics emphasizes power flowing upward incrementally from the smallest to the largest political unit within confederal arrangements. Governments that are not grounded in communities which themselves are rooted in their natural surroundings are dangerous to stability and security. Sale contends that bioregionally based government can better provide for the liberty, equality, efficiency, welfare, and security that are currently promoted as the legitimate goals of government. The division of power among bioregions promotes liberty in that it prevents the concentration of power and allows individuals in each bioregion to shape their own destinies. Equality is similarly promoted by the dispersion of power both politically and economically within the bioregion and is enhanced by the strong sense of community and sharing that is part of bioregional culture. Efficiency is promoted by the ability of bioregional citizens and institutions to respond to problems which are localized and about which there is accurate information. Welfare is better served on a bioregional level because communities know their members and can address their needs more quickly and efficiently. Security is enhanced because communities foster a cohesiveness and loyalty that discourages crime and internal disruption and because the political and economic institutions are under local control and thus subject to timely correction by the citizens of a bioregion themselves. As in nature, so in the bioregions, hetarchy, which involves distinction without rank, prevails over hierarchy, which bases power and rank on distinctions of gender, race, age, wealth, birth. If power exists in a bioregion, it rests with the totality of citizens, not with a specific group, institution, or office. Unlike the superficial notion of citizenship, which prevails in the modern nation-state, citizens of a bioregion can regularly participate in the ongoing deliberations of the community which center on the ever-evolving interactions between the human and the natural environment. Citizenship in a bioregion brings forth the multifarious talents, energies, and insights that constitute the human resources of a bioregion.

> Where all individuals are citizens . . . the true powers of comple-
> mentarity are revealed. The strong hues and delicate tints, the
> bold splashes and slender lines, the full range of color and value,
> of shape and pattern, are evident in the canvas of a community's
> civic life, all parts contributing to the smoothness, the strength,
> even the magnificence of the whole. There is no meaning, no
> value, to hierarchy here; it would only be stifling and enervating,
> scorned as the impediment to community that it is.[105]

America historically has been a nation of regions, a fact which according to Sale has not escaped the notice of some historians, city planners, and government commissions. Among those understanding the importance of region in American life were Frederick Jackson Turner who recognized that national legislation was determined more by sectional interests than party voting; Lewis Mumford who advocated regional planning for permanent human communities protecting their social and physical environments;[106] Howard Odum who defined regionalism as the philosophy and technique of self-help and self-development; and the National Resources Committee commissioned by the federal government in the 1930s to provide a report on the regional factor in national development and planning which concluded that the problems to be treated did not follow state lines but resolved themselves into regional elements which were not amenable to treatment through existing state and national political institutions.

Bioregionalism is connected to present concerns about the environment; to feminism with its focus on nurturing and communality; to distrust of bigness in government and in the economy. According to Sale, bioregionalism offers the possibility of uniting the Left and the Right in America because its values of local control, self-reliance, decentralization, and community power represent traditional or Jeffersonian values which can be shared by the National Rifle Association hunter in Pennsylvania and the environmentalist in Colorado.[107] Bioregionalism does not take aim at the national government by organizing constituencies on a national scale and nominating candidates for national office. It aims at local action where the problems are more tractable precisely because they are local and can be addressed through the human resources of the bioregion. Bioregionalism represents gradualism, evolution, not revolution which all too frequently has the unpleasant habit of continuing, albeit in altered form, the very institutions and conditions it was meant to erase. People have to be educated to understand the potentialities of the human and natural resources in their bioregion. They have to learn the active mode of citizenship. They have to come to believe that they themselves can help themselves and shape a decent future from their own resources. Bioregionalism, says Sale, is a realistic project since it does not demand a new human nature or revolutionary new technologies, including those which would enable humans to live on space stations once the planet is rendered uninhabitable by current economic and political practices. Bioregionalism has another important feature. It is the space where green politics can flourish, because it is in the bioregion that the principles of green politics can be applied: human-scale economics, self-government, the preservation of nature, conservation of natural resources, and the interdependence of nature and human communities. Given the results of the Green Party campaign in the 2000 election and the strategic question of what is to be done during the next four years, Sale's comment on green politics is quite prescient:

> . . . [T]o be successful it [Green politics] will perforce be region-
> ally grounded and it will have to understand itself in bioregional
> terms, as bioregionalism's political face. It will need to take the
> bioregional message into all the niches of the established system,
> whether that means appearing before a township planning com-
> mission, or running candidates for a county water board, or elect-
> ing an ecologically oriented slate to a city council, or petitioning
> a regional air-pollution authority, or lobbying the state fish-and-
> game office. . . .[108]

The Green Party and Ecological Political Economy

The Green Party Platform 2000[109] reflects the focus on decentralization, empowerment of citizens at the local level, economic self-reliance, and pro-tection of the environment typical of ecological political economy. The Plat-form Preamble states that democracy is practiced most effectively in local communities; calls for environmental and economic sustainability, which balances the interests of the market and business with the interests of the community, the land, and living and future generations; and urges the creation of a diverse social environment characterized by a sense of community.

Green Key Values include grassroots democracy ("Every human being deserves a say in the decisions that affect their lives and not be subjected to the will of another"); ecological wisdom ("Human societies must operate

with the understanding that we are part of nature, not separate from nature");
decentralization ("Centralization of wealth and power contributes to social
and economic injustice, environmental destruction, and militarization"); and
community-based economics and economic justice ("We support . . . cooperatives and public enterprises that distribute resources and control to more
people through democratic participation").

Under Political Reform, the platform calls for campaign finance reform
and adoption of various proportional representation voting systems. It states
that the Green Party will move toward bioregional confederations that address
regional issues based on ecosystem boundaries instead of the traditional
political boundaries. The support of citizen involvement at all levels of the
decision-making process is extended to the creation of "children's parlia-
ments" through which children would elect their peer representatives to meet
with and make proposals to city councils and school boards. Under Tax
Justice/Fairness, the platform urges a tax policy that encourages small and
socially responsible business and ends subsidies to large corporations. Environmental taxes, such as taxes on environmental pollution, would assist in
achieving the full cost pricing of industrial goods and processes and would
partially replace income taxes. Under Management-Labor Relations, the platform states that because the decisions a company makes affects its employees, consumers, and the surrounding communities, "people in each of these
groups must be empowered to participate in economic decision-making."
Under Environmental Sustainability, Land Use, the platform states that "Greens
are advocates for the Earth. All the rivers, lakes, landscapes, forests and
wildlife" and calls for restructuring economic and political institutions to
conform to bioregional realities of scale and resources. Ownership and use of
land should be social at the community and regional level in the form of
community land trusts under covenants of ecological responsibility.

Communities must be designed with a focus on energy efficiency, appropriate or human scale, and integrated land use which provides easy access
between residences and work, school, local food supply, cultural and medical
facilities, and recreation and natural areas. Individual motorized transport
should be minimized through the provision of mass transit and bicycle and
pedestrian paths. Urban sprawl can be countered by such policies as urban
growth boundaries, tax base sharing between urban and suburban areas, fair
housing policies, and metropolitan mass transit. Under Environmental
Sustainability, Agriculture, the platform calls for the "establishment of an
ecologically based sustainable agricultural system that moves as rapidly as
possible toward regional/bioregional self-reliance," thus regionalizing the food
system and decentralizing agricultural lands, production, and distribution.
Under Economic Sustainability, Eco-nomics, the platform calls for a mixed
economic system with private business, democratic cooperatives, publicly

owned enterprises, and alternative economic structures,[110] so that human and ecological interests balance the profit motive. Community-based economics is seen as an alternative to both corporate capitalism and state socialism and reflects the Green commitment to diversity and decentralization. "Humanizing economic relations is just one aspect of our broader objective to consciously and deliberately (albeit gradually) shift toward a different way of life—characterized by sustainability, regionalization, a more harmonious balance between the natural ecosphere and the human-made technosphere, and a revival of community life."

Under Community Involvement, the platform advocates policies which will promote locally owned small businesses, local production and consumption and consumer cooperatives, credit unions, microloan funds and local currencies, and other institutions that assist community economic development. Such policies will enable municipalities to approve or disapprove proposed large economic developments on a case by case basis utilizing such criteria as environmental impact, local or outside ownership, reinvestment in the community, wages and working conditions. Endorsed are town meetings "which express a community's wishes on economic decision-making directly to local institutions and organizations." Under Small Business and Job Creation, the platform favors making loans available to small businesses at rates which are competitive to those offered to large corporations. Opposed are disinvestment practices whereby financial institutions move money deposited in local communities out of the same communities. "As lending institutions have obligations to the health of their local communities, we oppose arbitrary or discriminatory practices which act to deny small business access to credit and expansion capital." Home and neighborhood based businesses should be encouraged by forward-looking planning, not obstructed by out-of-date zoning ordinances.

Under Rural Development, the platform calls for a rural development policy that aims at protecting and sustaining the family farm which is "the backbone of a sustainable rural economy."[111] Family farms are more likely than corporate agribusiness to be ecologically sensitive to the land, use more labor than energy-intensive farming practices, and support agricultural biodiversity. Because of their smaller scale and farming practices, they are also more likely to produce foods that are healthier for consumers. The platform urges state-assisted product marketing efforts and rural development banks to provide low-interest loans and capital expansion funds to family farms and encourages cooperative efforts to broaden markets for local producers. Under Banking for People, the platform calls for the extension of the Community Reinvestment Act which provides public information on housing loans, small business loans, loans to minority-owned businesses, investment in community development projects, and affordable housing. Recommended

is Congressional legislation to charter community development banks, capitalized with public funds, to meet the current needs of local communities.
Under Pension Reform, the platform states that working people who own
over three trillion dollars in pension monies should have control over where
their money is invested. "The irony of investing pension funds in corporate
decisions that undercut workers' rights, employment and retirement while
hugely rewarding nonproductive speculation should no longer be ignored."

The Green Party Platform 2000 thus clearly focuses on the major themes
of an ecological political economy: political and economic self-determination, political and economic decentralization, community empowerment,
bioregional scale, economic and environmental sustainability, and balanced
and harmonious interactions of human and ecosystem communities of life.

Ecological Political Economy and Environmental Politics

It is necessary at this point to differentiate sharply between ecological political economy and what, as in Walter A. Rosenbaum's book, is referred to as
environmental politics and policy.[112] The latter operates within the context of
a capitalist growth economy ideologically founded on the dominant techno-
industrial paradigm. It is within this context that government regulations to
address environmental degradation must be understood. On the one hand, the
private economy is the chief engine of economic growth and employment. In
this role, the private economy receives government support and encouragement through various policies. A failing economy inevitably costs the party
in office the national election. On the other hand, to maintain its legitimacy
with the public, the government needs to respond to the most serious and
increasingly obvious environmental problems created by an expansive economy
which focuses on profit, not environmental protection. Since regulations or
outright prohibitions on economic processes which would materially dampen
the very economic growth government depends on for social and budgetary
stability are, ipso facto, ruled out, government responses to environmental
problems must perforce not damage continued economic growth while persuading the concerned public that effective action has been taken to address
the problems caused by such growth. Within this context, environmental
protection tends to be seen as a policy supported by a particular interest
group, environmentalists, which engages in the political process along with
other interest groups utilizing such standard political tools as lobbying, supporting candidates for office, and contributing to election campaigns. Environmental politics accordingly has to do with getting environmental issues translated
into law and administrative policy and the study of environmental politics, as
in Rosenbaum's book, focuses on how an issue gets on the legislative agenda,

how it becomes a law, how it is interpreted and administered by relevant executive agencies, how it meets its objectives and how it eventually is amended or terminated if it does not meet the original legislative intent.

The analytic model for viewing legislation as a reflection of special group interests is pluralistic democracy or interest-group liberalism.[113] This model views actually existing democracy as the competition of various organized groups for access to government and the translation of private group interests into government policy. The model also requires the assumption that a rough parity of power exists among organized groups so that all government policy represents

> bargaining and compromise among institutions and actors all sharing some portions of diffused power. . . . Bargaining and compromise often purchase consensus at the cost of disarray and contradiction in the resulting policies. "What happens is not chosen as a solution to a problem but rather results from compromise, conflict and confusion among officials with diverse interests and unequal influence," notes Graham Allison.[114]

From this analytic perspective, policymaking, except under rare instances of national crisis, is incremental, working at the margin from existing policy and avoiding significant alteration or innovation. Accompanying policy incrementalism is the jurisdictional fragmentation that exists in the national legislative and executive branches. Thirteen congressional standing committees and thirty-one subcommittees currently have some form of jurisdiction over the EPA. Twenty-seven federal agencies have environmental regulatory responsibility.[115] From the analytic perspective of interest-group liberalism, the American political system displays no political direction. Interest groups vie with one another and since there is no dominant interest group, policy represents compromise and bargaining among competing groups all of which get only something of what they want. From this perspective, environmental issues are the issues supported by environmental groups. Like other issues, they must compete for attention in the political marketplace and must expect to be compromised as they work their way through the political process.

The interest-group model, however, is not the only analytic perspective by which to understand American politics generally and environmental issues specifically. It is true, of course, that different interests compete in the American political marketplace. There is competition, for example, between import and export businesses, among domestic businesses, between domestic and overseas businesses, between supporters of fortress America and internationalists, between business and labor, between business and environmental interests, between local/regional and national interests of one kind and another. None of this, however, necessarily gainsays the possibility that there may be a dominant interest at work. To use a sports analogy, in the NBA, for example, there are many basketball teams competing. Different teams have different resources to bring to the game; individual players have different skills and styles; and uniforms serve to give each team a distinct group appearance. Basketball experts focus on the mechanics of the game, on the quality of the coaching staff, and the level of support by the owners of the team. All of these factors are open to scrutiny and analysis. What is not open to scrutiny and analysis is the game itself. The game is the taken-for-granted reality which is never brought into question. Similarly, the existence of competing interest groups in the political marketplace can be squared with the assumption that all such groups are playing within the rules and goals of one game only, a game that rules out any actions or policies that would undermine a growth economy. If such is the case, then regardless of interest-group competition, there is a direction to national policy and what from one perspective is compromise, incrementalism and confusion, can be seen, from another perspective, in the case of environmental policy, as the expected outcome of the privileged position of business in government, given its role in promoting economic growth and the strategic resources which this role allows business to bring to bear in the political process.

Given the overall record of state and federal environmental protection and remediation since the passage of the National Environmental Policy Act of 1970, there is some reason to view environmental policy, as Matthew A. Cahn does,[116] as symbolic politics designed to placate the public when environmental problems reach such a scale as to be noticed by the public but not to curb the economic engine that drives environmental destruction. " . . . [E]nvironmental policy is often characterized by discourse that seeks to satisfy public anxiety while maintaining a commitment to traditional . . . economic development."[117] Thus, current environmental policy represents "words that succeed and policies that fail."[118] From the perspective of symbolic politics, the overloading of EPA, the key federal environmental agency, with mandates it cannot fulfill, becomes more understandable.

> The growing disparity between the EPA's administrative responsibilities and its resources has reached a point at which many observers believe the Agency is, or will soon be, mired in "a pathological cycle of regulatory failure." . . . The Agency is years, or decades, behind in complying with many of the most important requirements in its ten major statutory programs and new jobs are always ahead. . . . Of the estimated 3,700 businesses that are required by RCRA [Resource Conservation and Recovery Act of 1976] to control their environmental releases of toxic substances, . . . by the late 1990s less than 9 percent had actually created the cleanup measures required by EPA.[119]

A review of Rosenbaum's study of air and water pollution regulation and toxic and hazardous substances regulation reveals that despite some significant improvements of environmental conditions in specific areas and sites, overall the major achievement has been to keep air and water pollution at lower levels than would have been the case if there had been no regulation at all. Former President Reagan's attempt[120] to emasculate the EPA for fear of its negative impact on the economy and the willingness of succeeding administrations to work deals with the business community to lessen the impact of environmental policy—witness George Bush's Council on Competitiveness chaired by Vice President Dan Quale which reviewed and often terminated environmental regulations approved and developed by independent regulatory agencies and cabinet-level departments—are evidence of the priority given to economic growth over environmental protection. Even if there were a full commitment to the full enforcement of environmental policies, an expanding economy based on fossil fuel energy and an increasing population socialized to maximize consumption cannot but undermine attempts to protect the environment. If twice as many cars are produced and sold, doubling the fuel efficiency of cars only maintains current urban air quality.[121]

In short, what is referred to as environmental politics and policy has little if anything in common with ecological political economy. Environmental politics and policy deals with the positioning of environmental issues within a constitutional and party system which separates power in the national government, provides a federal sharing of power between states and the national government, often gives one party control of Congress and the other control of the presidency, provides numerous access points to government for interest groups, and usually generates compromise legislation which offers only incremental policy approaches to problems. This constitutional and party system is itself, however, subordinated to an economic system which gives economic interests a privileged relationship with government and insures that no environmental policy that is seen as undermining economic growth will be effectively applied. To the extent that environmental policy and regulation have no serious impact on the economy or may even be beneficial to economic interests in terms of profitable ventures in new environment-enhancing technology, environmental improvements can be attained.[122] The question of limits to growth raised by ecological economics is, of course, not part of environmental politics and policy discourse.

While Rosenbaum concludes his book with the statement that "Environmentalism at its best is a challenge to develop the moral and ethical sensibilities to leaven this [technological and scientific] power with an enlightened stewardship of the earth,"[123] his own, very comprehensive, treatment of environmental politics and policies does not suggest how from the existing dominant paradigm political and economic structures and institutions such "enlightened stewardship" is to emerge. Ecological political economy sharply differentiates itself from environmental politics and policy by directly confronting and challenging the contemporary dominant political and economic institutions. It rejects the validity of an interest-group interpretation of American democracy just as it rejects the notion that a political democracy can coexist side by side with an economic oligarchy. It maintains that while interest-group liberalism is an accurate description of the politics of actually existing democracy in America, this perspective ignores the deep economic structures that shape a system which cannot offer significant forms of participation to its citizens and cannot follow a path of environmental and social sustainability into the future. Ecological political economy is based on several fundamental postulates, all of which can be found in the writings of Morrison, Robertson, Bookchin, Sale and the Green Party Platform 2000 discussed here.

One postulate is that individuals are capable of solving problems which are proximate to them, providing they have the necessary resources, that is, are empowered politically and economically. Local communities can maintain, if encouraged and supported, sustainable economies which are not dependent on exterior market forces. A second and related postulate is that democracy can only be practiced at a local or, at best, regional level where face-to-face contact with other citizens makes possible that civic discourse that moves the individual from a narrow self-interested view of events to a broader and more inclusive public or community view. While confederal structures can provide for democratic decision making beyond the community level,[124] democracy does not flourish when confederal arrangements are replaced by a system of representation such as exists in the United States where national and transnational economic interests dominate the political scene and remain well positioned regardless of which party is in power. A third postulate is that empowered communities will not despoil their environment. The defining term here is empowered for without empowerment members of local communities will have no choice but to work for firms that maximize profit, not environmental protection, or be forced to exploit what meager resources they have in the manner of peasants pushed off private land and forced to ruin the rain forest in order to survive.[125] While there have been preindustrial societies that ruined their own environment and thus destroyed the physical foundations on which they existed, there have also been preindustrial societies and there are currently such societies in existence, that maintained and still maintain centuries-long equilibrium between their human communities and the surrounding physical environment. Can members of an advanced industrial society such as is the United States maintain a similar equilibrium with their environment? The writers discussed here say yes they can provided that they live in democratically organized communities in which social and economic institutions and activities are fully integrated with the natural environment. All the writers discussed here believe that environmental degradation is largely the result of large-scale political and economic institutions that have no community ties or loyalties and can avoid the consequences of environmental degradation by utilizing relatively unspoiled environments anywhere on the globe, while leaving to others the environmental destruction they create. The assumption is that individuals and communities will not foul their own nest voluntarily since, unless as individuals they have the means to leave the area, they will have to live in that fouled nest. A fourth postulate is that human society and the natural environment are not at war with one another. Human society and the natural environment have co-evolved, each shaping the other. Free human beings, participating fully with their fellows in community relationships are more likely to perceive that they are a part of nature and sharers in the evolutionary process, and may be expected to enhance, rather than degrade, the diverse life forms that constitute the living natural environment. Self-determination, decentralization, democracy, community, empowerment, self-reliance, and respect for nature are the goals of ecological political economy, and they can only be met by transforming the currently dominant political and economic systems which create political and economic dependence and environmental degradation.

Ecological political economy contains a social ethics which emphasizes community self-determination and democratic decision-making processes in both politics and economics. The practice of this social ethics is expected to promote communities which are socially and environmentally sustainable. Despite frequent references to human communities whose activities harmonize with the natural environment and respect nature, the social ethics of ecological political economy addresses itself mainly to appropriate relationships among humans. The following chapter examines the principles of an ecological ethics that addresses appropriate relationships between humans and nonhumans.

Chapter 3

Ecological Ethics

*It follows that, if the biocentric outlook forms the basis of our
perspective on human life, we will see ourselves as an
integral part of the system of nature. We will then recognize
that our faring well or poorly depends to a great extent on
the role we choose to play in the web of life. We will realize
that if we try to break our connections with that web . . .
we will thereby destroy our chances for pursuing
our uniquely human values.*

—*Paul W. Taylor,* Respect for Nature

Moving Toward an Ecological Ethics

All economic interactions of humans with the natural environment exact a
cost to the latter. Hunter-gatherer societies have driven some megafauna to
extinction. Agricultural societies alter the topography of the land, eliminate
native plant species and also drive out megafauna. These preindustrial economies, however, had a limited negative environmental impact, one that was
typically local or regional, and they operated in what has earlier been described as an empty-world scenario.[1] Moreover, the cultural context within
which these preindustrial economics functioned included either animistic
attitudes[2] toward nature or social norms against aggressive wealth seeking
and unlimited material accumulation, all of which tended to reduce the actual
damage inflicted on the environment.

89

The capitalist (and until recently the Soviet socialist) industrial economy represents an economic interaction with the natural environment that for the first time in human history is free from any cultural restraints in its use of the natural environment.[3] The natural environment for modern industrial societies represents an ensemble of animate and inanimate resources useful for economic production purposes. Inanimate resources are mined or timbered or harvested and animate resources are increasingly catalogued for genetic characteristics which have possible commercial uses. Animate resources are, of course, other life forms on the planet and the manipulation of their genetic structure for commercial purposes represents, in fact, an attempt to transform all forms of nonhuman life into economic resources used in the production of market goods.

Ecological economics has recognized the resource limits to economic growth in a full-world scenario.[4] It has reconnected economic activity with the entropy law and it has rejected the unlimited growth dogma that man-made capital can be endlessly substituted for natural capital. It has demonstrated that natural capital is now the limiting factor in economic production and that industrial economies can escape natural capital limits only be importing natural capital from less industrially developed nations. Ecological economics has characterized the globalization of unlimited growth economics under existing national and international conditions as a policy which accelerates and generalizes environmental degradation on a planetary scale. It has sharply differentiated between an economics of sustainable development that operates within its environmental carrying capacity and an economics of unlimited and therefore unsustainable growth which destroys its natural capital base. Ecological economics has joined ethical considerations to economic concerns and has rejected an economics that discounts the well-being of future human and, with much less emphasis, nonhuman generations. Accordingly, it has strongly suggested that citizens of the industrialized nations reexamine their life-styles and personal values and recognize their personal responsibility for the environmental degradation to which these life-styles and values contribute.

Ecological political economy has called for decentralization of economic and political institutions on the grounds that only such decentralization can restore authentic democracy, community, and a balance between human activities and the natural environment. For ecological political economy, decentralization of economic and political institutions is the only means by which the principles of ecological economics can be put into practice. Centralized governments allied with global corporations in the pursuit of an ever-expanding economy cannot be expected to support ecological economic principles which undercut the rationale for such an expanding economy. Along with the emphasis in ecological political economy on the empowerment of local communities and bioregions and the restoration of participatory democracy, there is the assumption that empowered and self-reliant communities and bioregions are far more likely to respect their natural surroundings than large-scale governmental and corporate entities, particularly the latter, that treat people and the natural environment as factors of production to be managed for profit and discarded when no longer profitable.

Both ecological economics and ecological political economy are, clearly, for different reasons, sensitive to limits of economic growth. For the former, the limits are represented by the entropy law and its impact on the use of nonrenewable and renewable natural resources for economic purposes.[5] For the latter, the limits are represented by the erosion of authentic democracy as a result of the increasing economic dependence of individuals, communities, and regions on global corporations and the global market. The same endless growth economy which transforms the natural environment into an economic resource also transforms citizens into factors of production on one end of the economic process and into consumers on the other end. This sensitivity to the environmental as well as social limits to economic growth does not translate, however, into a systematic ecological ethics. Recognition of the importance of natural capital for a sustainable economics and of the role that political and economic decentralization can play in maintaining a balance between human activities and the natural environment, does not automatically translate into an ethical concern for other life forms.

Leopold: The Land Ethic

In *A Sand County Almanac*, Aldo Leopold defined ethics generally as a limitation on freedom of action in the struggle for survival, reflected in human society by social norms and laws regulating relations among individuals and between individuals and social organizations such as government. Ethical constraints on the way individuals relate to one another, whether enforced by social norms or the law, are essential if the community of which individuals are members is to exist and prosper. An ethics that regulates relationships between individuals and the government is essential to the development of democracy, a form of social organization that offers greater governmental legitimacy and stability and greater sensitivity to the needs of the general public than do other forms of social organization. Leopold notes that while a social ethics has been in place, in one form or another, for at least two millennia

> there is as yet no ethic dealing with man's relation to land and to the animals and plants which grow upon it. Land, like Odysseus' slave girls, is still property. The land-relation is still strictly economic, entailing privileges but not obligations. . . . The land ethic simply

enlarges the boundaries of the community to include soils waters, plants, and animals, or collectively: the land. . . . In short, a land ethic changes the role of Homo sapiens from conqueror of the land-community to plain member and citizen of it. It implies respect for his fellow-members, and also respect for the community as such.[6]

The "fellow-members" that Leopold refers to are the plant and animal life forms that live on the land; the "community" refers to the ecosystem which these life forms constitute in interaction with one another and with the non-animate elements of the physical environment. Leopold's land ethic does not disregard the economic consequences of land degradation. Plant and animal species that are threatened by extinction may have played an important role in building the soil and their preservation is not an "aesthetic luxury,"[7] but a recognition of the complexity of agronomy and the danger involved in allowing any part of the land to be lost. The land ethic, however, moves beyond the anthropocentric/economic focus which characterizes the industrial approach to the land typical of agribusiness, and expresses an appreciation of the intrinsic value of the land as a community of life.

It is inconceivable to me that an ethical relation to land can exist without love, respect, and admiration for land, and a high regard for its value. *By value, I of course mean something far broader than mere economic value; I mean value in the philosophic sense.*[8]

Valuing the Natural Environment

It is the purpose of this chapter to explore through various writings what it means to value nonhuman life forms in the "philosophic sense." One important conceptual distinction must be made at this point, the distinction between the terms "anthropocentric" and "anthropogenic." The first term refers to a form of valuing which places primacy on the satisfaction of human interests. Thus, maintaining a national park is valuable because it provides for human recreation; placing wolves in Yellowstone National Park is valuable because the wolves reduce the elk herd numbers, thus mitigating overgrazing which interferes with other uses of the park. Saving tropical rainforests is valuable, because many species of plants that may have significant medical application for humans have not yet been catalogued and collected. Addressing pollution of a waterway is valuable because clean water provides recreation possibilities and allows the reappearance of fish with possible commercial value. A cleaner river flowing through a city encourages waterfront development which provides jobs and more revenue for the city. These examples of anthropocentrically focused environmental concern are familiar ones; there is no doubt that such concern can lead to positive environmental results along with the associated economic benefits. When human interests are served by protecting or improving the natural environment, an anthropocentric valuation of the environment does not contribute to environmental degradation. When, however, the natural environment is valued only as an economic resource and the logic of the market overwhelms all other possible valuation, an anthropocentric valuing of the environment takes on a deadly form and becomes a major contributor to environmental degradation.

The second term, "anthropogenic," refers to the fact that only humans self-consciously attribute value to things. People value trees; trees do not value people. Whether a tree is valued for the wood it supplies a paper mill or because it is seen as a thing of beauty, the source of the valuation is a human being. The crucial question is not the source of the valuation, but the nature of the valuation, that is, whether it is exclusively anthropocentric/ economic or whether other characteristics of the object are valued.[9] On one end of the spectrum of environmental valuation is the solely economic valuation which judges all other characteristics of the object as irrelevant; on the other end of the spectrum is the attribution of non-economic or even intrinsic value to an object, in which case it is valued simply because it exists. Between these two polar valuations are the examples cited above where human interests are addressed and a specific part of the environment is improved. It is this middle range of environmental valuation that constitutes the basis for the claim that economic growth and environmental protection go hand in hand and that current life-styles can be maintained within a so-called green economy. Despite increasing sensitivity to the environmental impact of economic activity as evidenced by U. S. environmental legislation and international conferences on global warming, CFCs, biodiversity and related topics, the dominant valuation of the environment remains strongly anthropocentric/ economic.

It is on the other end of the valuational spectrum, the recognition of non-economic and even intrinsic value, that ecological ethics is positioned. The reasons offered for assigning non-economic and intrinsic value differ and will be discussed in the following sections. It must be emphasized, however, that both the anthropocentric/economic and the non-economic and intrinsic value positions are anthropogenically derived, that is, both positions, however antithetical to one another, originate in the way human beings look upon the natural environment. The different outlooks can be the result of differences in an individual's economic location (whether an individual has substantial vested interests in the economy and enjoys significant social status), education, socialization within a specific socioeconomic grouping, personal experiences in childhood,[10] and the influence of a significant other individual, even a nonhuman individual.[11] All valuations of the environment reflect the interest of the valuer *vis à vis* the environment, and all valuations stem from human judgments (shaped by reason, emotion, and cultural influences) about what is important, beautiful, worth saving, open to economic exploitation, not worth saving, or useless. As noted above, however, there is a substantial difference between a valuation of the environment in exclusively economic terms and a valuation of the environment in terms of non-economic and intrinsic value. The former valuation, which is integral to the dominant techno-industrial paradigm, reduces the entire natural environment, animate and inanimate, to an economic re-source, actual or potential. As an economic resource, natural capital or some part of it may be protected so that it can be reproduced for future economic use. Protection, however, is contingent on economic considerations and if market tastes or product processes change the rationale for protection ends.

This exclusively anthropocentric/economic valuation acknowledges no limits to economic expansion and thus no boundaries beyond which the natural environment is off limits to economic exploitation. This form of environmental valuation subordinates the natural environment to the decisions of those who control the economic system, and it implicitly recognizes no life form, other than human beings,[12] as having a non-economic or intrinsic value. On the other hand, the valuation of the environment in terms of non-economic value circumscribes the economic exploitation of the environment by recognizing that important non-economic values such as beauty or diversity can be destroyed by economic exploitation. When intrinsic value is attributed to either nonhuman life forms or the physical environment limits to further economic exploitation are clearly indicated.

An ecological ethics that recognizes the non-economic and intrinsic value of nonhuman life forms and even elements of the physical environment,[13] runs counter to the dominant anthropocentric/economic valuation of the natural environment which provides the intellectual warrant for the trans-formation of the natural environment into a resource for the economics of unlimited growth. That so much damage could be inflicted on the planet's biosphere, so many species exterminated, so many landscapes devastated, so much pollution let loose in the environment, bespeaks a mind set that is closed to any consideration of the possible moral responsibility humans may have for the well-being of nonhuman life forms. Eating habits that accelerate the destruction of tropical rainforests and the overgrazing of grasslands, and promote the development of factory farming which turns millions of animals into consumable commodities, are rarely questioned. Energy-intensive life-styles that require continued depletion of nonrenewable fossil fuels and ratio-nalize nuclear energy as a "clean" alternative to fossil fuels are accepted as an American birthright while ignoring the environmental devastation caused by both nuclear and fossil-fuel energy. The widespread assumption that humans stand at the apex of the evolutionary process with all other life forms subordinated to human desires and purposes and the commonplace notion that there is an unbridgeable gulf between humans and nonhumans represent an arrant speciesism[14] that like racism renders its adherents incapable of ever taking the viewpoint of the other. There are, of course, many examples of individual humans' affection for and kindness to nonhumans, especially household "pets,"[15] and there are various organizations that promote concern for the welfare of animals, including those used in various forms of research.[16] Such individual and group concerns for nonhumans are not unimportant, but they are manifested within the context of a society driven at this time by the dominant paradigm commitment to an expanding economy which requires an overwidening circle of resources to fuel its expansion and can tolerate no permanent barriers to its sources of energy and matter. More often than not, the individuals and groups that display an ethical concern for nonhumans participate as consumers in the very economic and political system that is devoid of any ethical concern for nonhumans. As Thomas Berry points out,[17] the U.S. Constitution in its present form recognizes only human rights and so along with the economic system is complicit in the general social consensus that excludes nonhumans from ethical consideration.

An ecological ethics can have only marginal influence within the bounds of the current economic and political system, however dedicated some individuals and groups may be to the welfare of nonhumans. An ecological ethics requires an ecological economics and political economy just as these require an ecological ethics. Each of these is a complement to the others, with each logically calling forth the others. An ecological ethics in a society dependent on an unlimited growth economy is a chimera, as is participatory democracy based on empowered communities in a global techno-industrial economy. An ecological economics without an ecological ethics and political economy has limited ethical motivation and little political energy. By itself, it cannot successfully contest the dominant economic system which is sustained and legitimated by its own ethics and politics, however environmentally pernicious these may be. If economics and politics are instrumentalities to achieve preferred ends and are not ends in themselves, an ecological economics and political economy must be understood as instrumentalities to achieve the ends envisioned in ecological ethics, among these, human existence viewed as membership in a community of life on Earth. This community of life includes both humans and nonhumans and requires of humans the love, respect, and admiration that Leopold spoke of for one another and for the nonhuman life forms that inhabit the land. An ecological ethics requires a respect for humans exhibited at the social level by empowered communities and participatory democracy and on the individual level by recognition of the moral worth of each person. It also requires, and here it departs from an anthropocentric ethics, love, respect, and admiration for nonhumans which will necessarily be expressed and institutionalized differently than it is for humans. Respect for humans requires that they participate on equal terms in the political process, for instance. Equal voting rights for nonhumans clearly does not follow as an ethical obligation on the part of humans. To express for nonhumans the love, respect, and admiration that an ecological ethics demands will require the best and most creative imagination and intellectual breath that humans are capable of. The challenge is made even more daunting by the dominant paradigm influences that have now reigned for more than two centuries and that have severely atrophied the moral imagination and thought required to formulate and put into practice an ecological ethics. However, it is a challenge that must be faced for what is at stake is a vision of the good life in the not-too-distant future, a good life based on an economy that sustains human communities without destroying its own physical base or undermining a good life for future generations of humans and nonhumans; on a political economy that decentralizes government and economic organization to empower individuals and communities and to create the conditions necessary for an authentic democracy; and on a cultural norm, ecological ethics, that respects in appropriate ways the nonhuman members of the community of life.

Wild nature defined as natural areas where human influence is marginal and evolutionary processes determine how or whether nonhuman life forms will flourish or not, will continue to disappear as human populations increase and the intrusive industrial process becomes global. The only limits on such intrusions will be those that are self-imposed by humans. An ecological ethics, as Leopold observed, represents a voluntary self-restraint on the part of humans, a willingness to refrain from activities which undermine the Earth's community of life. Such self-restraint may be motivated by scientific evidence that the Earth's biosphere is experiencing traumatic and possibly fatal shocks and the realization that the present course of industrial society is not physically sustainable. It may be motivated by what E. O. Wilson calls "biophilia,"[18] a natural affinity that humans have for nature; it may arise from a sense of wonder and awe at the beauty of creation, much as a masterpiece of art elicits emotions of wonder and awe from one generation to another; or it may stem from the conviction that the exploitation and degradation of nature goes hand in hand with the same processes that exploit and degrade humans, in which case the liberation of nature is a necessary condition for the liberation of humans. It is this argument for an ecological ethics that is raised by Herbert Marcuse.

Marcuse: The Liberation of Nature

Herbert Marcuse, a leading member of the German Frankfurt School,[19] developed a critical theory of contemporary techno-industrial society in such works as *Eros and Civilization*,[20] *One-Dimensional Man*[21] and *An Essay on Liberation*,[22] utilizing selected ideas and themes from Marx and Freud. Marcuse's critique focused on the social, political, psychological, and epistemological consequences of advanced industrial societies. He noted the preeminence of what he termed "instrumental reason" which provided technically efficient means to reach social goals that were themselves not subject to critical examination of their long-term consequences, as in the case of chemical farming which brings short-term economic gain but ruins the soil in the long run. He noted the tendency to reduce humans and the environment to factors of production in the economic system and the linkage of science with specific economic and political interests. Science and technology in contemporary society were applied not to serve their historic promise of liberating humans from the limitations of a short, nasty and brutish condition but to serve the imperatives of an ever-expanding economy.[23] Rather than providing the material conditions under which humans could self-consciously and freely, that is, democratically, construct their own history, science, and technology were increasingly instrumentalities for achieving the purposes of the economic system. The historical a priori, as Marcuse referred to it, of science and technology was the conquest of nature, the Baconian enterprise of wresting from nature its secret powers to use for the empowerment of humanity. The mechanical and chemical processes that were derived from the scientific investigation of the natural environment were from the very beginning applied to the industrial processes of mining, refining ores, transforming ores to industrial metals, and machine production.

The Industrial Revolution incorporated a series of scientific and technical applications to industry which progressively brought the natural environment into the circuit of industrial production and made possible the transformation of ever larger portions of the natural environment into an economic resource. The Industrial Revolution thus made possible a volume and variety of production never before possible and, at least in the West, created a material standard of living never before achieved by so many. But the very success of the Industrial Revolution, in its original and later stages, provided the impetus for further transformations of the natural environment and created societies deeply committed to the accumulation of material goods as a cultural goal. The power over nature represented by science and technology and expressed through an ever-expanding economy required that no limits be placed on such material accumulation and that the chief life activities of most members of industrial societies be production and consumption. The domination of nature in both its capitalist and later Soviet industrial forms required control of a vast labor force and a vast consumer market. The first was secured in capitalist economies by the disappearance of an agrarian employment alternative and increasing dependence on industrial employment. The control of a consumer market in capitalist economies was secured through a ubiquitous network of advertising and the creation of what Marcuse calls "a second human nature" in which the values of the industrial society and the industrial-technological mode of dealing with humans and the natural environment are introjected and come to be felt by individuals as authentic, even biological, needs.[24]

The focus on production and consumption creates a one-dimensional techno-industrial society characterized by one form of reason, instrumental-industrial; one form of human activity, production-consumption; and one view of reality, material-quantitative. The psychological one-dimensionality of this second nature is the result of the reduction of sensory stimuli through the standardization of the social environment and the physical destruction of the natural environment. As the volume of production and consumption expands, the phenomenological field which humans could potentially experience shrinks. Cultures not based on techno-industrial values are marginalized or destroyed. Employment opportunities outside of or unrelated to techno-industrial occupations are severely diminished. The amount of work time significantly increases as people work longer or at more than one job to obtain the means to purchase the commodities defined as essential for the good life, or simply work longer hours because those are the conditions of employment set by the employer.

Just as free time is an essential prerequisite for freedom so it is a prerequisite for engaging in activities other than production and consumption, in activities and experiences which challenge what Marcuse called the "reality principle" of techno-industrial society. By reality principle Marcuse meant the social paradigm that defined for individuals who they were, what they were to do, and what was meaningful in life. This reality or performance principle, so called because techno-industrial society demands from its members continuous production and consumption performance, represented what Marcuse termed "surplus" or "unnecessary repression." Human society cannot exist without socializing and disciplining its members to follow social norms, particularly those that deal with economic functions that insure human survival. Hard and unremitting labor of one kind or another is a social necessity as long as the conditions for human survival have not been permanently established. Marcuse's reference to surplus repression in techno-industrial society points to the fact that presently the conditions for human survival have been permanently established by the science, technology, and industrial processes that first appeared some three centuries ago and in their contemporary form can more than satisfy the basic material foundation for a decent life.

The system in place, however, is propelled by an expansionist dynamic that has no limits of production and consumption[25] and no way of providing for the equitable distribution of what it produces. The result is that despite the productive capacity of the techno-industrial apparatus, most people do not work shorter hours, do not have more free time, and spend what free time they have not engaging in experiences which lie outside the techno-industrial realm but in the consumption of commodified recreation provided by television, computers, and related electronic goods, the purchase of which requires further participation in the techno-industrial cycle of job-production, income-consumption.

> The so-called consumer society and the politics of corporate capitalism have created a second nature of man which ties him libidinally and aggressively to the commodity form. The need for possessing, consuming, handling, and constantly renewing the gadgets, devices, instruments, engines offered to and imposed upon the people, for using these wares even at the danger of one's own destruction, has become a "biological" need. The second nature of man thus militates against any change that would disrupt and perhaps even abolish this dependence of man on a market ever more densely filled with merchandise—abolish his existence as a consumer consuming himself in buying and selling.[26]

For Marcuse, the psychological one-dimensionality created by the techno-industrial society could be countered only by a "new sensibility" capable of recognizing such one-dimensionality and reaching out to sensory, aesthetic, and imaginative experiences excluded from the shrunken phenomenological realm that defines techno-industrial reality. The new sensibility is "receptive to forms and modes of reality which thus far have been projected only by the aesthetic imagination"[27] and represents the claims of the human mind and body for a sensory and aesthetic fulfillment denied by a one-dimensional society.

In *Counter-Revolution and Revolt*, Marcuse arrived at the conclusion that the expression of human sensibility beyond the established perceptual and sensory realm of techno-industrial society requires the liberation of nature from its total subordination to the purposes of ever-increasing production and consumption. The liberation of nature thus calls for the end of its abusive exploitation by a science and technology which serve the interests of a system that dominates and exploits both human and nonhuman nature.

> In the established society nature itself, ever more effectively controlled, has in turn become another dimension for the control of man: the extended arm of society and its power. Commercialized nature, polluted nature, militarized nature cut down the life

environment of man, not only in an ecological but also in a very existential sense. . . . Liberation of nature is the recovery of the life-enhancing forces in nature, the sensous aesthetic qualities which are foreign to a life wasted in unending competitive performances: they suggest the new qualities of *freedom*.[28]

Human freedom is rooted accordingly in the ability of the human senses to discover new aims and new qualities of experience in nature, aims and qualities which are outside the ambit of techno-industrial production and consumption. Marcuse posits the existence of objective qualities in nature which exist independently of humans and can either be destroyed, as they are in the techno-industrial society, or assisted to obtain their full manifestation by new, appreciative human sensibility. To assist nature in the full manifestation of its objective qualities is to recognize that the animate elements of nature possess a *telos,* or ultimate end, which if realized would represent the actualization of all qualities inherent in any animate entity. Each living organism is a form of life with qualities that define its mode of existence. Under the most favorable of conditions an organism actualizes its capacity to be fully that form of life which it is. To give a familiar example, the *telos* of an acorn is to become a specific kind of oak tree, to be as fully that oak tree as possible. The diversity of nature is such that it offers to perceptive human senses a kaleidescope of forms, colors, patterns, sounds, and aromas. Marcuse refers to the Kantian notion of the aesthetic judgment in which the beautiful object is perceived as exhibiting a definite form or inherent purpose or *telos,* free from any consideration of its utility for humans.[29] The second nature of individuals in techno-industrial society represents a stultification of the human senses vis à vis the natural world and an intensification of sensitivity to the sounds and objects of the market. This second nature

. . . deprives man from recognizing nature as a *subject* in its own right—a subject with which to live in a common human universe. The deprivation is not undone by the opening of nature to massive fun and togetherness, spontaneous as well as organized—a release of frustration which only adds to the violation of nature.[30]

To recognize nature as a subject in its own right is to recognize nature as a complex of subjects in their own rights, a community of life in which humans are members. The notion that nature exists for human exploitation as merely matter for economic uses is a notion that belongs to a specific form of society, techno-industrial. A society characterized by a new sensibility would be a society in which science and technology are applied to the protection of the totality of life viewed as a network of interacting subjects with inherent qualities that enrich the sensory and aesthetic experiences of humans. A new sensibility emerging as a generalized social psychology implies new social institutions: a new economics that acknowledges limits to economic growth; a new political economy that supports economic and political decentralization, loosening dependency on government and corporate bureaucracies and the techno-industrial reality principle they represent; and a new ecological ethics that recognizes nature as a subject in its own right with inherent qualities that constitute an experiential reality far richer than the one offered by techno-industrial society.

> Our world emerges not only in the pure forms of time and space, but also, and *simultaneously*, as a totality of sensuous qualities— objects not only of the eye (synopsis) but of *all* human senses (hearing, smelling, touching, tasting). It is this qualitative, elementary, unconscious or rather preconscious, constitution of the world of experience, it is this primary experience itself which must change radically if social change is to be radical, qualitative change.[31]

For Marcuse, nature represents unadministered space filled with the myriad inherent qualities of diverse life forms, a space which allows human senses and imagination to perceive possible life experiences other than those provided by a one-dimensional society. The sounds, shapes, and smells of nature are not those associated with the production, distribution, and consumption sounds, shapes, and smells of techno-industrial processes. The notion of nature as a subject in its own right functions as an ongoing critique of a society which in reducing nature to raw materials for production and consumption inflicts a sensory and aesthetic deprivation on the majority of its citizens.

Marcuse was not unaware that some form of appropriation of nature was necessary for human survival and welfare. The new sensibility which perceived nature as a subject in its own right would go far in reducing the violence and, toward life forms, cruelty inflicted on nature by the techno-industrial society. The institutions associated with a new economics and political economy would aim at the reduction, not the increase, of environmental destruction. Yet, there would apparently remain that irreducible minimum[32] of human violence necessarily inflicted on the natural world.

> To treat nature "for its own sake" sounds good, but it is certainly not for the sake of the animal to be eaten, nor probably for the sake of the plant. . . . In the face of the suffering inflicted by man on man, it seems terribly "premature" to campaign for universal vegetarianism or synthetic foodstuffs. . . . And yet, no free society is imaginable which does not, under its "regulative idea of reason"

make the concerted effort to reduce consistently the suffering which man imposes on the animal world.[33]

The term "regulative idea of reason" refers to those paradigmatic principles arrived at by philosophic reasoning which determine the goals of a society and provide both an explanation for and justification of its institutions. One preeminent principle that emerges from the regulative idea of reason of a society based on the new sensibility is the aesthetic principle which requires that beauty be a major criterion in determining the appropriateness of human institutions and human behavior.

Beston: Ecological Aesthetics

A tour de force in the application of the aesthetic principle to the perception of nature as a subject in its own right is Henry Beston's *The Outermost House*.[34]

> Nature is part of our humanity, and without some awareness and experience of that divine mystery man ceases to be man. When the Pleiades and the wind in the grass are no longer part of the human spirit, a part of very flesh and bone, man becomes as it were, a kind of cosmic outlaw, having neither the completeness and integrity of the animal nor the birthright of a true humanity.[35]

Beston spent one year on the great beach of Cape Cod, immersing himself in the sounds, shapes, colors, and smells of the beach with its inhabitants, permanent and transitory, and the ocean. He experienced and recorded a solar year.

> My year upon the beach had come full circle. . . . Seeing the great suns, I thought of the last time I marked them in the spring. . . . Now, once again the Hunter rose to drive summer south before him, once again autumn followed on his steps. I had seen the ritual of the sun; I had shared the elemental world.[36]

He identified the three elemental sounds in nature: the sound of rain, of wind, and the waves on the beach.

> Listen to the surf, really lend it your ears, and you will hear in it a world of sounds: hollow boomings and heavy roarings, great watery tumblings and tramplings; long hissing seethes, sharp, rifle-shot reports, splashes, whispers, the grinding undertone of stones,

and sometimes vocal sounds that might be the half-heard talk of people in the sea.[37]

While he described the sound of the ocean as the most awesome, he did not slight the sounds of lesser beings such as the insects, "Those trillions of unaccountable lives, those crawling, buzzing, intense presences. . . . But all those little fiddles in the grass, all those cricket pipes, those delicate flutes. . . . "[38] He observed the changing shapes of the dunes driven by the wind and altered in texture by changing temperatures. He noted the effect the lengthening day with its increased light had on the beach.

> Under this April light the mound and landward slopes of the great wall have put on a strange and lovely colour which lies upon them with the delicacy of reflection in a pool. This colour is a tint of palest olive. . . .[39]

He celebrated olfactory sensitivity, noting the disappearance of smells like that of a newly ploughed field or a warm morning after an April rain, in the stench of contemporary civilization.

> We ought to keep all senses vibrant and alive. Had we done so, we should never have built a civilization which outrages them, which so outrages them, indeed, that a vicious circle has been established and the dull sense grown duller.[40]

He noted the manner in which modern society progressively distanced itself from contact with nature, ignoring circadian rhythms, and insulating itself from the night.

> Our fantastic civilization has fallen out of touch with many aspects of nature, and with none more completely than with night. . . .
> Are modern folk, perhaps afraid of night? Do they fear that vast serenity, the mystery of infinite space, the austerity of stars? Having made themselves at home in a civilization obsessed with power, which explains its whole world in terms of power, do they fear at night for their dull acquiescence and the pattern of their beliefs?[41]

He witnessed the instantaneous formation of bird constellations with mass changes of direction in which individual birds responded as if members of one organic body. He rejected Descartes' description of animals as mere machines, uttering sounds, and exhibiting movements as would a machine. In one of his most widely quoted statements, he called for a deeper understanding of nonhuman life.

> We need another and a wiser and perhaps a more mystical concept
> of animals. Remote from universal nature, and living by compli-
> cated artifice, man in civilization surveys the creature through the
> glass of his knowledge and sees thereby a feather magnified and
> the whole image in distortion. We patronize them for their incom-
> pleteness, for their tragic fate of having taken form so far below
> ourselves. And therein we err, and greatly err. For the animal shall
> not be measured by man. In a world older and more complete than
> ours they move finished and complete, gifted with extensions of the
> senses we have lost or never attained, living by voices we shall
> never hear. *They are not brethren, they are not underlings; they are
> other nations*, caught with ourselves in the net of life and time,
> fellow prisoners of the splendour and travail of the earth.[42]

In this passage Beston speaks to the core principles of an ecological ethics. Animals and other nonhuman life forms are not our brethren and so our relationship with them cannot assume the legal and institutional forms that shape human relationships.[43] They are not underlings and therefore cannot have their existence self-evidently subordinated to human purposes. They are other nations and thus our relationship to them, as relationships among human nations, must be based on internationally recognized norms of conduct. An ecological ethics rests on a recognition of nature as a subject in its own right; on a deeply aesthetic appreciation of the qualities of nature: the sounds, shapes, colors, smells, the sensuous totality of that experiential realm called nature which Beston celebrated in the September fortnight that turned into a year on the great beach.

> My house completed . . . I went there to spend a fortnight in Sep-
> tember. The fortnight ending, I lingered on, and as the year length-
> ened into autumn, the beauty and mystery of this earth and outer
> sea so possessed and held me that I could not go. The world to-day
> is sick to its thin blood for lack of elemental things, for fire before
> the hands, for water welling from the earth, for air, for the dear
> earth itself underfoot. In my world of beach and dune these el-
> emental presences lived and had their being, and under their arch
> there moved an incomparable pageant of nature and the year.[44]

In the foreword to the 1949 edition of *The Outermost House*, Beston commented that in retrospect what caught his attention in the book was the "meditative perception of the relation of 'Nature' . . . to the human spirit."[45]

Though not expressed in the usual language of religion, Beston's perception of the relationship of nature to the human spirit is essentially religious in its emphasis on creation. If asked what he had learned from his year on the beach, Beston says

> I would answer that one's first appreciation is a sense that the creation is still going on. . . . *Creation is here and now.* So near is man to the creative pageant, so much a part is he of the endless and incredible experiment, that any glimpse he may have will be but the revelation of a moment, a solitary note heard in a symphony thundering through debatable existences of time. Poetry is as necessary to comprehension as science. *It is as impossible to live without reverence as it is without joy.*[46]

It is this sense of awe and reverence, this sense of the magnitude and beauty of the creative forces that gave rise to human and nonhuman life, that constitutes the new sensibility that Marcuse spoke of, the new sensibility that is the motive power of an ecological ethics. Beston ends his book with a paean to nature and the creation.

> Touch the earth, love the earth, honour the earth, her plains, her valleys, her hills, and her seas; rest your spirit in her solitary places. For the gifts of life are the earth's and they are given to all, and they are the songs of birds at daybreak, Orion and the Bear, and dawn seen over ocean from the beach.[47]

Maguire: The Relationship of Religion to Ecological Ethics

Daniel C. Maguire in *Ethics for a Small Planet* speaks directly to the relationship of religion to an ecological ethics.[48] In 1992, sixteen hundred scientists issued a declaration, "Warning to Humanity," calling on religious communities to help address the environmental threats to the planet. The question Maguire raises is whether in the Western nations the mainstream Christian communities are theologically prepared to sponsor a new ecological ethics. The changes that need to be effected in economics, political economy, ethics, and education will necessarily transform Western societies and those non-Western societies that have adopted the institutions integral to a techno-industrial order. Profound social changes, however, do not occur as an automatic response to scientific data showing, for example, global warming or species extinction. Radical changes in the way people perceive and value things and events are propelled less by cerebral than emotional and visceral forces. As Maguire says, "Values perceived as sacred are the ultimate motivators. Values worth dying for are what religion, at root, is all about."[49] Few are disposed to die for scientific truths. If the sacred is the motor for all social reform, the question to be asked is whether a theistic conception of the sacred assists or hinders religion's contribution to an ecological ethics.

> What happens when we see the world and say "God" rather than seeing it and saying "Wow!" Is *appreciation* shortcircuited by *ratiocination* and cause-effect calculation? Does creation-theology not belittle nature by reducing this primal miracle to an artifact, prompting us to worship the purported cause while draining us of wonder at "the effect?" If the earth could speak, would it say it would have been better off without our distracting theism?[50]

The imagining of God as supreme master and masculinized owner of all he surveys helps create attitudes of domination over nature and can justify human improvidence given the divine providence of an almighty God who can redeem humanity from its destructive acts. Moreover, biblical monotheism with its notion of the reign of a universal law mandated by a single deity contributed to the emergence of a science which disenchanted nature, a disenchantment which "opened the way for the demeaning instrumentalization of nature and the human alienation from our biological matrix."[51] The conventional imaging of God is clearly anthropomorphic. Christian theologians such as Saint Augustine and Saint Thomas Aquinas rejected such anthropomorphism, declaring that what is understood about God cannot be about God since the nature of God is unknowable. If it is not possible to describe God in human terms without engaging in an espistemologically flawed anthropomorphism, then it is not inplausible to speak of God "as an imaginative construct of human making, not as a distinct 'being.' "[52] The term God becomes, in this latter construction, an adjective that describes the sacred or that which we find indescribably and unqualifiedly valuable.

> . . . [F]rom the viewpoint of ecology, to project the experience of the sacred onto an immaterial God is to shortchange sacredness as a dimension of material life and turn it into an object of worship that is beyond our world and thus alien to life. Sacrality hypostatized (or reified) can easily be sacrality lost.[53]

For Maguire, the notion of an afterlife further removes the sacred from this Earth by making life on earth merely a prologue to another and immaterial existence. "*Earth as prolegomenon* and *earth as destiny* are the ultimate in divergent world views and divergent ethics."[54] The notion of an afterlife creates a metaphysical gulf between humans and plant and animal life forms. The common practice of burying the dead in metal coffins to insulate them from the earth reinforces the perceived gulf between humans and nonhuman life forms. If humans have a supramundane future not shared by any other life forms and if human burial practices symbolize the separation of humans from the Earth even in death, then it is difficult to see how traditional Western religion can contribute to an ecological ethics. The salvationist element in traditional Christianity, especially, tends to minimize reverence for the sacred on earth. A thought experiment illustrates this point. Imagine that one day the deity manifests itself to humanity and demonstrates to all, without the shadow of a doubt, that it is indeed God. The deity then declares the following: "For ages you have worshipped me because you believed that through such worship you would be granted eternal life in the hereafter. I tell you now that you have worshipped me for the wrong reason. While you are a special species endowed with self-consciousness, language, and ability to understand and control many natural processes, you are, like all earth's life forms, a part of the earth and you share the finitude of all earth's living creatures, a finitude which serves the purposes of creation. I ask now that you worship me not because I will grant you life after death but because I am the source of all of earth's beauty. Love the earth as you would love me. Love the earth because you are part of it. Love the earth because you of all its species can perceive its beauty, and remember that the earth alone is your destiny, as it is the destiny of all those species with whom you share the earth."[55] One can only surmise the effect of such an epiphany on the religious faith of traditional theists. If, however, as Maguire states, religion in the generic sense is the experience of the sacred, then such an epiphany would strengthen the religious sense of the earth's sacredness.

> Monotheists for whom nothing else makes sense could still be modest and learn to respect the religious spirit of those whose response to the sacred in our midst, to the sanctity of life, is sincere and even heroic . . . but not theistic. The nontheistic may be more reverent of the mystery of life.[56]

That religion can be nontheistic; that God can be an adjective, not a noun; that the awe and reverence typically directed in religion toward a deity should be directed to the earth; that life on earth is destiny and not prolegomenon to an afterlife; that there is no metaphysical or ontological gulf between humans and nonhuman life forms; that religion as the experience of the sacred is at the core of ecological ethics—these propositions can shake the foundation of traditional Western religion. Yet, says Maguire, if Western religion is to respond to the call of the world's scientists to assist in addressing environmental threats to the earth, these propositions cannot be dismissed out of hand.

Berry: The Universe Community

Thomas Berry has also examined the relationship of religion to an ecological ethics and, like Maguire, has centered on the elements of the sacred in both religion and ecological ethics. For Berry, an ecological ethics must be based on the understanding that the universe forms a single, integral community: "the sacred community is primarily the universe community."[57] The universe is the only self-referent mode of being. All other beings are universe-referent, that is, the meaning of their existence is bound up in their relationship to the universe. In a similar manner, the Earth is the basic referent for all life existing on it. "Every mode of being must be understood within the Earth context."[58] Berry quotes Saint Thomas Aquinas who says in his *Summa Theologica* that the whole universe manifests the divine more than any single being, the great multiplicity of beings insuring that the perfection lacking in any one being will be provided by the others. Contemporary cosmology reveals an emergent universe in which creative processes unfold and the biological sciences demonstrate that humans are integrally connected to the earth community. The denial of this connection represents, for Berry, a pathology which is at the heart of the ecological crisis. Since the Earth is a component of the universe, human membership in the Earth community suggests membership in a more inclusive universe community.

> Even beyond the earth the sense of community would extend throughout the entire universe seen as a single coherent community that has emerged into being with a total dependence of each component on all the others. Indeed we need to think of the universe as the supreme norm of reality and value with all component members of the universe participating in this context, each in accord with its own proper role.[59]

Berry maintains that the sense of community with the universe and the Earth operates to counter the pathological cultural disjunction between the human and the nonhuman. The entire universe is to be seen as a "communion of subjects, not a collection of objects,"[60] with each subject having inherent value and the right to those conditions necessary for the full manifestation of its particular mode of being. Religion presently does not act to strengthen the sense of human membership in the universe and earth communities. Religion focuses excessively on the process of redemption, neglecting the ongoing process of creation evident in the universe and on Earth. Religion has not effectively taught that the natural world is the primary revelatory experience. "Emphasis on verbal revelation to the neglect of the primary manifestation of the divine in the natural world is to mistake the entire revelatory process."[61] Like Maguire, Berry defines the religious as the sense of the sacred in the natural world and the universe itself. Humans can fulfill their imaginative, spiritual, aesthetic, and emotional needs only within the larger context of the surrounding earth and universe.

> There is no inner life without outer experience. The tragedy in the elimination of the primordial forests is not the economic but the soul-loss that is involved. For we are depriving our imagination, our emotions, and even our intellect of that overwhelming experience communicated by the wilderness. For children to live simply in contact with concrete and steel and wires and wheels and machines, for them never to experience any primordial reality or even to see the stars at night; this is a soul deprivation that diminishes the deepest of our human experiences.[62]

Impediments to an Aesthetically and Religiously Based Ecological Ethic

Aldo Leopold found it inconceivable that an ecological ethics could exist without love, respect, and admiration for the land seen as a community of life and without a high regard for its intrinsic value. The aesthetic and religious arguments for an ecological ethics assert that humans have the emotional and cognitive capacity to sense the sacred in nature, to experience love and reverence for natural creation and to recognize and protect the objective, aesthetic qualities in nature which enable the perceiving individual to break through the one-dimensionality of techno-industrial society and the limited sensory and emotional fulfillment it provides. An ecological ethics founded on love and reverence for the natural environment with a deeply felt appreciation for the objective, aesthetic values in nature, would, indeed, be energized by powerful human emotions and highly regarded ethical values. The question remains, however, whether a sense of the sacred and appreciation of the aesthetic qualities in nature can reasonably be expected of individuals who live in artificial or built environments where even the night sky is obscured, where the economic system which employs them treats nature only as a resource, and where the educational system by and large ignores issues relevant to an ecological ethics.

Despite the Copernican revolution in astronomy, satellite photographs of the Earth in space, and the new cosmology of an expanding universe, there is no substantial cultural sense of kinship with other life forms co-evolving with humans on a small planet located in a vast universe with no evidence to date of another planet so richly endowed with life. The fact that the Earth is a small planet in a vast space is generally known but only as other geographic facts about the Earth are known. Such factual knowledge carries no larger philosophic implications and does not lead to a cultural metanoia, a transformation of the way humans look at themselves and their relationship to the Earth and its life forms. Not only has the techno-industrial paradigm closed off alternative social visions; it has also relegated contemporary cosmology, along with ecology, to an irrelevancy.[63] As this dominant paradigm has promoted a narrow, materialist, and solitary notion of what human existence is about, so it has promoted an equally narrow, materialist, and solitary notion of the nature of the Earth which ignores the genetic commonalities that link all life on Earth and the relationship of planet Earth to the galaxy in which it is located. The awe and reverence that accompany a sense of the sacred are lost in the commodification of nature and human society itself in the techno-industrial society where, for the most part, even leisure time is spent in the consumption of so-called recreational goods. Instead of awe and reverence as a response to the natural creation, there is what Berry refers to as the "autistic inability" to establish intimate rapport with the natural world.[64]

If, as Maguire and Berry maintain, an ecological ethics must be rooted in the sense of the sacred and energized by the profound emotions which this sense evokes, then the existing economic, political, and pedagogical institutions, which represent the institutionalization of the dominant paradigm, must be replaced by institutions consonant with the new ecological paradigm. Just as daily contact with the dominant paradigm institutions atrophies the individual's capacity for experiencing awe and reverence, so daily contact with new paradigm institutions would strengthen this capacity. With very few exceptions, life in techno-industrial society disconnects individuals from nature and focuses their attentions and efforts on the premier goals of that society: employment, income, consumption, identity through acquisition of commodities. Reflective, not consumptive or acquisitive, enjoyment of nature is ruled out for the most part and any sense of frustration generated by the increasingly administered activities in which individuals engage in is mollified by further consumptive activities.

The difference between reflective and consumptive enjoyment is crucial. The aesthetic sense described by Marcuse and Beston and the sense of the sacred described by Maguire and Berry are reflective senses which perceive intellectually and emotionally those qualities in nature which connect with these senses. Aesthetic and religious experience transforms the individual and the way he or she responds to nature, Earth, and the universe, and strongly suggests ethical responsibility on the part of the individual toward nonhuman life. This aesthetic and religious experience is not primarily directed at transforming the natural environment, unlike the dominant economic and technological valuation of the world which is intended to transform nature and the entire planet into one globally administered and commodified system for the purpose of maximizing production and consumption. Presently, the churches which could be a countervailing force against the reductionism of the dominant paradigm are, as Berry observes, much too pious and too focused on redemption to resist the progressive deterioration of creation on Earth. Colleges and universities could also constitute a countervailing force against this reduction of nature to an economic resource. Instead, the vast majority of colleges and universities, as Berry states, prepare "students for their role in extending human dominion over the natural world, not for intimate presence to the natural world."[65] Since government is now largely the political ally of the techno-industrial economy, all four basic institutions which shape human life and activity under the dominant paradigm—the economic, political, intellectual, and religious establishments—support, directly or indirectly, the prevailing reductionist view of nature. Under these circumstances an ecological ethics based on an aesthetic sense and a sense of the sacred appears hopelessly romantic and is likely to be rejected out of hand.

Deriving Ecological Ethics from Human Ethics

Given the seeming utopianism of the attempt to construct an ecological ethics on a sense of the aesthetic and the sacred, on what other grounds can an ecological ethics be constructed? Deriving an ecological ethics from the principles that inform human ethics offers several foundational possibilities. One such possibility is to make ecological ethics a subset of human ethics and to gauge human behavior toward nature in terms of good or bad consequences for humans. Because humans value recreational activities in nature, protecting recreational areas becomes ethically obligatory since it serves human interests. Similarly, humans value natural resources for commercial and industrial activities. Natural areas which provide these resources, particularly if they are renewable, would therefore receive protection since their destruction would damage present and future human interests. In this context, what is good for humans determines how nature will be used. Nature has only instrumental value as determined by contemporary human needs and wants. All of nature is subordinated to human preferences and what is not preferred has no value and may be either ignored or disposed of. Clearly, an ecological ethics in its own right cannot be derived from a purely instrumentalist view of nature. One way to establish an independently standing ecological ethics which is derived from the principles that govern human ethics is to locate in nature those living entities that share in some degree or other the characteristics that humans possess which entitle them to ethical consideration.

One such approach is known as "moral extensionism" and has two leading representatives, Peter Singer[66] and Tom Regan.[67] Both agree that certain kinds of animals are entitled to moral consideration since they are moral subjects, that is, they possess the same characteristics that entitle humans to moral consideration. For Singer, any animal capable of experiencing suffering and enjoyment has an interest in avoiding suffering and pursuing enjoyment. Sentience or the ability to suffer and enjoy is a necessary condition for having interests and having interests is a necessary condition for receiving consideration as a moral subject. Accordingly, all sentient animals are moral subjects, entitled to moral consideration from humans. Such moral consideration means that it is ethically reprehensible for humans to cause the suffering of animals in order to satisfy their convenience or needs when such can be satisfied in ways that do not cause animal suffering. Under the rule of assigning ethical consideration to sentient animals

> we would be forced to make radical changes in our treatment of animals that would involve our diet, the farming methods we use, experimental procedures in many fields of science, our approach to wildlife and to hunting, trapping and the wearing of furs, and areas of entertainment like circuses, rodeos, and zoos. As a result, a vast amount of suffering would be avoided.[68]

All human decisions in this approach would have to take into consideration the interests of sentient animals, minimizing wherever possible the amount of suffering imposed on animals by human actions. Since the interests of humans differ from those of sentient nonhumans, the interests of humans can and will on different occasions trump the interests of sentient nonhumans. Such trumping will not be ethically reprehensible provided the interests of all parties, human and nonhuman, are taken into consideration. The calculation of total suffering and enjoyment caused by human action on other humans, and in moral extensionism on nonhumans as well, has always plagued a utilitarian approach to ethics, requiring the kind of felicific calculus that Bentham proposed with all its attendant difficulties.[69]

Tom Regan has rejected Singer's utilitarian approach, arguing that an ecological ethics requires assigning rights to sentient animals on the grounds that such animals have inherent value. To have inherent value is to have value independent of the needs or interests or uses of anyone else. Any sentient animal has inherent value, because it is the subject of a life which is to say that it has a sense of the present, initiates action in pursuit of goals and interests, can suffer pain and experience enjoyment, and has an individual welfare that can prosper or decline independently of its utility to others. For Regan, the ethical issue at the heart of animal farming, for example, is not the suffering of the animals per se.

> But the fundamental wrong isn't the pain, the suffering, isn't the deprivation. These compound what's wrong. Sometimes—often— they make it much worse. But they are not the fundamental wrong. The fundamental wrong is the system that allows us to view animals as *our resources*, here for us—to be eaten, or surgically manipulated, or put in our cross hairs for sport or money.[70]

Thus, animal farming uses sentient animals as things, useful because they serve as food for people. But sentient animals that are subjects of a life have, as do humans, an inherent value that must be respected by moral agents. This inherent value creates a right for its holder, a right to have its life respected simply because it has a life. Entities with inherent value are ends in themselves, not means for the realization of others' purposes. Even though sentient animals cannot behave as moral agents since they cannot recognize the inherent value of others, they are to be considered moral patients or subjects, entitled to respect, entitled to a right to exist as subjects of a life. A rights approach to an ecological ethics excludes utilitarian considerations since no amount of enjoyment on the part of rights violators, even if conjoined with the elimination of any pain on the part of the violated, can ethically justify violating the right of a sentient animal to be the subject of its own life. While Singer's class of sentient beings ranges from mammals to crustaceans, Regan restricts sentiency to "mentally normal mammals of a year or more."[71]

Both Singer and Regan have derived an ecological ethics from human ethics, maintaining, in essence, that only those nonhumans that share the relevant characteristics that make humans the paradigm holders of moral value, are entitled to consideration as moral subjects. For Regan, moral standing derives from the inherent value of a subject of a life. For Singer, moral standing is derived from the capacity to suffer and enjoy and thus to have an interest to avoid pain and seek enjoyment. Both Singer and Regan extend ethical consideration to a category of nonhumans for an anthropocentric reason, namely, the possession by certain nonhumans of morally relevant characteristics as these are understood by humans. Kenneth Goodpaster has challenged an ecological ethics founded on such patently anthropocentric principles.

> Neither rationality nor the capacity to experience pleasure and pain seem to me necessary (even though they may be sufficient)

conditions on moral considerability. And only our hedonistic and concentric forms of ethical reflection keeps us from acknowledging this fact. Nothing short of the condition of being alive seems to me to be a plausible and nonarbitrary criterion.[72]

Taylor: Biocentric Ecological Ethics

Paul Taylor's *Respect for Nature* is a comprehensive effort to construct an ecological ethics based on Kenneth Goodpaster's plausible and nonarbitrary criterion of simply being alive,[73] an ecological ethics based on biocentric principles.[74] Taylor's ecological ethics is concerned with relations between humans and the natural world, the latter defined as natural ecosystems free of human intrusion and changing only through genetic mutation and natural selection. Two types of natural ecosystems can be distinguished. One type has never been exploited by humans and has undergone no major changes brought on by human culture and technology. The second type has undergone major changes as a result of human activity but has returned to a natural condition as in parts of New England where former farm land has reverted to forest. Unlike Singer and Regan, Taylor does not base his ecological ethics on an extrapolation of morally relevant human characteristics. Nor is his ecological ethics based on the aesthetic and religious motifs found in the writers previously described or on so-called moral intuitions derived from social conditioning. Humans as moral agents must engage in ethical inquiry "to establish the rational grounds for a system of moral principles by which human treatment of natural ecosystems and their wild communities of life ought to be guided."[75] Questions raised by ethical inquiry are whether humans have an ethical relation to nature or only to humans; if humans do have ethical relations to nature, on what grounds do such relations rest; how are such grounds to be justified; and what guidelines are there to resolve conflicts between duties humans owe to nature and duties they owe to each other. While a wholly anthropocentric environmental ethics derives all duties to nature from duties to humans, a biocentric ecological ethics grounds duties humans have to nonhuman life forms on the inherent worth of all sentient and living entities. Like Singer and Regan, Taylor distinguishes between moral agents and moral subjects. Moral agents, the class of which includes all mentally competent humans, are capable of making moral judgments based on ethical rules of conduct and bear responsibility for their actions. Moral subjects are all entities that can be harmed or benefited. All moral agents can take the standpoint of moral subjects and are themselves, in relationship to other moral agents, moral subjects.

An ecological ethics must, like all ethical systems, satisfy both formal and material conditions necessary for the postulation of valid moral principles. Formal conditions describe a valid moral principle with no reference to the empirical conditions to which the principle or rule applies. The principle must be general in form, universally applicable to all moral agents, applied disinterestedly and must be taken as overriding all nonmoral principles or rules, including the laws of the state. Material conditions for the application of a valid moral principle describe the actual existing entities to which moral principles apply. In human ethics, moral principles are applied to humans treated as persons, that is, as centers of autonomous choice and valuation. Human ethics, thus, is based on a belief system which regards all humans as persons with the capacity for self-realization and conscious preference for those elements which contribute to the attainment of a good life. An ecological ethics also entails a belief system and like human ethics requires an attitude of respect for moral subjects and a set of rules and standards to guide the behavior of moral agents in their relations with moral subjects.

For Taylor, the belief system of an ecological ethics is biocentrism which maintains that every human is a member of the Earth's community of life and that the very existence of humans depends on the health of the biological system of nature. Each organism in this community of life has a *telos* or ultimate goal which is to become as fully the form of life it is as possible. This *telos* is not confined to conscious and self-reflective organisms, nor is it manifested in a hierarchy of life forms with some at the top of the evolutionary process and others at the bottom. Biocentrism recognizes and respects wild life forms for themselves, not for their usefulness to humans. Taylor differentiates between wild organisms and those bred for human purposes. Ecological ethics is directed to wild nature only. A separate ethics, an ethics for what Taylor refers to as bioculture, needs to be applied to domesticated plants and animals since the instrumental value of plants and animals bred for commercial and research purposes does not eclipse the inherent worth of such organisms. The institutions and practices of the bioculture rest on the unconditioned power of humans but neither power nor the lack of personal feeling absolves humans of moral consideration for the animals and plants of the bioculture. Some sacrifice of human interests is entailed in the practice of a biocultural ethics as it is in the practice of an ecological ethics.[76]

The attitude of respect for nature which represents the second of the three components that constitute an ecological ethics is incumbent on all moral agents who recognize that wild organisms have a good of their own which is independent of their usefulness for humans. To have a good of its own does not require that a wild organism be conscious of that good. Plants and simple forms of animal life have a good of their own as do more complex forms of life. Moral agents can recognize an objective good for wild organisms even if the latter cannot. The good of an entity can be ascertained empirically. The decision to respect the good of an organism is an ethical choice made by a moral agent who recognizes the inherent worth of the organism. Such an attribution by a moral agent recognizes that the organism is a moral subject. The attitude of respect for nature requires a set of dispositions on the part of moral agents: valuational or valuing wild organisms for their inherent worth, conative or desiring to avoid harming organisms and wanting to adopt policies to preserve wild life, practical or judging and willing specific actions, and affective or feeling pleased when wild life flourishes.

Thus, it can be said that actions are right and character traits are morally good when these express and embody the moral attitude of respect for nature. Without the valuation of inherent worth required by an attitude of respect for nature, actions that in fact benefit wild life are not expressions of respect for nature and are incidental to the pursuit of human interests. Personal feelings for nature do not in themselves express a moral attitude of respect for wild nature. The obligation of moral agents to recognize the inherent worth of wild nature, that is, to assume an attitude of respect, is not based on personal feeling. Scientific, aesthetic, and hedonistic attitudes toward nature can never supercede the attitude of respect for nature since nonmoral grounds cannot supercede moral principles, but such attitudes may not be incompatible with the attitude of respect for nature if they do not exploit nature. The attitude of respect for nature is not founded on a more fundamental moral principle and cannot be justified by giving moral reasons for it since any such reasons are determined by the attitude of respect. Taylor maintains that to justify the attitude of respect for nature it must be demonstrated that the entire ethical system entailed by it is a valid one in that the belief system, biocentrism, that underlies the attitude is acceptable to all who are rational, factually informed, and have a developed sense of reality awareness.

The reality that biocentrism is based on is the ecology of life on Earth. Humans are members of Earth's community of life in the same way as nonhuman organisms are members of that community. The natural world is a system of interdependent relations of diverse life forms and necessarily includes humans and their artifacts. Humans have an increasing capacity to affect significantly the natural environment, particularly as their economic activities approach the carrying capacity of the planet, and therefore have a choice to promote or destroy the necessary conditions for the survival and well-being of the Earth's community of life. Human activities are presently causing air and water pollution, species extinction, soil erosion, deforestation, desertification, global warming, and stratospheric ozone depletion. Given that humans and other species are integral elements in a system of interdependence in which the survival and well-being of each living thing is determined by the physical conditions of its environment and its relation to other living things, a rational individual who is factually informed and has a developed sense of reality awareness will adopt an attitude of respect for nature.

While humans have free will, autonomy and social freedom, they are not inherently superior to other life forms. Like other living things, humans, too, face constraints on their freedom to preserve their existence and further their own good: external positive constraints such as physical violence directed at them; external negative constraints such as the absence of sufficient food, medical services, and other material conditions essential to well-being; and internal negative constraints such as the absence of health. Such constraints represent barriers for humans and nonhumans alike in the way of achieving the fullness of life as that life is expressed in different life forms. Rational individuals can approach nonhuman life from an objective and holistic perspective. Objectivity means seeing the animal or plant not in its relationship to human purposes (the coyote as seen through the eyes of a sheep owner or the deer as seen through the eyes of a hunter) but as life forms that possess a unique form of existence, the full manifestation of which goes well beyond any economic or cultural relations to humans. "Certainly our acquiring scientific knowledge about certain kinds of animals and plants can help us enormously in the attempt to understand objectively the everyday existence of particular individuals of those kinds."[77] Wholeness of vision about nonhuman life forms requires rejecting the one-sided understanding that most humans have of animals and plants, for example, the hunter who sees the deer as only game, the researcher who sees laboratory animals as research tools, the logger who sees a tree as only so many board feet.

> The animal or plant is not seen through a screen of abstract forms, categories or stereotypes imposed by humans interests and purposes. Insofar as we are able to achieve wholeness or vision in our grasp of an organism's uniqueness, we come to know the life of that individual as it is lived by it. We then conceive of it as a complete, many-faceted being carrying out its own mode of existence, responding in its own way to the particular circumstances confronting it.[78]

Objectivity and wholeness of vision regarding animals and plants provide a heightened awareness on the part of moral agents which makes possible the capacity to take the standpoint of animals and plants and make judgments as to what actions and conditions can harm or benefit them. Recognizing the full reality of the existence of animals and plants means conceiving of each such entity as a teleological center of a life pursuing its own good in its own way in the world. Objectivity, wholeness of vision, and recognition of animals and plants as teleological centers of their own lives are the elements of a developed sense of reality awareness and provide the capacity for humans, acting as moral agents, to recognize animals and plants as moral subjects with a good of their own.

> Shifting out of the usual boundaries of anthropocentricity, the world-horizon of our moral imagination opens up to encompass all living things. Seeing them as we see ourselves, we are ready to place the same value on their existence as we do our own. If we regard ourselves as possessing inherent worth, so will we be disposed to regard them.[79]

To affirm the inherent worth of all living things, to recognize them as teleological centers of their own life and to view them as moral subjects deserving of moral consideration, requires the denial of human superiority. That humans have reason, autonomy, and the freedom to change their social institutions while nonhumans do not possess these characteristics, does not entail the conclusion that humans are morally or otherwise superior. All life forms have their own species-specific characteristics. That a cheetah can run faster than any human does not make it superior to a human. Assigning superiority to a species because of its species-specific characteristics is to commit the category fallacy of judging one group by the standards of another group. Human characteristics are valuable only from the human standpoint. Such characteristics have made humans a dominant species but domination of nonhumans is a physical fact, not a ground for declaring the superiority of humans. The human capacity to reason makes it possible for humans who are factually informed and possess a developed sense of reality to act as moral agents, take the standpoint of an animal or plant and treat it as a moral subject. This human capacity for moral agency is a unique characteristic not shared by other animals, but since animals cannot be moral agents they cannot logically be judged to be morally inferior to humans. Taylor concludes, therefore, that humans do not have greater inherent worth despite the several traditional arguments designed to prove that humans have greater inherent worth and are superior.

The Greek essentialist argument[80] that human reason endows humans with greater inherent worth illustrates the category fallacy. Reason is important for human good but the absence of the reasoning capacities of humans in nonhumans does not validate claims of human superiority. The Christian argument that humans are higher than animals and plants in the universal chain of being, below only God and the angels, rests on suppositions of faith and, for Taylor, by assigning nonhumans to a lower scale of value, brings into question the Creator's moral virtues of love, mercy, and justice.[81]

The Cartesian argument for human superiority,[82] distinguishing humans who are both mind (soul) and matter (body) from all other life which is merely matter extended in space assumes a metaphysical gulf between humans and nonhumans which no scientific evidence or objective observation supports. Other more recent arguments for human superiority based on the greater range of human capacities (from opera to calculus) or the possession of moral rights are further examples of the category fallacy.[83] Whatever the range of human capacities, whatever moral rights humans possess in their relations with their fellow humans, these capacities and moral rights are characteristics of humans and their absence in nonhumans does not establish the greater inherent worth of the former. The biocentric outlook demands species impartiality. Every living entity has a good of its own and possesses the same inherent worth as every other living entity. *Ceteris paribus*, the good of nonhumans is to be given as much weight in moral deliberations as human good.[84]

The biocentric position which justifies the attitude of respect for nature and the concomitant attribution of inherent worth to all living things meets the formal criteria for judging the acceptability of any philosophic world view: comprehensiveness and completeness; systematic order, coherence and internal consistency; and freedom from obscurity, conceptual confusion and semantic vacuity.[85] Under ideal conditions of rationality of thought and judgment, factual enlightenment and a developed capacity of reality awareness which is consistent with all known empirical truths, moral agents will choose biocentrism as the world view underlying an ecological ethics of respect for the inherent worth of all life.

Moral agents who accept biocentrism and the attitude of respect for nature which it entails require specific rules to guide them in meeting their moral duty to nonhuman moral subjects. Taylor proposes four rules to guide moral agents when dealing with wild nonhuman life in situations where moral duties to nonhumans are not in conflict with moral duties to humans. The primary rule is nonmaleficence which requires that moral agents never harm an entity which does not harm them. This rule does not require of moral agents the positive duty to prevent harm or alleviate suffering. A second rule is noninterference which entails two negative duties: no restrictions are to be placed on the freedom of any individual organism and a general hands-off policy is to be followed with regard to individual organisms and their environment . The rule of noninterference is in line with the biocentric valuing of the autonomous functioning of the natural order and the upholding of species impartiality. A third rule is fidelity or the prohibition of actions designed to deceive animals such as hunting using calling devices,[86] fishing, and trapping. The rule may be broken as a temporary expedient justified by the fourth rule of restitution which requires that a moral agent who harms a nonhuman organism owes that entity some form of compensation for the moral wrong committed. If an individual organism is killed, the compensation under the rule of restitution must be to that organism's species to advance its good. If the species itself has been decimated, compensation goes to the remaining members in the form of protection and a secure habitat. Major forms of restitution are the setting aside of wilderness areas, protecting endangered species, restoring the quality of a degraded environment, and assisting animals and plants to regain a healthy state after they have been injured by human actions. Injuries to individual organisms or to species and the destruction of habitat by natural causes lie outside the range of duties that moral agents owe to nonhuman life.

> In one sense to have the attitude of respect toward natural ecosystems, toward wild living things, and toward the whole process of evolution is to believe that nothing goes wrong in nature. Even the destruction of an entire biotic community or the extinction of a species is not evidence that something is amiss. If the causes for such events arose within the system of nature itself, nothing improper has happened. In particular, the fact that organisms suffer and die does not itself call for corrective actions on the part of humans when *humans have had nothing to do with the cause of that suffering and death.*[87]

Of the four rules to guide moral agents in their relations with nonhuman organisms, nonmaleficence overrides both fidelity and restitution if the application of these latter two rules results in harm to nonhuman organisms. There can be no conflict between nonmaleficence and noninterference since refraining from intruding on the natural environment cannot bring harm to any nonhuman organism. Depending on the circumstances in specific situations, the rule of fidelity may override noninterference and restitutive justice may override both noninterference and fidelity. The primary duty of moral agents is nonmaleficence:

> Our most fundamental duty toward nature . . . is to do no harm to wild living things as far as this lies within our power. Our respect for nature primarily expresses itself in our adhering to this supreme rule.[88]

The four rules to guide moral agents in their behavior toward wild organisms necessarily operate in a world where nature and humans interact and where industrial societies particularly have a severe negative impact on the natural environment as they increasingly reduce nature to resources to be processed by the economy. Under such circumstances, duties to wild nature and duties to humans lead to competing moral claims. That only humans have moral rights does not justify human domination of nature or denial of the inherent worth of nonhuman life.[89] Yet, humans, too, have inherent worth, are moral subjects, and have a good of their own which they are morally entitled to pursue. To deal with conflicting moral claims faced by moral agents who adopt an attitude of respect for nature and for humans, Taylor provides five priority principles for resolving such conflicting claims. The first principle of self-defense permits a moral agent to harm or kill wild organisms that threaten his or her life. Since both the moral agent and the wild organism have inherent worth, the former is not obligated to exchange her life, if in danger, for that of the threatening organism.

The second principle of proportionality is based on the distinction between basic and nonbasic interests of humans and nonhumans. Basic interests of humans and nonhumans override nonbasic interests. The former refer to the conditions and needs which must be satisfied if an individual organism is to function as a teleological center of its own life. In the case of humans, nonbasic interests which are necessarily deadly to basic interests of nonhumans, as listed by Taylor,[90] include killing elephants for their ivory tusks to carve items for the tourist trade, capturing tropical birds for sale as caged pets, trapping and killing reptiles for their skins to be used in making fashion products, killing leopards and jaguars for the luxury fur trade, and all hunting and fishing done for sport and recreation rather than for needed food as in native subsistence hunting and fishing. To satisfy such nonbasic human interests, the basic interest and inherent worth of the animal trapped or killed are disregarded in order to pursue activities which are not essential for the flourishing of human life. Such nonbasic human interests clearly negate the attitude of respect for nature.

The third principle of minimum wrong guides the action of moral agents when nonbasic human interests which are pursued in the context of social values and cultural goals conflict with the basic interests of nonhumans. Nonbasic human interests shaped by dominant cultural norms include the building of a hospital or museum on a natural habitat, the construction of a highway or airport which causes serious disturbance of a natural environment, and damming a river for a hydroelectric power plant. Unlike the killing of elephants for their tusks and sport hunting and fishing, the building of a hospital or the construction of a highway is not in itself incompatible with an attitude of respect for nature. Such activity does not of necessity require the killing of a wild organism and could, with proper precautions, be carried out with minimum harm to the natural environment.[91] Accordingly, moral agents involved in such activities must recognize the harmful consequences to nature that are likely to occur and make the best effort to minimize the harm. Since harm, however mimimal, will occur, moral agents must apply the principle of restitutive justice to compensate for the harm done.

The fourth principle of distributive justice applies when the basic interests of humans and nonhumans conflict, as they will when both exist in the same land area and require access to indigenous resources. Patterns of accommodation suggested by the principle of distributive justice include setting aside permanent wilderness areas closed off to human activity; common conservation or the sharing of common resources with nonhumans such as a lake which serves as a breeding habitat for migratory birds and also provides recreational opportunities for humans; environmental integration which involves the building of human residences in a way that permits the coexistence of nonhuman life;[92] and rotation by which humans and nonhumans alternate in their use of a specific environment as in the case of an area used for strip mining and then restored to the extent that habitat is available for various animals and plants.

The fifth principle of restitutive justice is applied when harm occurs to nonhumans under the principles of minimum wrong and distributive justice which allow moral agents to override the basic interests of nonhumans.[93] The greater the harm done, the greater the reparation required. Despite the focus on individual organisms in biocentrism, the most effective form of reparation, according to Taylor, is to tend to the well-being of the ecosystem in which the harmed organisms exist.

> [We need to] focus our concern on the soundness and health of whole ecosystems and their biotic communities, rather than on the good of particular individuals. As a practical measure this is the most effective means for furthering the good of the greatest number of organisms. Moreover, by setting aside certain natural habitats and by maintaining certain types of physical environments in their natural condition, compensation to wild creatures can be "paid" in an appropriate way.[94]

Taylor's ecological ethics is based on biocentrism as a belief system and on an attitude of respect which is entailed by biocentrism and which recognizes the inherent worth of all life forms and accords each moral consideration. As with human ethics, an ecological ethics requires that moral agents autonomously accept the principles and rules that it postulates. Moral agents view wild nature as inhabited by life forms with inherent worth not because the law, supported by sunctions against violators, requires that they do so but because their reason and a developed sense of reality awareness require that they so act. Since moral agents treat wild animals and plants as moral subjects with inherent worth that must be respected, the argument, advanced by some, that an ecological ethics must assign moral rights to wild animals and plants adds nothing, according to Taylor, to the moral considerability of such entities and even introduces linguistic usages appropriate only to human ethics. Moral rights exist in human society within a common moral context of rights-holders and rights-recognizers who are simultaneously moral subjects and moral agents. Each bearer of moral rights is recognized by others as an equal among equals. Plants and animals cannot logically be conceived as bearers of moral rights since they are not moral agents with the capacity to recognize and respect the moral rights of other moral subjects. Instead, plants and animals may be considered to have a general moral right in a biocentric ecological ethics to the preservation and protection of their good as their specific life forms require. As Taylor says, a valid system of ecological ethics can be maintained without emphasizing the language of rights especially when this language is understood according to the paradigm provided by the rights of humans. That nonhumans for the reasons presented cannot be said to have moral rights does not prevent human society from assigning legal rights to plants and animals as in the case of the Endangered Species Act of 1973.

> Once the people of a nation come to regard all wild living things as possessing inherent worth, they will enact such laws as are needed to protect the good of those wild creatures as far as that is compatible with the rights of humans. . . . In the light of the ethics of respect for nature . . . we can add that a society that gives recognition to wild creatures as bearers of legal rights is one which more completely fulfills valid moral principles concerning the relation between humans and the natural world than a society which does not.[95]

Taylor's system is an impressive example of a rationalist-deontological approach to the construction of an ecological ethics.[96] Moral agents who are rational, factually informed and fully cognizant of the reality of the ecology of life will choose to do their moral duty as called for by the attitude of respect for nature. They will do their moral duty, says Taylor, because they will possess both the general and special virtues needed to carry out their moral obligations.[97] The general virtues are those of moral strength and concern. Special virtues are specific character traits that enable the moral agent to carry out specific moral duties. For example, the special virtue of consideration or empathy is required to carry out the duty of nonmaleficence; for restitutive justice, the specific character traits of fairness and equitable dealing are needed. Each person, therefore, has the duty to strive to become a fully moral being by making his or her inner (private) motivational life congruent with the outer (public) life of action. Right conduct is the public counterpart of the inner structure of character. That wild nature expands the sensory experiences that techno-industrial society stifles and makes possible a sense of the beautiful and the sacred largely ruled out in urban areas, is a contingent fact for Taylor's ecological ethics. Moral agents do their moral duty toward wild life because it is the rationally warranted right thing to do. Feeling good about doing one's moral duty adds a pleasant fillip to the situation but is neither a necessary nor a sufficient basis for an ecological ethics. To know what is right through philosophic reasoning and to do what is right despite social norms and laws to the contrary, to persevere in one's moral duty because both reason and character demand no less, requires a very high standard of moral agency and one not likely to be met by most individuals in a society where the consumer culture renders self-restraint and other-regarding behavior economically counterproductive.[98] Taylor, however, is not unaware that an attitude of respect for nature may be established on other than rationalist-deontological grounds.

> Whether a culture accepts a mystical view of the identity of the human soul with the world-soul or looks at the relation between human and other forms of life in some nonmystical way (. . . religious transcendentalism, animism, Earth-stewardship . . .) the *belief-system in question must allow the attitude of respect for nature to be adopted and put into practice.* The biocentric outlook is a rational and scientifically enlightened way of conceiving of the place of humans in the natural world, but it need not be the only world view accepted by cultures when the ethical ideal of harmony between human civilization and nature is achieved.[99]

The harmony between human civilization and nature that Taylor refers to is understood as the preservation of a balance between human values and the well-being of animals and plants in wild nature. This concept of harmony between humans and wild nature is presented as an ethical ideal which provides a long-range moral purpose to guide the day by day decisions of moral agents in specific settings: a world that contains as much good, human and nonhuman, as it is possible for it to contain.

> Most of us in the contemporary world have been brought up in a thoroughly anthropocentric culture in which the inherent superiority of humans over other species has been taken for granted. Great effort will be needed to emancipate ourselves from this established way of looking at nonhuman animals and plants. But it is not beyond the realm of practical possibility. Nothing prevents us from exercising our powers of autonomy and rationality in bringing the world as it is gradually closer to the world as it ought to be.[100]

The Individual and the Ecosystem in Ecological Ethics

While Taylor's ecological ethics is not based on the moral extensionism that shapes the ecological ethics of Singer and Regan and limits moral consideration to sentient animals, his ethics is based on a logical extension of what he considers to be at the center of human ethics, an attitude of respect for individuals who are seen as teleological centers of their own life. Taylor extends this attitude of respect to all nonhuman life, especially wild but including domesticated nonhuman life. A major criticism of any ecological ethics that extends moral consideration to individual life forms is that it gives moral priority to the well-being of individual organisms, rather than the ecosystem in which such individual organisms exist through a network of interaction and interdependency with other life forms. Giving preference to the individual over the ecosystem community appears to inject into an ecological ethics the individualistic focus typical of the market society and to ignore the value and importance of community just as it is ignored in the market society. This criticism of an organism-centered ecological ethics is related closely to another criticism, namely, that an acceptable ecological ethics cannot be an extension of human ethics. Thus, Thomas Berry:

> The ecological community is not subordinate to the human community. Nor is the ecological imperative derivative from human ethics. Rather, our human ethics are derivative from the ecological imperative. The basic ethical norm is the well-being of the comprehensive community and the attainment of human well-being within that community.[101]

Aldo Leopold's dictum that a thing is [ethically] right when it tends to preserve the integrity, stability, and beauty of the biotic community and wrong when it does otherwise is the foundation stone of an ecocentrically focused ecological ethics which gives moral consideration to the ecosystem as a community of life. An ecocentric ecological ethics requires moral agents to become factually informed about the objective conditions necessary for the integrity, stability, and beauty of the ecosystem and act to maintain or reinstate such conditions. The science of ecology is the primary source of information about such ecosystem functions as exploitation, conservation, release and reorganization, the role of keystone and insurance species, and the role of biodiversity generally. Once the status of an ecosystem has been determined, moral agents may be required to act against the welfare of individual organisms and even species if either threatens the integrity, stability and beauty of an ecosystem and to condemn human actions that undermine the health of an ecosystem as violations of an ecocentric ethics. Such an ethics can be said to be derived from the objective needs of ecosystems themselves and not from psychological or logical extensions of a human ethics. Thus, Holmes Rolston III:

> The ecologist finds that ecosystems are objectively satisfactory communities in the sense that organismic needs are sufficiently met for species long to survive, and the critical ethicist finds (in a subjective judgment matching the objective process) that such *ecosystems are satisfactory communities to which to attach duty.* . . . Duties arise in an encounter with the system that projects and protects these member components in biotic community. . . . We follow nature, this time ecologically.[102]

While biocentric and ecocentric approaches to an ecological ethics are, arguably, derived from different principles, the ecocentric approach ostensibly removing all anthropocentric vestiges from its ethical norms,[103] the practical, real world difference between Leopold's dictum and Taylor's biocentric rules of conduct and priority principles to settle conflicting moral duties to humans and wild nature, may not be that wide. The first two duties in Taylor's rules of conduct are nonmaleficence and noninterference. Both of these duties require moral agents to adopt a hands-off policy toward wild nature. If such duties are violated for whatever reason, moral agents must provide appropriate reparation, including, as Taylor says, furthering the soundness and health of whole ecosystems and their biotic communities as the most effective means of contributing to the welfare of the greatest number of organisms. The priority principles for addressing conflicting moral duties to humans and wild nature are also not at odds with an ecocentric ecological ethics. The principles of proportionality, minimum wrong, and distributive justice are aimed at reducing the impact of human activities on wild nature and are all supplemented, as are the rules of conduct, by the principle of restitutive justice, which requires reparation for any harm done to wild nature by a moral agent. Here again reparation as noted can effectively take the form of furthering the health of the ecosystem in which the affected animals and plants live. With ecosystems as with humans, an ounce of prevention is worth a pound of cure. If complete human noninterference in ecosystems were possible, the integrity, stability, and beauty of ecosystems would be assured. Since it is currently difficult to find ecosystems anywhere on Earth that have not been interfered with, Taylor's rules of conduct and priority principles offer guidance to moral agents on how to minimize harm to wild nature and how to proceed to offer restitution if harm is done. What ecocentric ethics adds to biocentric ethics is the understanding that individual organisms are what they are because of their interactions with other organisms in an ecosystem.

Ecocentric ethics assigns ontological primacy to the systems and relationships which shape the individual organism. Predator and prey naturally shape each other and are shaped by the matrix of relationships which is an ecosystem. But understanding the relationships that constitute the biotic community of an ecosystem does not mean that individual organisms or species are to be ignored by moral agents.[104] The ecocentric and biocentric approaches to an ecological ethics should be seen as complementary, not mutually exclusive, approaches. A moral agent who understands the role of ecosystems in shaping individual organisms has a more fully developed sense of the complex reality of the community of life of which the moral agent is a member and to which she owes moral duties.

The Social Implications of Ecological Ethics

Whether derived from elements of human ethics or from the ecology of ecosystems, an ecological ethics with widespread acceptance as a cultural norm and translated into law and administrative regulation would have a profound impact on the dominant institutions of society. An economics that treats all of nature as a resource for production would have to be abandoned and replaced by an ecological economics that recognizes physical and ethical limits to growth and undertakes to provide optimal conditions for the well-being of present and future generations of humans and nonhumans. Full-cost accounting which involves monetizing environmental stocks and services would be required of all proposed projects and, under the principle of restitutive justice, would include the cost of mandatory compensation when harm is inflicted on animals and plants and the ecosystem they inhabit. An ecological ethics also requires a profound change in the U.S. Constitution.

> [The devastation of the natural world] is due also to the American Constitution, which guarantees to humans participatory governance, individual freedoms, and rights to own and dispose of property—all with no legal protection for the natural world. The jurisprudence supporting such a constitution is profoundly deficient. It provides no basis for the functioning of the planet as an integral community that would include all its human and other-than-human components. Only a jurisprudence based on concern for an integral Earth community is capable of sustaining a viable planet.[105]

General recognition that humans are moral agents owing moral duties not only to one another but to nonhumans would dramatically alter the prevailing cultural psyche which now reflects the dominant paradigm values of economic reductionism, short-term maximizing policies of individuals and governments, and a materialist carpe diem solipsism which divorces the life of the individual from any deep and lasting relationships with the Earth's community of human and nonhuman life. An ecological ethics would connect the welfare of individual humans and the human community with the welfare of the natural environment. Social approbation would go to individuals who exhibited the character traits essential for the exercise of moral agency: self-control, conscientiousness, integrity, patience, courage, objectivity of judgment, perseverance, and steadfastness-in-duty.[106] Under the dominant paradigm such character traits or virtues stand in the way of an expanding economy and a one-dimensional consumer culture that marginalizes the human capacity to engage in other than accumulation and consumption activities.

The paradigm shift in economics, politics, and cultural values that an ecological ethics would effect would not leave untouched the aims, processes, and instrumentalities of an educational system which currently serves the purposes of the dominant techno-industrial paradigm by training students for required work and consumer skills and by reproducing through the various curricula the taken-for-granted norms of the dominant paradigm and the language and concepts in which these norms are embedded. What an ecologically oriented educational system would involve is the subject of the next chapter.

Chapter 4

Ecological Pedagogy

*The fact that we see [social and environmental decay] as
disconnected events or fail to see them at all is . . .
evidence of a considerable failure that we have yet to
acknowledge as an educational failure. It is a failure to
educate people to think broadly, to perceive systems
and patterns, and to live as whole persons.*

—*David W. Orr,* Earth in Mind

The Problem of Contemporary Education

From the perspective of ecologism most criticisms of American education
and proposals to correct its failings miss the point because both criticisms and
proposed reforms assume that what is of concern are problems in education
rather than problems of education. Voucher plans and calls for accountability
and outcome testing, smaller classes, merit pay for teachers, construction of
new buildings, computerization of classrooms, and secure schools deal with
the mechanics and logistics of the existing public educational system, rather
than with the issue of curriculum substance and purpose. The problem of
education, from an ecologistic perspective, is that it continues to reproduce,
explicitly or implicitly, the taken-for-granted assumptions of the dominant
techno-industrial paradigm. From grade school to university, the educational
system functions to reproduce the cognitive and psychological features of a
culture whose values are largely derived from the techno-industrial paradigm.

While there are disagreements among mainstream educators as to the most effective pedagogic techniques for enhancing classroom teaching (cooperative learning, direct instruction, assertive discipline, multiple intelligences, outcome-based education, critical literacy), and disagreements about the goals of education (providing computer literacy and related technical knowledge essential for successful competition in the business world, encouraging free expression of creative potential, enabling critical reflection and capacity for civic participation), such disagreements over techniques and goals are less significant than they appear because of the taken-for-granted pedagogic assumptions shared by most if not all the ostensible antagonists.[1]

These culturally driven assumptions or root metaphor ways of thinking permeate all the social institutions of the contemporary American techno-industrial society, education included, and necessarily form the cognitive background of the great majority of educators, regardless of differences in pedagogical technique and purpose which, taken in isolation, would appear to divide educators into separate and irreconcilable camps. Such shared, taken-for-granted assumptions include an anthropocentric view of the world reflected in textbooks and courses; the high status of technology and technology-induced change; the individual seen as an autonomous source of judgment and valuation when rationally informed and free of the constraints of tradition; social development viewed in terms of economic growth spurred by science and technology; the purpose of human life defined by the self-interested activities of individuals; techno-industrial culture viewed as the highest expression of human development; and machines, particularly the computer, used as analogues to explain the life processes and cognitive capacities of humans.[2] Within the context of the dominant techno-industrial paradigm, which emphasizes individual self-seeking, the conversion of nature into resources for economic growth, the relativization of all values except economic growth, and the application of human intelligence, particularly in its instrumental/technological form, to the mastery of the natural environment, the taken-for-granted assumptions of most educators are quite understandable. From an ecologistic perspective, however, these assumptions guarantee that mainstream education will continue to reproduce the dominant culture and its social and environmental consequences. Within an ecological pedagogy, terms such as intelligence, creativity, understanding, judgment, and learning take on meanings quite different from the way these terms are understood within the dominant paradigm. Similarly, new constructions must be assigned to the knower-known relationship, to the relationship between the individual and the community, and to the relationship between the educational enterprise and the natural environment within which all human institutions and activities, perforce, take place. While it is naive to believe that educational institutions can unilaterally initiate profound cultural changes, the

potentially significant role that education can play in assisting the ascendance
of a new social paradigm must be recognized. Whatever the forces that will
shape a new social paradigm, ultimately that paradigm will have to be incorporated in appropriate ways in educational curricula from grade school to
colleges and universities. The literature examined here represents both an
assessment of the failure of contemporary education to educate ecologically
literate citizens and a proposal to prepare American education to meet its
ecological responsibilities in the twenty-first century.

Orr: Principles of Ecological Education

David W. Orr, currently the director of environmental studies at Oberlin
College, has provided a trenchant critique of the ecological shortcomings of
American education as well as a number of specific proposals to address such
shortcomings. In *Earth in Mind* and *Ecological Literacy*,[3] he has emphasized
that he is addressing not only problems in education, but also the problems
of contemporary education. His comments, therefore, are, as he says "not a
call to tinker with minutiae, but a call to deeper change."[4] He lists six principles to guide efforts to rethink the whole educational enterprise, measured
against the agenda of human survival. All six principles are discussed in some
detail in what follows.

The first principle is that all education is environmental education, which
is to say that even in the absence of courses dealing with environmental
issues, a form of environmental education is taking place. The absence of
environmental courses in a college curriculum, for example, conveys to students the unimportance of a subject that is not discussed. Similarly, the absence of institutional efforts either to maintain any campus's natural
environment, or to refrain from using pesticides and herbicides on existing
landscapes, signals to students and faculty alike that what the institution does
not practice is not worth being concerned about. Other seemingly trivial acts
of non-performance on the part of the institution, such as leaving lights on in
unoccupied classrooms, habituate students and faculty to dismiss the urgency
of efforts to conserve energy. A president of a college who at commencement
sums up the purpose of a four-year liberal arts education as preparation for
job competition, clearly announces the irrelevancy of environmental education to graduates and their parents. The construction of a new building on a
college campus in typical twentieth-century style, sans passive and active
solar energy technology, sited on a formerly wooded area now cleared of all
trees, utilizing non-biodegradable materials, including wood from nonsustainable timbering practices, monumentalizes for students, faculty, alumni,
and visitors the disconnectedness of campus architecture and the natural

environment. What the college in its instructional programs and institutional practices ignores or is indifferent to becomes part of the campus culture and functions as an implicit educational curriculum.

The second principle Orr derives from the Greek concept of *paideia*, defined as the training of the physical and mental faculties in such a way as to produce a broad enlightened mature outlook harmoniously combined with maximum cultural development.[5] From this perspective, the goal of education "is not mastery of subject matter but mastery of one's person."[6] Mastery of one's person suggests an understanding of limits for one's self and for society as a whole, an understanding made possible by the multidimensional and transformative outlook which is the goal of *paideia*. The principles of ecological economics, political economy, and ethics are all based on concepts of limits: to economic growth within a finite globe, to centralized politics and economics given the spatial constraints on meaningful human interaction and accountability, and to self-seeking and self-aggrandizement given the moral considerability of other humans and nonhumans. To recognize such limitations and to strive for a full and rich life within such limitations is an indication that one's education has succeeded in producing an understanding of interconnections and interdependencies. How far contemporary education is from the *paideia* norm is measured by its failure to educate for any mature sense of limits, be these personal, economic, political, or cultural. The technocratic focus on technical education as certification for the job market has no place for a sense of limits on economy activity and expected personal rewards. The neo-romantic focus on the full expression of individual emotions and sensibilities carries with it no reference to the individual's place in the community and responsibility to others. The emancipatory focus on providing the individual with critical analytic skills and capacity for civic participation while addressing the economic reductionism of the technocratic approach and the solipsistic individualism of the neo-romantic model, places no limits on human activities if they are rationally informed and carried out by way of a democratic political process. The emancipatory model suggests, in fact, that the utilization of critical, scientific inquiry combined with an active democratic citizenry can remove any impediments to ongoing human progress defined as a rising, largely material standard of living.[7] It is difficult to find anywhere in public and private higher education academic or other experiences that equate an informed and mature outlook with a clear sense of limits. Those students who are provided with and expect an education that will give them a competitive edge in the job market place no limits on expected income and an expected life-style. Nor will they take seriously any suggested limits to economic growth since the growth of the economy is synonymous with their economic security and the expectations associated with such security. If contemporary education does not provide that mature outlook which recognizes and accepts limits to personal and collective activity, then one cannot expect that any other contemporary cultural, economic, or political institutions will address this failing.

Mainstream economics envisions the economy as a box in infinite space, expanding without limit. The Channel One program provided by corporations to public schools indoctrinates school children into a consumer culture where any notion of limits to self-gratification is taboo. The de facto expurgation of the concept of limits in the educational system and in the techno-industrial culture has produced not the mature outlook of the *paideia* ideal, but a generalized immaturity of the population characterized by a vastly reduced sense of responsibility on the part of the individual to a community, a place, the polity, and the natural environment. In an empty world scenario, this kind of cultural immaturity with its attendant economic and social consequences would not inflict a disaster on the natural environment, except on a local or regional scope. In a full-world scenario, the absence of any sense of limits in economic and political policy and cultural values portends a large-scale disaster, particularly with the globalization of the policy of unlimited economic growth.

As a third principle, Orr proposes that "knowledge carries with it the responsibility to see that it is well used in the world,"[8] that is to say knowledge should "be used responsibly, safely, and to consistently good purposes."[9] To use knowledge well and to consistently good purposes requires that the possessor of knowledge have a moral sense of what is right and what is wrong in the application of knowledge. Such a moral sense incorporates a notion of limits, along with an understanding of how the application of knowledge affects a specific locality or specific situation. Typically, most education today takes the form of conveying or incorporating in the student whatever information is deemed relevant to the course by the instructor and the standard textbook writer. For the most part, students are passive recipients in this process, acquiescing to the course requirements as established by the instructor. Rarely, if ever, is the course justified on the basis of its contribution to a wider body of knowledge which in turn is justified in terms of its contribution to some aspect of human welfare. Since students are either in no position to demand such justification or do not expect it, the only justification a course needs is to be included in the curriculum. Under these circumstances, each course stands on its own, no attempt is made to connect one course content with another, and most "knowledge" becomes a multiplicity of facts and pieces of information rather than a unified set of concepts constituting a body of knowledge the uses of which can be critically evaluated. When the knowledge in question is a technology, the inability to assess the consequences of its application means that it probably will not be used responsibly, safely, and to consistently good purposes in either the social or natural environment. In selling "knowledge" to students with little or no explanation of its purposes and consequences in use, the educational system reflects the practices of the market economy which focuses on the commodification of the results of scientific research and its technological applications. The question for the market is not what the social and environmental consequences of a given marketable product may be but whether there is a demand for it that justifies research, development, and promotion expenses. If the economy itself is visualized as a box in infinite space without any temporal, ethical, or physical relations to social and natural environments, then the notion that knowledge is to be used responsibly, safely, and to consistently good purposes makes no sense. A moral compass is useless in infinite space.

The fourth principle proposed by Orr follows from the third and states that "we cannot say that we know something until we understand the effects of this knowledge on real people and communities"[10] and, one might add, real natural environments. An education which assumes no limits to social progress defined as unlimited economic growth and unlimited individual maximization of utilities does not put a premium on understanding the impact of such collective and individual behavior on real people, human communities, and the natural environment. The globalization of an unlimited growth economy makes such understanding still more problematic, even if educational institutions made an effort to promote the skills and information required for such understanding.

In Orr's terms, what consumer of a hamburger in a fast food establishment "knows" the environmental, economic, social, and health impacts of the transaction? Does she "know" the wages and working conditions of employees of slaughterhouses? Does she "know" the kind of sadistic treatment that is often inflicted on animals in the slaughterhouses? Does she "know" that the grain used to feed the animals that provide the meat for the hamburger could significantly alleviate hunger in areas where millions are undernourished? Does she "know" that raising beef cattle in southern nations often results in the devastation of rain forests and other fragile environments and undermines the livelihood of peasants and small farmers? Does she "know" that the globalization of trade globalizes disease? Does she "know" that the globalization of Western economies further aggravates the per capita income disparities between the industrialized and developing countries? Such forms of knowing are not on the agenda of an educational system which reproduces the taken-for-granted assumptions of the techno-industrial paradigm. Knowing, as Orr defines it, is possible only under circumstances promoted by economic and political decentralization, under policies of full cost pricing, under policies which transform free trade into fair trade, in short, under conditions which make visible the effects of applied knowledge on real people, human communities, and natural environments. Under such conditions, individuals and communities affected may be able to respond in a way they cannot respond when the effects are rooted in decisions made by invisible corporate and government elites. Given such decentralization and localization, educational institutions could help students develop the intellectual and practical skills needed to understand the effects of applied knowledge on their lives and on their communities. As long as the educational curriculum is located within the institutional framework of the techno-industrial paradigm, it will continue to prepare students to function within that framework. It will not prepare them to know and question the effects of the system on real people, communities, and natural environments.

Knowing, as Orr understands it, is really ecologically informed knowing, a form of knowing in which the emphasis is on how things are related, how doing one thing results in affecting many other things. An unlimited growth economy which globalizes its activities rests on an epistemology which is linear, which gives primacy to objects and not relationships, and ignores or marginalizes its impacts on social and natural environments. Contemporary education for the most part implicitly accepts this epistemology which is reflected in the linear, disconnected nature of the various subject matters taught and in the inability of graduates to understand the larger effects of such personal activities as, for example, the purchase of a hamburger in a fast food store or reliance on an automobile as the chief mode of transportation in urban areas. The paradigm form of knowing for Orr requires the articulation of goals and purposes to which all applied forms of knowledge are subordinated as means are to ends. To know the effects of economic and political policy on real individuals, communities, and natural environments assumes that the effects known are to be evaluated within a larger framework of valued ends. Simply cataloguing the effects perceived would not result in any meaningful response to problems. Ecological education would, unlike the current system, articulate the ends promoted by an ecological economics, political economy and ethics and provide the instrumental skills and knowledge needed to achieve these ends.

In the current techno-industrial society the only generally acknowledged end is constant economic growth. Thus, there is no limit to the proliferation of instrumental skills and knowledge designed to promote this end. Since the dominant paradigm takes as self-evident the desirability of constant increases in the mass of man-made capital and consumer goods, educational institutions operating within this paradigm will privilege those skills and forms of knowledge which serve the growth economy. Unlike a society based on the principles of the ecologistic paradigm which would be rich in examined human developmental ends and supplied with a sufficient number of appropriate instrumentalities to support these ends, the techno-industrial society is rich in an unending stream of technical means to accomplish the taken-for-granted goal of increasing without limits the mass of manufactured goods in existence. Under these circumstances, the current educational system will not provide a unified and coherent body of knowledge aimed at articulating transeconomic growth goals, supplying the requisite instrumental skills and knowledge, and eliminating from the curriculum those instrumentalities whose known effects on real individuals, communities, and the natural environment are incompatible with such social goals.

The fifth principle requires that students be in contact with "faculty and administrators who provide role models of integrity, care and thoughtfulness and . . . institutions capable of embodying ideals wholly and completely in all of their operations."[11] This principle in its application to ecological education calls for faculty and administrators who are committed to ecologistic economic, political, and ethical values, demonstrate these values in the educational curriculum and operations of the institution, and shape their public and personal behavior by these values. As Peter Singer has written. "[There] is something incoherent about living a life where the conclusions you come to in ethics did not make any difference to your life."[12] Professing convictions while acting in disregard of them is hypocrisy and students, as Orr states, soon learn "without anyone ever telling them, that they are helpless to overcome the frightening gap between ideals and reality."[13]

There are a number of major impediments to the actualization of this fifth principle. In higher education the Balkanization of the academic community into separate disciplines, subdisciplines, and subsets of subdisciplines has resulted in confining academic discourse to the narrowest, most specialized and, frequently, most arcane issues. Faculty in the same department may be worlds apart in terms of their specialties, teaching even basic courses which are designed to introduce the foundational concepts of the discipline from the perspective of their specialized field. Faculty, reflecting the market ethos, often behave like entrepreneurs selling their courses to a college administration and department. They advertise themselves, in most cases, by publishing in journals that cater to their specialized research. Whether the research done and published contributes to the quality of teaching and thus helps educate students, or whether it contributes to the solution of some pressing social problem is not the issue. However narrow (the more specialized the more likely it can find a niche in some specialized journal) the research and however small the intended readership, the goal of serving notice to the college that the faculty member is engaged in scholarship is achieved. This disciplinolatry,[14] which is the result of both the nature of graduate education and the publish or perish dictum in colleges and universities, has no bearing on ecologically informed knowledge and prevents faculty from acting as a role model of "integrity, care and thoughtfulness," personifying for students commitment to the concepts and values they teach in class. The narrower the specialty taught, the less likely that socially significant values and issues will be discussed and that the instructor will be in a position to demonstrate personal commitment to important values. Page Smith's comment on the overall educational impact of the research output of atomized academics ensconced in their specialties and sharing no common frame of reference is apropos:

> [T]he vast majority of the so-called research turned out in the modern university is essentially worthless. It does not result in any measurable benefit to anything or anybody. . . . It is busy work on a vast, almost incomprehensible scale. . . . [I]t deprives the student of what he or she deserves—the thoughtful and considerate attention of a teacher deeply and unequivocally committed to teaching.[15]

Smith is describing a situation of academic anarchy in higher education characterized by fiefdoms of specialized knowledge whose raison d'être is the protection of their territory. Smith's critique focuses on the intellectual vacuity of much of the research done in this Balkanized academic context and the resulting diversion of attention from the quality teaching which Smith insists is the major responsibility of college faculty.[16] The academic scene that Smith describes is one of drift without direction, with no consensus on what is or is not worth knowing and with little or no moral fervor and social commitment to any cause.[17] One might assume that under such circumstances no dominant set of beliefs shapes the academic agenda and students simply learn the separate esoterica of the various academic specialities. In fact, however, the separate academic specialities do exist in a commonality of shared values and assumptions derived from the dominant techno-industrial paradigm. All the academic specialities that Smith criticizes have in common their disregard of the natural environment within which individuals and societies exist and function. Terms such as "ecosystem," or "biosphere" are not an integral part of the academic vocabulary. If in economics references are made to "resources" and "environment," such references are linked to strategies for unlimited economic growth. While mainstream economics explicitly champions growth and its globalization and directly supports the techno-industrial paradigm, other disciplines and their associated specialities have a more implicit connection to the dominant paradigm beliefs.[18] Such implicit connections nevertheless ensure that the dominant paradigm remains free from the criticism that might be expected from disciplines that claim to be scientific and objective.

> Where intellectuals once addressed the public, they now talk mostly to each other about matters of little or no consequence for the larger society. To the same degree that it is obscure, jargon-laden, and trivial, professionalized knowledge has come as a great windfall to the comfortable, serving to divert attention from behavior

that is egregious, criminal, or merely embarrassing. When did an
issue of the *American Political Science Review* cause the comfortable in Congress to squirm? When did an issue of the *American
Economic Review* ever cause the barons of Wall Street to tremble?
And when did philosophy "cease to be 'the love of wisdom' and
aspire to be a science?"[19]

Not only does professionalized knowledge provide a windfall for the comfortable, that is, those who do well under the dominant paradigm institutions,
but for the most part the practitioners of specialized knowledge, outside of
their academic roles, pursue the standard forms of institutional recognition
and reward that make possible the consumer life-style of the more affluent.
As their disciplines have no clear moral content and direction, so their personal lives reflect the materialism of the market culture.[20] Thus, the fifth
principle underlying ecological pedagogy, namely, that faculty provide students with role models of integrity and care and that institutions embody
ideals in all of their operations is currently rendered inoperative by the moral
incoherence of specialized education and of the public and private lives of
many of its practitioners.

The sixth principle proposed by Orr is that process is important for
learning and that "the way in which learning occurs is as important as the
content of particular courses."[21] Pedagogy within the dominant paradigm is
not threatened by student passivity, lecturers who present information which
is to be memorized rather than questioned, and campus buildings and classrooms that implicitly teach the irrelevance of the natural environment to learning, indeed that learning requires that the natural environment be excluded. One
of the ironies experienced by the small minority of environmentally-oriented
faculty is that classes dealing with environmental issues are taught, on occa-
sion, in windowless rooms or rooms where existing windows cannot be opened.
Even non-urban campuses where every square foot of space is not occupied by
buildings do not integrate into the curriculum whatever natural environment
still exists. Few college seniors if asked to name five different species of trees
on the campus as a condition of graduation could do so. The sense of place so
important in making possible the reversal of environmental devastation is sorely
lacking in college students who "reside" for four years on a college campus.
Not only do students typically not know anything about the history, flora, fauna,
and soils of the place in which a college is located but the faculty and administrators are equally ecologically ignorant despite their normally much longer
tenure at the college.

A March morning is only as drab as he who walks in it without
a glance skyward, ear cocked for geese. I once knew an educated

lady, banded by Phi Beta Kappa, who told me that she had never
heard or seen the geese that twice a year proclaim the revolving
seasons to her well-insulated roof. Is education possibly a process
of trading awareness for things of lesser worth? The goose who
trades his is soon a pile of feathers.[22]

If biology departments where an increasingly molecular approach is
replacing field studies cannot be expected to counter this place ignorance, no
help can be anticipated from other science departments and departments in
the social sciences and humanities. An ecological pedagogy requires education within as well as about the natural environment and the former requires
that students and faculty work with hands as well as heads, learning "practical things necessary to the art of living well in a place: growing food,
building shelters, using solar energy. . . ."[23] Ecological pedagogy must encourage and train students to complement their intellectual comprehension of
environmental issues with a mental and manual competence needed to restore
the vital relationships between humans and the natural environment that have
been sundered by the dominant social institutions. Such institutions collectively operate to create a kind of generalized social amnesia concerning the
effects of human activity on the natural environment and the dependence of
healthy individuals and communities on healthy ecosystems. Treating students as computers programmed by instructors may provide the cadres of
technically literate workers required by an unlimited growth economy, but it
is not a process which can educate for an ecologically and democratically
responsible citizenship. Recalling Orr's first principle that all education is
environmental education, the process or how students are taught becomes as
important as what they learn. In fact, what they are taught even in an environmental issues lecture course, can be vitiated by the contradiction between
the course content and the denatured classroom in which the course is taught.

The application of these six principles within the framework of an ecological pedagogy would address the failings of American higher education as
noted by Page Smith: the flight from teaching, the largely useless research
which replaces teaching, and the "spiritual aridity"[24] of the higher education
enterprise. Within an ecological pedagogy research from whatever disciplinary
source would be aimed at providing solutions to the problems now confronting
human society: unsustainable economic growth, human impairment of ecosystem services essential to life, unsustainable population growth, increasing income disparities between individuals and between nations that cannot be reduced
through unlimited economic growth, accelerating rates of species extinction
and destruction of habitat, decreasing accountability of economic and political
institutions to those who are significantly affected by the policies of these
institutions, the fragmentation of communities and the resulting withdrawal of

individuals from participation in any meaningful civic life, and a general cultural malaise in which consumerism fills the moral vacuum. Teaching within an ecological pedagogy would, at its best not only ensure the ecological literacy of students, but also would empower them as moral agents to become active participants in the effort to advance the ecological paradigm. Such a sense of empowerment and moral agency on the part of students and faculty alike would substantially counter the spiritual aridity in higher education which for Page Smith is "the most depressing aspect of all."[25]

The six principles enunciated by Orr are aimed at promoting ecological literacy, defined as a basic understanding of fundamental ecological concepts, the current extent of environmental destruction, the economic and political causes of environmental destruction, and alternative economic and political models which are more environmentally benign. Such understanding must be complemented by practical skills needed to assist in environmental remediation in specific places and to engage in specific political and civic activities. Basic ecologically relevant concepts as listed by Orr include the laws of thermodynamics, carrying capacity, least-cost and end-use analysis, limits of technology, appropriate scale, sustainable agriculture and forestry, steady-state or sustainable economics, environmental ethics, the role of international institutions and national governments in addressing environmental problems, the appropriate degree of political and economic centralization, the distribution of land, wealth, and income, and processes to strengthen democratic participation and government accountability.[26]

Ecological literacy represents for Orr intelligence rather than the cleverness which passes for intelligence in mainstream education today. Cleverness focuses on the short term and on fragmented facts. Intelligence deals with the long run and integrates facts. Intelligence or ecological literacy can distinguish cause from effect and the question "how" from the question "why." Intelligence enables one to maintain a harmonious relationship with one's surroundings and to stay within the bounds of morality which is to say that intelligence does not "in the name of some alleged higher good, demand the violation of life, community, or decency."[27] Intelligence depends on character and is congruous with moderation, compassion, truthfulness, and justice and with a sense of limits and human fallibility.[28] Cleverness can enable one to get all As but flunk life. Cleverness or pre-ecological intelligence can develop complex computers, land humans on the moon, clone animals and yet devastate natural environments and leave unaddressed issues such as inner-city decay, increasing violence, suburban sprawl, urban traffic congestion, de facto political oligarchy, and environmental discrimination. Since intelligence in the ecological sense derives from human contact with nature, the ongoing destruction of nature may lead to the destruction of the wellsprings of intelligence itself.

Could it be that the conquest of nature, however clever, is in fact
a war against the source of mind? Could it be that the systematic
homogenization of nature inherent in contemporary technology
and economics is undermining human intelligence?

. . . We have good reason to believe that human intelligence
could not have evolved in a lunar landscape, devoid of biological
diversity. . . . Elemental things like flowing water, wind, trees,
clouds, rain, mist, mountains, landscape, animal behavior, changing seasons, the night sky and the mysteries of the life cycle gave
birth to thoughts and language.[29]

As ecological intelligence is linked to character so is it linked to love
or the emotional bond between humans and nature. As Stephen Jay Gould has
said, "We will not fight to save what we do not love."[30] A pre-ecological
intelligence, that is, intelligence as defined in the techno-industrial paradigm,
"dispassionately" reduces the natural environment to lifeless material elements to be processed as resources for production and consumption. Nature
in this context is a collection of animate and inanimate objects all potentially
economically useful, and emotional bonding with nature would, from the
perspective of a pre-ecological intelligence, violate the canons of a scientific
methodology which rules out human emotions in the study of phenomena.
Despite claims of dispassionate and disinterested objectivity, however, techno-
industrial science with its technological applications is quite passionate about
promoting economic growth, quite interested in the rewards that accompany
corporate-subsidized research, and quite insistent in its claim that the metaphysical gulf between humans and nature makes it impossible for humans to
bond with nature. The problem with such fundamentalist science, as Orr
refers to it, is that it is not scientific enough. Humans share with animals
many common physiological and behavioral features and both humans and
animals depend for their existence on their membership in Earth's community
of life, with each member's survival and well-being determined by the physical conditions of its environment and its relation with other living things. An
ecological intelligence necessarily respects the very environment which makes
possible human existence and is not embarrassed to couple the best professional science with a love of life and a sense of awe and mystery before the
immensity of creation.

What does the art of love have to do with the discipline of science?
On one side of the question, love is not a substitute for careful
thought. On the other side, when the mind becomes . . . "a merce-
nary of our will to power . . . trained to assail in order to plunder

rather than to commune in order to love," ruin is the logical result.
In either case it is evident that personal motives matter, and different motives lead to very different kinds of knowledge and very
different ecological results.[31]

The willingness of ecologists and environmentalists to recognize the
connection between the best professional science and love of life and to
communicate that connection to students, meets the requirement of Orr's fifth
principle that faculty and administrators provide role models of caring, integrity, and thoughtfulness for their students. Educators who act as such role
models will also make their students aware of the difference between a career
and a calling and the consequences of choosing the first without a commitment to the second.

> A career is a job, a way to earn one's keep, a way to build a long
> resume, a ticket to somewhere else. . . . [A] career is too often a
> way to support a "lifestyle" by which one takes more than one
> gives back. In contrast, a calling has to do with one's larger
> purpose, personhood, deepest values, and the gift one wishes to
> give to the world. A calling is about the use one makes of a
> career. . . . A career is planned with the help of "career develop-
> ment" specialists. A calling comes out of an inner conversation.[32]

Within the mainstream educational system, students in high school,
particularly those who are going on to college,[33] are counseled, tested for
specific aptitudes and advised as to career choices by counselors who for the
most part view a career as a niche, well paid preferably, within the techno-
industrial system of unlimited economic growth. Students are groomed for
job interviews where they will be expected to sell themselves to potential
employers. The term job market is an apt one for it describes the coming
together of buyers and sellers, in this case employers who buy labor skills and
individuals who sell their labor skills. Career counselors do not distinguish
for students forms of employment which are socially and environmentally
responsible and those that are not. In accordance with the norms of the
techno-industrial paradigm students are seen as maximizers of utility engaged
in the same goal of material acquisition as are all other members of society.
If matching aptitude with the appropriate career does not bring a sense of
personal fulfillment, it is expected that such fulfillment can be found outside
of the job through leisure and recreation activities which themselves are
increasingly implicated in forms of consumerism. There is little or nothing in
this process of career counseling that enables the student to have that inner
conversation with herself out of which might come that sense of purpose,

personhood, deepest values, and a gift one wishes to give the world, as Orr describes it.

Within the dominant paradigm, the overarching purpose of all social institututions, expressed through the action of individuals, is to support unlimited economic growth. Neither mainstream education nor career counseling can be expected to challenge this paradigm norm. While some students may have a sense of themselves, which is at odds with cultural expectations of a career, the messages from the educational establishment, from career counselors, from, in many cases, parents and from the various media all reinforce the notion that accommodation must be made to the demands of the "real world," that is, the economic system. Without the encouragement of adults who in their teaching and public and private lives display commitment to values that constitute the elements of a calling, young people will necessarily pursue a career that serves the interests of those who direct the growth economy. While the financial rewards of some careers may provide strong personal satisfaction to those so employed, such personal satisfaction cannot in the aggregate counterbalance the real harm to humans and nonhumans that has resulted and will continue to result from an economic system that in the long rum is inherently unsustainable in terms of environmental and social stability. The consequence of not distinguishing between a career and a calling is "that without significant precautions, education can equip people merely to be more effective vandals of the earth."[34]

Given the six principles that Orr provides for reconstructing education to serve ecological goals, it becomes necessary to rexamine the way in which institutions of higher learning are ranked today. Indices currently in use to rank colleges, for example, reflect the bias toward quantitative measures typical of the techno-industrial paradigm: number of faculty with Ph.D. degrees, number of faculty publications, faculty-student ratio, per capita endowment, dollar value of grants received by faculty and the college itself, number of students receiving graduate school scholarships, value of capital plant, extent of proposed capital investment, dollar value of alumni giving, the wealth of members of the board of trustees, and the level of faculty salaries. Such indices fit well into the expectations that students, faculty, alumni, board members, and the public generally have about the role of colleges and universities. Highly ranked colleges and universities connect successsful students with well-established businesses, which frequently recruit the bulk of their new employees from selected schools. The more prestigious the school the more likely, or so the concerned parties believe, it will be a conduit to lucrative employment. As the cost of higher education increases,[35] tuition is seen as a necessary investment or defensive expenditure to ensure a bright future in the economy.

From the perspective of an ecological pedagogy such indices for ranking institutions of higher learning may largely measure only the incapacity of these institutions to provide their students with the comprehensive ecological literacy required if the twenty-first century is not to repeat the mistakes of the twentieth century. The posession of a Ph.D. degree is by itself no guarantee of ecological literacy. Faculty publications, as Page Smith has observed, can represent in the main academic busywork and research may be frequently under contract for corporations which expect such research to provide expanded market shares and profit. Large endowments, depending on their source, may commit a college or university to the curriculum preferences of corporations and individual donors. The standard indices used for ranking also reflect the predilection for the larger over the smaller, for more rather than less. More books, more Ph.D.'s, more students, larger endowments, more research contracts are all assumed to indicate superior assets that lead to superior education. Yet, none of these indices necessarily reflects a resource usable for ecological education. More books in a college library do not promote ecological literacy if they are all different disciplinary expressions of the same techno-industrial paradogm. Nor does the acquisition by a college library of a collection of ecological literature ensure their use and incorporation into a college curriculum which is shaped by the assumptions of the dominant paradigm.

Orr suggests ranking institutions of higher learning based on whether or not the institutions and their graduates help to move the world in a more sustainable direction. An institution would be ranked in terms of the carbon dioxide emitted annually per student as a result of its energy consumption. Consumption of other items such as water, paper, and electricity, and per capita waste production would be other measures of college resource use. Institutions with higher per capita numbers would receive low marks for such destructive impacts on the natural environment. Rankings would also reflect institutional management policies for waste disposal, recycling, landscaping practices, and construction of new buildings. Institutions that do not recycle, use toxic chemicals on lawns, do not equip new buildings with passive or active solar technologies, and are not sensitive to energy efficiency measures would be ranked low because of such environmentally unsustainable practices. Institutions would be ranked according to their success in promoting ecological literacy throughout the curriculum. Adding environmental courses or creating an environmental major or minor does not by itself promote ecological awareness among all students and certainly does not guarantee that graduating seniors are "suited for a responsible life on a planet with a biosphere,"[36] and that they have had instilled in them "knowledge, love, and competence toward the natural world. . . ."[37]

Ecological literacy is not simply the result of indoor classroom lectures. Out-of-door experiences are needed which connect students with the realities of the natural environment, animate and inanimate. Students must learn to distinguish between natural environments that are characterized by stability, integrity, and beauty and those that have been despoiled and require remediation and restoration efforts by commiitted individuals. Ecological literacy becomes an integral feature of a college when students, faculty, and administrators take part in regular energy, waste, and materials audits of the campus; when faculty monitor energy use in their offices; when students do the same in their rooms; when no one walks past an empty classroom with the lights on without turning the light switch off; when littering on the campus becomes a social taboo; when a sizable number of students and faculty know the difference between economic growth and development, between the environment conceived as a subsystem of the economy and the economy seen as a subsystem of the environment and recognize the underlying assumptions of the dominant techno-industrial paradigm; when the flora and fauna on campus can be identified as discrete species of life and treated with respect; and when honors convocations and commencement exercises publicly recognize and reward those on campus who in various ways have helped to move the college and the surrounding community in a more environmentally benign and sustainable direction. An institution which allows its students to graduate unprepared to resist those activities which are unraveling the fabric of life on Earth, has failed its responsibility to educate for ecological literacy and should be ranked accordingly.

Institutions would be ranked on the use of their "buying power to help build sustainable regional economies"[38] by purchasing food from neighboring farms and goods and services from local suppliers, merchants, and crafts people. Institutions would be ranked by their investments in companies that treat employees responsibly and minimize their impact on the environment by recycling, conserving energy, and internalizing all their costs of production. Investments in unsustainable business enterprises would result in a low ranking. Institutions would be judged by the impact their graduates have on the world and how they use the education they received in various programs of study to provide a decent life for themselves and their families without jeopardizing the welfare of future generations of humans and nonhumans.

> How many [graduates] work through business, law, social work, education, agriculture, communications, research . . . to create the basis of sustainable society? Are they part of the larger ecological enlightenment that must occur as the basis for any kind of sustainable society, or are they part of the rear guard of a vandal economy? Most colleges make serious efforts to discover who among their alumni have attained wealth. I know of no college that has surveyed its graduates to determine their cumulative environmental impacts.[39]

As an ecological pedagogy requires a new way of ranking institutions of higher learning in terms of their educating for ecological literacy, so it requires a new way of recruiting and retaining the faculty who bear the chief responsibility for educating ecologically literate students. Reflecting the current intense professionalization of the intellectual landscape, faculty who have a Ph.D. from a recognized graduate school, whose graduate training in some specialized niche of a particular discipline fits the needs of a department, and who have published in an appropriate peer-reviewed professional journal are given preference. While teaching experience is one factor considered in the decision to hire, it is rarely a primary consideration. Moreover, for younger candidates prior teaching is viewed as a time when the transition from graduate student to instructor occurs, a process in which the recent graduate, now instructor, learns to present information to a group of students who know little or nothing about the subject matter of the course. Once hired, the new faculty member is expected to publish in his or her specialized field as a condition of tenure and promotion. Since there is normally no ongoing observation of classroom teaching by senior department members or department chairpersons, there is no way to ascertain whether a new faculty member's research is in any way related to his or her lectures. In most instances, the research is meant to result in a publication in a professional journal and is focused on a specialized topic which rarely fits into a classroom lecture designed for undergraduate college students. Even if by chance there were a fit between research designed for a professional journal and classroom lectures, the subject itself is a fragment of information disconnected from the larger social, political, and economic issues associated with the techno-industrial paradigm.

> Educational institutions and professionalized schools do tend to seal themselves off from the unpleasant and less rewarding challenges [addressing vital and controversial issues] around them. And when they do engage these challenges, they do so as "research," not as serious efforts to solve real problems.[40]

The present system of recruiting new faculty in institutions of higher learning ensures that for the most part the academic scenario described by Page Smith will continue. Students will not meet faculty who can serve as role models of thoughtfulness, caring, and commitment to values expressed in teaching, and faculty will continue to publish research which as Page Smith has said is essentially worthless in that it does not result in any measurable benefit to anything or anybody and represents busy work on a vast scale. While such research does not serve students well, it also fails in another crucial way: it ignores environmental realities and undermines the prospect of educating for ecological literacy. By ignoring the increasingly stressed relationships between human activities and the natural environment and by treating what research is done in this area as simply a means to justify tenure or promotion, the colleges and universities clearly signal to young faculty applying for positions what the hiring institutions consider to be important.

David Orr has suggested several ways of providing the faculty and staff needed for colleges and universities that are serious about providing an ecological education for their students. One proposal which Orr directs at tenure decisions but which can also be applied to the initial hiring process, is to require that all candidates for tenure appear before an institution-wide forum to answer questions which do more than assess a peer-reviewed publication record or the standard evaluations of departmental and other colleagues.

> Where does your field of knowledge fit in the larger landscape of learning? Why is your particular expertise important? For what and for whom is it important? What are its [the particular expertise] wider ecological implications and how do these affect the long-term prospect? Explain the ethical, social, and political implications of your scholarship.[41]

Such questions, if posed to candidates applying for a position and those faculty up for tenure review, would encourage those questioned to consider the broader intellectual implications of their specialized fields and to explain themselves in a way free of specialized jargon. The hiring and tenuring of candidates who display a grasp of transdisciplinary issues would help to create a balance in the faculty between those who are sensitive to the issues that lie outside their academic specializations and those who are narrowly specialized. Institutions that ask these questions could continue to hire and tenure those faculty who will confine their scholarship to a specialized field or who will provide a needed technical service within the curriculum,[42] but given this procedure there would be a much stronger sense of the proper mix of faculty required if an institution is to succeed in providing a substantial ecological education for its students. If all hiring and tenure decisions were made on the basis of evaluation framed by such questions, the faculty and administrators involved in these decisions would also be impelled to examine for themselves their own and the institution's capacity to serve the larger and transdisciplinary purpose of educating for ecological literacy. Institutions which screen candidates in this way might also consider hiring and retaining individuals who do not necessarily hold a Ph.D.

> . . . [W]e can suspend the implicit belief that a Ph.D. is a sign of intelligence and draw those who have demonstrated a high degree of applied ecological intelligence, courage, and creativity (farmers,

foresters, naturalists, ranchers, restoration ecologists, urban ecologists, landscape planners, citizen activists) into education as mentors and role models.[43]

If the questions proposed by Orr seem designed to impose an intellectual orthodoxy on faculty hired and tenured, one must consider the set of questions currently typically addressed to candidates.

> Do you have a Ph.D. from a recognized graduate school? Do you have references from your graduate school professors certifying that you have the potential to publish in your specialized field? Is there evidence that you can communicate your expert knowledge in a way appropriate to your audience? Are you aware that the policy of this institution is to grant tenure and promotion based on publication in peer-reviewed journals and the recommendations of the senior professors of the department?[44]

These questions screen candidates for their commitment to research in a specialized field and publication in professional journals, and for their ability to fill a niche in a department's course offerings. Since many major programs do not establish prerequisites for courses taken within the major, departmental courses need not connect with one another and members of a department need not review with one another how and whether the different courses serve a common departmental objective.[45] Thus, the questions now being asked and the expectations raised select for those candidates whose research and teaching will perpetuate the Balkanization of knowledge and the moral vacuum that characterizes much of the present system of higher education.

Ecological pedagogy does not require that the faculty be of one mind on environmental issues or that they transform all their courses or direct all their research efforts in order to advance ecological literacy. There are many sectors of knowledge and subject matters that provide important insights into the human situation and stand on their own, independent of any connection to environmental issues. To understand, for example, the Civil War period, its antecedents and consequences and the role of Abraham Lincoln in that context, is to understand the moral dilemmas faced by Americans at that time. While military actions had some effect on local environments, a meaningful account of the Civil War would not be served by considerations of environmental impact. Orr's point is not that all of higher education is to be fashioned into an instrument of ecological literacy, but that the contemporary professorate be encouraged to search beyond its specialized boundaries for answers to problems which are increasing in scope and intensity and stem from the stress imposed on the natural and social environments by the functioning of the techno-industrial paradigm. Unlike the older generation of faculty who received their graduate degrees in the 1950s, 1960s, and 1970s, the younger faculty are more familiar with environmental issues, if not through their graduate work then through the media and the greater visibility generally of the environmental movement. Ecological pedagogy requires that all faculty but particularly younger faculty be encouraged to explore important environmentally related issues typically outside of their own specialized fields and to be protected against a system that not only discourages such exploration, but also penalizes it by withholding rewards afforded to those who stay strictly within a specialized field. Contrary to some conventional notions, ecological literacy requires at least as much intellectual effort and scholarship as the traditional specialized fields. Ecological literacy entails an intellectual competence in both depth and breadth and a capacity for understanding interrelationships among data, events, and disciplines that are ostensibly unrelated.

> For those willing to do it, the task of mastering a particular field in depth while acquiring a broad and contextual knowledge demands time, patience, intellectual skill, and great commitment. It demands scholars who pay attention to large issues and who have loyalties to things higher than the profession. These people deserve to be protected from both capricious administrators and from what Page Smith . . . has called "academic fundamentalists. . . ."[46] The world has always needed a dangerous professorate and needs one now more than ever. It needs a professorate with ideas that are dangerous to greed, shortsightedness, indulgence, exploitation, apathy, high-tech pedantry, and narrowness.[47]

A major impediment to the development of a sizable professorate that engages in social issues and is "dangerous" to the techno-industrial paradigm, is the fallacious notion that "neutrality" and "objectivity" are synonymous terms. Objectivity means that judgments about events are based on the best available information, that all data and sources of information are subjected to rigorous scrutiny according to the accepted canons of inquiry, and that earlier judgments are modified or rejected if contravened by new evidence. Neutrality represents a decision not to take sides on an issue. If the decision to be neutral is based on a lack of conclusive evidence one way or another and if there is no moral imperative[48] that requires immediate action or judgment, then the decision to remain neutral on an issue makes sense. If, however, the preponderance of evidence is on one side of an issue, the evidence is the result of objective analysis and impartial inquiry, and there is a moral imperative that calls for immediate action or judgment, then the decision to remain neutral in the name of objectivity and scientific rigor constitutes a misunderstanding or misinterpretation of the nature of objectivity and scientific rigor. As often as not, remaining neutral under such circumstances is the result of motives that have little to do with maintaining scientific rigor and much to do with self-interest, as exemplified by researchers working for tobacco companies who never voluntarily disclosed their findings on tobacco-related health problems. A professional discipline can meet its self-defined criteria of objectivity without committing itself to perpetual neutrality. In the case of political science, for example, an objective study of federal environmental policy and its administration reveals the role that business groups play in the shaping of environmental legislation and in the subsequent administration and enforcement by the Environmental Protection Agency and the Justice Department.

Where there is clear evidence that contributions to the election campaigns of House of Representative members and Senate members have resulted in environmental legislation tilted to private rather than public interest or in no legislative action at all on an environmental issue, no canons of scientific and objective inquiry would be violated if the American Political Science Association were to support efforts in the United States Congress to severely curb if not eradicate the influence of private money in the shaping of national legislation. Similarly, the American Political Science Association would not violate standards of objectivity if it vigorously supported efforts to reduce carbon dioxide emissions in the United States, basing its action on the recent findings of the United Nations Intergovernmental Panel on Climate Change whose one thousand-page report stated that "projected climate changes during the 21st century have the potential to lead to future large-scale and possible irreversible changes in Earth systems with continental and global consequences."[49]

The failure of various professional organizations such as the American Political Science Association to support policies which are aimed at addressing serious threats to social stability and the integrity of the natural environment can be explained to some extent by such internal political considerations as avoiding antagonizing the major political parties and administrations in office from whom flow grant monies, as well as avoiding a possible polarization of the membership when the organization takes a stand that supports one party over the other. It should be noted that the public policy section of the APSA includes

> a strong representation of political scientists interested in environmental politics and policy, as does the section on science, technology, and environmental policies. Each section has its own newsletter. The *APSA itself now records environmental policy as one of the standard specializations for its members.*[50]

While acceptance by the APSA of the academic legitimacy of research on environmental policy represents an advance in the recognition of the existence of environmental policy issues, the creation of another "standard specialization" within the discipline adds to the fragmentation of knowledge already endemic in the prevailing system of higher education. The larger environmental issues cannot be addressed by way of a specialized subdiscipline viewed as one of many such specialized subdisciplines, each pursuing its own research ends, competing with the others for available grants, and providing college and university departments justifications for increasing staff in order to offer courses in the subsdiscipline.

> The great ecological issues of our time have to do in one way or another with our failure to see things in their entirety. That failure occurs when minds are taught to think in boxes and not taught to transcend those boxes or to question overly much how they fit with other boxes. We educate lots of in-the-box thinkers who perform within their various specialities rather like a dog kept in the yard by an electronic barrier. And there is a connection between knowledge organized in boxes, minds that stay in those boxes, and degraded ecologies and global inbalances.[51]

If some of the intellect now locked up in boxes could escape such confinement and begin to recognize the environmental and social damage inflicted by the techno-industrial paradigm and an educational system which from grade school to the university abets this paradigm, progress could be made in addressing what Bruce Wilshire describes as the "strange detachment from crucial human realities"[52] in which colleges and universities find themselves. Some psychologists, for example, might free themselves from the fixation on animal experimentation as a way of discovering important knowledge about humans and begin to examine the human pathology that characterizes obsessive consumerism. They might investigate the psychological consequences for humans of denatured urban environments, of disappearing communal life, of forms of human alienation that lead to various addictive behaviors. Some sociologists might explore the changes needed in American society to restore a semblance of community and a more social sense of self on the part of the individual. Some historians might correlate specific periods of American history with their environmental impact on both the animate and inanimate natural environment. Some theologians and scholars in religion might follow the lead of those who are assessing doctrinal changes needed to make the major religions proponents of the ecological paradigm, rather than supporters by default of the dominant paradigm. Some philosophers who specialize in explicating and interpreting the philosophic system of an individual thinker might consider the ecological implications of that system. Some specialists in seventeenth-century English literature, for example, might consider how the natural environment was being altered in Shakespeare's England.

Some political scientists who specialize in the functioning of the United States Congress might examine the role various United States Congresses have played in the protection or degradation of the natural environment.[53]

Education for ecological literacy does not require that all faculty specifically address environmental issues in their research and teaching. It does, however, require a critical mass of faculty committed to teaching and research that advances ecological literacy, along with a broader faculty constituency that is increasingly self-consciously aware of the possibility of foregrounding environmental concerns that their research and teaching have heretofore ignored or marginalized. An ecological pedagogy requires the replacement of the current taken-for-granted assumption that the natural environment is only a resource base for a techno-industrial society by the very different taken-for-granted assumption that the natural environment is the matrix within which all life exists and is, as Thomas Berry has stated, " the basic referent for every being on the Earth [with] every mode of being on the Earth . . . understood within the Earth context."[54] If the latter assumption is accepted, the exclusively anthropocentric focus which shapes most higher education must give way to an ecological perspective which measures all human activities, projects, and institutions within the Earth context, which is to say by their impact, sustainable or not sustainable, on the Earth's natural environment.

Bowers: Critique of High-Status Knowledge

The prevailing denial of the centrality of the natural environment for all human projects and institutions which characterizes contemporary higher education in the United States is examined by C. A. Bowers in *The Culture of Denial*.[55] His basic theme is that public schools and colleges and universities promote what is currently deemed to be high-status knowledge, a form of knowledge which legitimates all applications of technology within the economy and promotes individual egocentricity, while treating as low status those forms of knowledge that connect individuals to viable communities and contribute to sustainable human relationships with the natural environment. High-status knowledge gives primacy to change and to the values and technologies that promote change, interprets social development in economic and technological terms, and promotes Western culture as the most fully evolved of all human cultures whose values and institutions deserve to be fully globalized. High-status knowledge supports what Bowers refers to as an "ongoing cultural experiment," namely, to bring all the worlds' cultures and natural environments into the orbit of the market and the process of commodification.[56] For high-status knowledge, machines serve as the analogue for understanding life processes, and technologies developed for maximum profit by experts who think in terms of standardized designs that can be reproduced throughout the globe are assumed to be instruments of progress. The sciences are an integral part of high-status knowledge and the conventional separation of scientific research from moral judgment, despite the evident impact of technological applications of science on social and natural environments, is a taken-for-granted principle. Within high-status knowledge the computer serves as the communication icon of the so-called information age and is often described as a thinking machine modeled after the processes of human thought. Given its iconic status, computers are rarely analyzed in terms of their cultural and environmental impact. Bowers acknowledges the familiar, positive uses of computers—simulation, information storage, solving complex problems—but notes that computers select for amplification only certain forms of knowledge and communication. Computers provide explicit, digitalized context-free data and their users are represented as autonomous individuals "surfing" through data and images to construct their own version of reality. The sense of time is reduced to the response capacity of computer technology whose time frames are very different from ecosystem time cycles. What is communicated through computers is represented as culturally neutral, objective, and value and context free, rather than, as Bowers describes it, a metaphorical construction of reality based on the root metaphors of the dominant cultural paradigm.[57] The cultural mediation process of the computer severely reduces the experience of participatory and communal relationships where context, memory and mutual responsibility for maintaining relationships are expressed through face-to-face contact. Computers also amplify an instrumental and anthropocentric approach to relationships with others and the natural environment.

The multiplicity of disciplines and disciplinary specialties creates the impression that there is no common conceptual foundation that is shared by all. In fact, the current educational enterprise with all its variety of disciplines rests on the assumptions of the dominant techno-industrial paradigm. Such assumptions are reflected quite clearly in professional schools of business administration and education. In the former, courses teach that economic growth and profitability are the primary criteria for business decisions, ignoring the impact of such decisions on the natural environment. The schools of education currently produce teachers imbued with the taken-for-granted assumptions of the techno-industrial paradigm: an anthropocentric attitude toward the natural environment; an individually centered way of understanding intelligence,[58] creativity and moral judgment; a view of science and technology as culturally neutral; a sense of time and events as linear and progressive; a privileging of literacy-based thought and communication[59] and of all that is new and innovative; and the acceptance of competitive relationships as instrumental in the promotion of economic growth and social progress. Thus, Bowers observes, despite the multiplicity of disciplines and the diverse approaches to learning, all disciplines and approaches share a set of common paradigm assumptions which ignores individuals as cultural beings dependent on natural systems.

Bowers maintains that the pedagogic alternative to the dominant paradigm will have to be found in the conceptual and moral categories and vocabulary of what he terms "cultural/bio-conservatism."[60] The several forms of pedagogical liberalism which are current cannot function as a source of a new educational paradigm. Technocratic liberalism emphasizes measurable outcomes of efficient classroom management,[61] with the outcomes defined in terms of skills relevant to a technology-driven economy. Emancipatory liberalism focuses on the need to educate for the critical reflection essential if students are to be active citizens in a participatory democracy and advocates for justice and a more egalitarian society.[62] Neo-romantic liberalism[63] places emphasis on encouraging the students to freely engage their curiosity and imagination in their interactions with nature and culture in order to "create their own ideas, values, and understanding of relationships."[64] Technocratic liberalism aims at providing the skilled cadres for the economic labor market. Emancipatory liberalism aims at providing the critically reflective citizens needed by an authentic participatory democracy. Neo-romantic liberalism aims at freeing the creative and imaginative powers of students, particularly young children, from various forms of cultural stultification, thus allowing for maximum freedom and self-expression. All three approaches, however, fail to educate for any moral responsibility on the part of humans to the natural world. Nothing in the three programmatic foci of these pedagogic liberalisms speaks to the needed sense of responsibility for the integrity of the natural environment. Individual self-expression, high-tech work skills, and the capacity for critical reflection do not by themselves lead to a questioning of the dominant paradigm values. All three of these outcomes can and in fact do function within the framework of the dominant paradigm, further destabilizing social and natural environments. Even emancipatory liberalism with its laudatory goal of freeing individuals from the intellectual tyranny of unexamined social and political dogmas falls short of challenging the anthropocentrism and ecological irresponsibility of the dominant paradigm. As Bowers notes, all three forms of pedagogic liberalism fail to recognize the appropriate relationships between humans and the natural environment that alone can provide the basis for sustainable human communities.

Unlike the varieties of pedagogic liberalism, cultural/bio-conservatism recognizes the importance of place and the community institutions that determine the carrying capacity of an area and define the rights and obligations of those who use the resources of the area. It recognizes that the interests of the individual must be balanced with the needs of the community. It acknowledges the value of traditional knowledge developed over generations of collective experience but understands that such knowledge must be subjected to ongoing cultural reflection and scientific inquiry. It rejects the notion that democracy is merely a shifting equilibrium among interest groups seeking their own partisan ends, as it rejects the notion that the goal of education is to train students to be competitive members of a skilled work force. Cultural/bio-conservatism radically reconceptualizes the dominant paradigm version of the knower as the autonomous individual, "a spectator who observes and acts on the external world. . . . [constructing] . . . ideas from data on the computer screen or from direct experience."[65] An ecologically informed concept of knowing locates the individual in a network of relationships and interactions with a social or natural environment. The individual responds within this network through a culturally derived cognitive and valuational framework expressed in a metaphorical or image-laden language. The dominant and non-ecological view of knowledge identifies it as a form of power asserted by the knower over an external and passive environment. Bowers refers to Gregory Bateson's critique of the dominant paradigm's non-dialectic concept of the relationship between the knower and the known and Gregory Bateson's very different explication of that relationship.

> Consider a man felling a tree with an axe. Each stroke of the axe is modified or corrected, according to the shape of the cut face of the tree left by the previous stroke. This self-correcting (i.e., mental) process is brought about by a total system, tree-eyes-brain-muscles-axe-stroke-tree; and it is this total system that has the characteristics of immanent mind. More correctly, we should spell the matter out as: (differences in tree)-(differences in retina)-(differences in brain)-(differences in muscles)-(differences in movement of axe)-(differences in tree), etc. What is transmitted around the circuit is transforms of differences. And, as noted above, a difference which makes a difference is an idea or unit of information.[66]

In Bateson's view, intelligence is coterminous with the boundaries, in this case, of the natural system within which the individual acts. An ecological view of intelligence and knowledge takes into account that humans cannot exist in the world without interacting with the social and natural systems in which they are located. Bateson's example of a man felling a tree with an axe as an illustration of how the human action (occurring by means of an axe, which is a technological application of human knowledge) on the tree both shapes and is shaped by the object, can be supplemented with an example of the application of pesticides to crops. Applying pesticides induces pest resistance and a secondary resurgence of new or more resistant original pests which in turn selects for new pesticides and a more systemic way of understanding pest control. From this ecological, coevolutionary perspective,[67] the network of relationships within which the spraying of pesticides occurs includes pests, pesticides, pesticide production, pesticide regulation and associated policymaking and policy-enforcing government institutions, the current state of knowledge about pest control, and attitudes about the use of chemicals in the environment. The coevolutionary perspective, unlike the dominant paradigm focus on short-term interactions with the environment in response to market signals, recognizes longer-term feedback loops between the environment and human interaction in it.

> To emphasize coevolutionary process is not to deny that people directly intervene in and change the characteristics of environments. The coevolutionary perspective puts its emphasis on the chain of events thereafter, and how different interventions alter the selective pressure and hence the relative dominance of environmental traits which, in turn, select for values, knowledge, organization, and technology and hence subsequent interventions in the environment.[68]

The values, forms of knowledge, technologies, and institutions of the dominant techno-industrial paradigm have coevolved around the fossil hydrocarbons which constitute the still primary energy base for techno-industrial society. A fossil-fuel dependent economy has not only transformed the natural environment but has selected for materialist, individualistic, and competitive social values. It has also selected for a reductionist and instrumentalist form of reason, as well as for centralized economic and political institutions. Machines and chemicals powered by or derived from fossil hydrocarbons transformed traditional agricultural practices which in turn selected for increased chemical production, new government agencies, research institutions, expanded road systems, large-scale shopping centers, standardized crops, and mass media advertising campaigns.

> Agriculture transformed from an agroecosystem culture of relatively self-sufficient communities to an agroindustrial culture of many separate, distant actors linked by global markets. The massive changes in technology and organization gave people the sense of having control over nature and being able to consciously design their future while in fact problems were merely being shifted beyond the farm and onto future generations.[69]

From an ecological perspective, the notion that individuals can think and act in isolation from cultural forms of knowing and from environmental realities results in individual and institutional behavior which accelerates the destabilization of human and natural environments. A cultural-ecological understanding of intelligence takes into account that humans necessarily interact with other systems in the environment in which they are located. If the systems humans interact with are living systems, human action is met with reactive responses which reverberate throughout the ecosystem. The non-ecological cultural maps with which techno-industrial societies negotiate the terrain of the natural environment leave out such biotic features of an area as the presence of rare plants and animals and ecosystems under stress from taken-for-granted human activities.

> The [dominant] cultural form of intelligence (conceptual maps) originally led individuals to respond to the information circulating through natural systems as a result of the use of DDT by interpreting it as an expression of scientific and technological progress. The disappearance of insects and the increase in crop yields were what they were culturally conditioned to recognize as evidence of the success of pesticide intervention. . . . [T]he cultural maps diverted attention from other "differences" in the patterns of natural systems—such as the changes in bird populations and the toxins in the groundwater. In effect, the cultural maps diverted awareness away from information exchanges (perturbations) set in motion by the use of DDT by putting into focus only the "positive" effect of the pesticide.[70]

In the context of a cultural/bio-conservatism, intelligence, creativity, self-expression, and individualism are understood quite differently than they are in the dominant techno-industrial paradigm. Intelligence is the capacity to think in terms of relationships, networks, long-term effects, and to develop policies that restrain the market-driven impulse to promote the immediate introduction and application of whatever technology comes on line. Intelligence carries with it a sense of responsibility for the transmarket consequences of human interaction with the natural environment. Intelligence also transcends the boundaries of any one discipline and can assess what forms of more traditional knowledge provide important insights in moving toward sustainable human/nature relationships.[71] Creativity is not automatically associated with the new and ecologically untested or with the supposedly autonomous individual who applies her genius to technological innovation. From an ecological perspective, creativity is the ability to innovate within a cultural framework that values a sustainable economy, supports democratic communities based on decentralized economic and political institutions, and extends moral consideration to nonhumans. Creativity, self-expression, and individualism as these are understood and manifested in a techno-industrial culture too often result in forms of egocentric behavior that provide individuals with economic rewards and social status while furthering the illusion of unlimited growth, adding little if anything to community welfare, and fueling the prevailing cultural notion that the economically successful individual is the hallmark of social progress.

For Bowers, an ecologically centered educational system from grade school to higher education will recognize the crucial importance of childhood socialization processes which provide the primary language and its root metaphors that are the initial basis for the child's understanding of its social and natural environments. An ecologically centered educational system will also maintain a constant interplay between the explicit language of instruction and the implicit background taken-for-granted cultural assumptions. It will understand that the claims of objectivity and factuality within courses need to be examined from a cultural and historical perspective. It will foreground the root metaphors and other symbolic maps that coevolved with the Industrial Revolution and now constitute the taken-for-granted assumptions and understandings that contribute to the destabilization of the social and natural environments.

> . . . [T]he cultural forms of consciousness reinforced in the educational institutions that help advance high-status forms of knowledge are immanent in the system of dams that obstruct the migration of salmon, in the air that carries the chemicals that are altering the forms of life that exist in the soil, lakes, and rivers, and in the shopping malls that depend on subsistence culture being economically and technologically "developed" in ways that integrate them into a commodity-oriented economy.[72]

Smith: Education for Future Limits

Gregory A. Smith in *Education and the Environment* examines how the current educational curriculum will have to be reconstructed if schools are to prepare students socially and intellectually for a transition to a sustainable economy.[73] Schools currently focus on norms of independence or accomplishing tasks alone without assistance of parents, teachers, or peers; on achievement or striving to exceed the accomplishments of others; on universality or viewing others as members of categorical groups;[74] and on specificity or relating to others in terms of the marketable services they can provide. Such norms emphasize individualism and competition and marginalize cooperative and community-oriented efforts. Despite pronouncements that education is about empowerment, cultural unification, and critical thinking, schools largely prepare students to participate in a competitive market society. Such preparation involves not merely training in computer and related skills but the implicit incorporation of taken-for-granted cultural assumptions typical of the dominant paradigm. Thus, it is assumed that individuals are judged by their skill in material accumulation; that in a society of competing and unrelated individuals there is no transindividual social purpose, only individual choice and opinion; and that individual priorities are focused on personal security and control, not on the well-being of a larger group or community. Students are exposed less to an intellectual curriculum and more to norms of the prevailing social form of organization and to the behavior appropriate for participation in a techno-industrial society. The transient relationships that students experience with teachers and to a large extent with their peers, prepare them for the transient relationships characteristic of a market society. Students are detached from local and personal knowledge which is deemed to be parochial and inferior to high-status knowledge. Students are disconnected from any direct personal interaction with significant sectors of the social and natural environments. Instead, such interaction is replaced by memorization of data that are not integrated into a larger pattern of meaning that would help explain to students how their lives are shaped by social interactions and by the interactions between humans and the natural environment.

> In a fundamental way, schools seem to separate knowledge from life, turning a majority of students into passive spectators of teaching activities who see little relationship between the events of their classrooms and the requirements of responsible participation in the broader community.[75]

The continuation of education based on what Smith calls the "industrial world view" would portend deadly consequences for a society that needs to confront environmental limits to economic growth. Currently, the curriculum ignores the interdependence of all life, regards individuals as competing atoms, implicitly endorses the existing centralization of politics and economics, and takes for granted that the pursuit of material affluence defines the good life. The result is that the curriculum promotes environmental irresponsibility; undermines conditions needed to create the common values that make stable communities possible; discourages the application of local knowledge to local problems; and offers no moral principles or values to counter the self-seeking materialism that permeates the contemporary society. A curriculum consonant with an ecological world view would teach that humans are embedded in a natural environment that functions more as an organism than a machine and that the aim of knowledge is to further the understanding, not the domination, of that living system. It would teach that security and social stability are better achieved when individuals contribute to one another's well-being through cooperative support rather than competition. It would educate for the interpersonal social skills and forms of appropriate knowledge required if students are to live as members of smaller human communities capable of addressing community problems with local skills, knowledge, and means. It would reclaim value systems that direct the attention of individuals to who they are or what they may be and away from what they have. Such value systems would encourage a personal maturation and transformation transcending the limited ego shaped by the narrow perspectives of a market society and make possible the identification of the individual self with the larger community of life, human and nonhuman.

If the unlimited growth economy that is the mainstay of the dominant paradigm institutions and values is, in fact, not sustainable, either socially or environmentally, then the educational system will have to prepare students to cope with the transition from the dominant techno-industrial paradigm to the emerging ecological paradigm. Schools will have to educate for a degree of interdependence never acknowledged by the dominant paradigm.

> Creating schools that affirm students' attachment to others and the natural environment and which teach them to act collectively will require the systematic disassembling and reformulation of the hidden curriculum. . . . [It] should not be assumed that altering the hidden curriculum will alone be enough to ground [students] in a new world view. Elements of the explicit curriculum will also need to be changed.[76]

Smith recommends a number of strategic changes in the current explicit curriculum. Experiences in the school, home, workplace, and natural environment must be connected in a way they are not presently. The cultural background of students who are not middle class must be recognized to create respect for values which unlike those of the dominant paradigm have the power to create a sense of collective identity and commitment.[77] To further develop social habits of cooperation and collective responsibility among students, smaller classes, volunteer tutoring, student-directed advising groups, students staying longer with teachers, student participation in the process of creating and shaping the learning environments, and evaluation strategies that reward student contributions to the group as well as individual achievement would be pedagogic strategies incorporated into the new curriculum. Smith recognizes that policymakers at the state and national levels cannot be counted on to align themselves with a world view that challenges the taken-for-granted assumptions of unending economic growth and the pursuit of individual self-interest. Parents, particularly middle-class parents, will resist changing the current educational processes and goals which serve to prepare their children for participation in the techno-industrial culture. Educators, given their stake in the current educational system, public and private, are likely to be the most difficult group to convince that profound changes are required in school organization, pedagogical techniques, and curriculum content. Smith believes that while a new, environmentally oriented paradigm vision is not sufficiently widespread to generate needed educational reforms, the present concerns over dropout rates and the consequent social costs, the possibility of a shortage of skilled labor needed in the economic sector and the demographic trends that will bring more nonwhite and non-middle-class students into schools, can lead to reforms in the educational system. Such reforms may provide a basis for a new educational paradigm, even if the intentions behind the changes are directed at inducting into the dominant culture students who for various reasons have fallen to the margins of the existing educational system.

> A small but growing number of programs . . . are taking on the task of educating children who otherwise are at risk of dropping out. Schools that achieve this end are often characterized by a set of behavioral programmatic regularities that run counter to those which foster the transmission of the norms of detached independence and competitive achievement encountered in most conventional schools. . . . In the process, they often replicate the social relations and forms of interaction and support encountered in well-functioning primary groups.[78]

Typically in schools for at-risk youth, there is at least as much focus on experiential as on incorporative learning. Classroom work demands participation rather than detached observation. The boundaries between the school and the community become permeable; students, as at the Media Academy[79] in Oakland, California remain with the same teachers in two or three-year programs, and cohort education aids in the development of a sense of community and shared tasks. If the forms of individual mobility and security that have flourished under the dominant paradigm are not sustainable given the environmental limits to unending techno-industrial expansion, then schools that prepare children for what Nel Noddings has described as "caring and being cared for in the human domain and full receptivity and engagement in the nonhuman world"[80] will be instrumental in educating a generation who as adults are capable of collectively addressing the challenging physical and social conditions that will confront them in the twenty-first century.

Berry: The Universe Story

Thomas Berry's critique of higher education parallels that of C. A. Bowers and Gregory Smith: the system essentially prepares students to participate in the institutions and functions of a techno-industrial society.

> As now functioning, the university prepares students for their role in extending human domination over the natural world, not for intimate presence to the natural world. Use of this power in a deleterious manner has devastated the planet. . . . So awesome is the devastation we are bringing about that we can only conclude that we are caught in a severe cultural disorientation, a disorientation that is sustained intellectually by the university. . . .[81]

Colleges and universities currently reflect the fragmentation of knowledge into specialized niches and the anthropocentrism of the techno-industrial culture. Together, the fragmentation and the anthropocentrism in the natural and social sciences and humanities prevent institutions of higher education from providing the intellectual leadership needed to make the transition from the destructive techno-industrial paradigm to a new ecological paradigm that reorients "the human community toward a greater awareness that the human exists, survives and becomes whole only within the great community of the planet earth."[82] If colleges and universities are to make the transition from a curriculum that encodes the norms of the techno-industrial paradigm to one that educates for a sustainable relationship between humans and the natural environment, then the foundation of the new curriculum must be ecology, defined by Berry as a functional cosmology or universe story which operates to integrate the sciences, humanities, social sciences, and religion in a common narrative of the origins of humans and their ongoing participation in a continuing evolutionary process.

The universe story itself is the product of science and represents "the greatest religious, moral, and spiritual event that has taken place" in the centuries since Western science developed.[83] The universe story is both scientific and mythic since the more scientific understanding of the origin and structure of the universe increases, the more such understanding reveals a process that defies rational explanation. This scientific, humanistic, and spriritual understanding expressed through the universe story must form the foundation of all modern education, particularly higher education which has the capacity to reflect on the relevance of the universe story, the functional cosmological narrative, for the full range of human activities.

> College should be a center for creating the more encompassing visions as well as for communicating such visions to students.

The college student . . . needs to be involved in a significant historical as well as significant personal process. Neither of these can function effectively without the other. College students should feel that they are participating in one of the most significant ventures ever to take place in the entire history of the planet.[84]

Berry suggests a set of core courses for a college program aimed at enabling students to understand the universe story and the place of humans in that story.

A first course would describe the fourfold evolutionary process: the evolution of the galaxies, the evolution of the solar system and the Earth, the evolution of life, the evolution of consciousness and the developmental stages of human society. " . . . [T]he student, looking at his or her hand and considering the time span of fourteen billion years that it took to produce such a hand, could feel a personal importance in the scheme of things."[85]

A second course would focus on the different phases of human cultural development from the Paleolithic to the now emerging ecological or Ecozoic stage. "Such an overview could enable students to discover their personal identity in historical time and cultural space."[86]

A third course would deal with the major classical cultures that have shaped human development over the millennia. "From these cultures the student should learn the powerful impact of the divine, the need for spiritual discipline, the majesty of art, the great literature and music and dance and drama which befits the human mode of being"[87]

A fourth course would involve the study of the scientific and technological phase of human development, the power that humans now exercise over the natural environment and the consequences, good or bad, of this power, particularly during the last two hundred years of the industrial and technological revolutions. The course should educate students to the ways in which the topography, the biological functioning, and the climate of the planet have been affected by the applications of science and technology guided by the norms of a techno-industrial paradigm.

A fifth course would focus on the emerging ecological age and the growing awareness of humans that they are members of Earth's community of life. All current institutions, policies and practices would be examined in terms of their necessary repositioning and restructuring within an ecological context. The legal profession, for example, would address its attention to the rights of nonhuman entities. Commerce would recognize that degrading the environment is not a sustainable or acceptable form of commercial and industrial activity. Religion "would perceive the natural world as the primary revelation of the divine, as primary scripture, as the primary mode of numinous presence."[88]

A sixth course would deal with the origin and identification of values, seeking to discover within the human experience of the universe a foundation for values. It would teach that values are to be found in the self-emergent processes of the universe which produce individuality, subjectivity, and communion in which "every reality of the universe is immediately present to every other reality of the universe and finds its fulfillment in this mutual presence."[89] This course would address the current failure to develop a capacity for communion, a failing that is one of the causes of the present planetary, social, and educational disarray.

> The educational process itself would have through this program a cultural, historical, and cosmological context of meaning that can be accepted on a broad scale by persons of different ethnic and cultural backgrounds. Within this context the American college could understand in some depth its role in creating a future worthy of that larger universal community of beings out of which the human component has emerged and in which the human community finds its proper fulfillment.[90]

While Berry believes that any American college grounding its curriculum in the universe story narrative should have an extraordinary future,[91] there is little evidence that American higher education institutions are sensitive and responsive to the role they must play in providing the intellectual foundation for the ecological pedagogy needed in the transition from the techno-industrial to the ecological paradigm. There are few signs that the taken-for-granted assumptions incorporated in the conventional curriculum are being scrutinized and there are even fewer signs that Berry's call for the reconstruction of all existing disciplines to meet the ecological standards of the universe story is occurring anywhere.

This is not to say that there is no movement at all to a more ecologically oriented curriculum. The Talloires Declaration of the Association of University Leaders for a Sustainable Future[92] represents a set of principles to guide colleges and universities as they engage in education, research, policy formation, and information exchange on population, environment, and development in order to move toward a sustainable future. The Declaration has been signed by officers of some two hundred and seventy education institutions from forty countries. The Declaration commits member institutions to use every opportunity to raise public, government, and industry awareness of the urgent need to move toward an environmentally sustainable future and to make their campuses models of environmental responsibility through programs of resource conservation, recycling, and waste reduction. Member institutions are expected to develop the ecological literacy of faculty so that they are capable of teaching environmental responsibility to undergraduate, graduate, and professional school students. Member institutions are expected to establish partnerships with primary and secondary schools to assist teachers in public schools to provide instruction about population, environment, and sustainable development issues. The Association publishes *The Declaration*, a biannual newsletter which provides information about environmental initiatives at member institutions. The Center for Respect of Life and Environment publishes a quarterly journal, *Earth Ethics: Evolving Values for an Earth Community,* which focuses on topics pertinent to environmental education in colleges and universities.[93] The Center also cosponsors conferences on environmental education issues with the Association of University Leaders for a Sustainable Future.

A recent case study by Christopher Uhl and Amy Anderson in *Bio Science* reveals the superficial response being made by most colleges and universities in their curricular and campus operations to the call to educate for ecological literacy.[94] Uhl and Anderson describe the results of an environmental audit by students and faculty at Pennsylvania State University. The audit measured the integration of sustainability concepts and practices into the operations and curriculum of the university using the following criteria: fossil fuel independence, conserving water resources, reducing materials waste, providing food products sustainably, abiding by a land ethic, creating sustainable alternatives to car-based transport, constructing "green" buildings, guaranteeing ecological literacy, and prioritizing research for a sustainable world. Based on the criteria, the audit depicted an institution "whose performance . . . was merely mediocre . . . [with graduates completing] their education with little sense of their ecological identity."[95] Uhl and Anderson did find a few colleges and universities that scored high in each criterion area,[96] but these schools represent a very small minority of all institutions of higher education. More often than not even affiliation with the Association of University Leaders for a Sustainable Future and signing of the Talloires Declaration leads to no more than a reference to the Declaration in the school catalogue and the addition of an environmental course to the curriculum. The issue of faculty environmental literacy remains unaddressed, recruitment of new faculty reflects no application of ecological literacy criteria, and students continue to graduate prepared only to further the purposes of the techno-industrial society.

The widespread acceptance of the principles of an ecological pedagogy would go far in addressing the concerns expressed by critics of the contemporary higher education scene. The dispiriting nature of the educational enterprise and the moral vacuum that accompanies it could be significantly ameliorated by the introduction of an ecologically oriented curriculum. The contemporary academic culture is the pedagogic counterpart of the dominant techno-industrial paradigm. It fosters the fragmentation of knowledge, encourages the arid pedantry of the nonsciences and the alliance of science with commercial interests, and offers as the overarching purpose of education the acquisition of work skills. This academic culture would wither if forced to accomodate to an ecological pedagogy whose purpose, as Orr, Bowers, Smith, Berry and others have said, is nothing less than the healing of the existing rupture between humans and the natural world. Ecological pedagogy is rich in moral purpose, provides authentic guidelines for meaningful scholarship, and invites all disciplines to contribute to "a future worthy of that larger universal community of beings out of which the human component emerged and in which the human community finds its proper fulfillment."[97] The ascendance of an ecological pedagogy is tied, of course, to that new social vision, the ecological paradigm, which entails not only a new pedagogy but a new economics, political economy, and ethics. All four constitute the foundation of a world view emerging from the growing realization that the two-hundred-year human experiment in attempting to live in an unsustainable relationship with nature is failing and that staying the course is a sure recipe for social and environmental destabilization.

Chapter 5

Conclusion

We are discovering today that several of the premises which are deeply ingrained in our way of life are simply untrue and become pathogenic when implemented with modern technology.

—*Gregory Bateson,* Steps to an Ecology of Mind

Perhaps the most telling argument against the dominant techno-industrial paradigm is that as it unravels the ecological systems of life it diminishes the moral, political, social, and aesthetic capacities of individuals by drawing, as it were, a curtain between them and the consequences of that paradigm. Moral agency or the capacity for making moral judgments is rendered moot when an individual cannot confront the consequences of his or her actions. Moral agency is possible only when an individual can identify a moral concern and take responsibility if harm occurs either directly through the individual's actions or through the institutions of the society of which she or he is a member. Individuals who eat meat, for example, but never see a slaughterhouse in operation, or a rain forest destroyed to provide temporary grazing area for cattle, or indigenous people forced off traditional commons, cannot exercise their capacity for moral judgment. Consumers who purchase the products of a global market and typically do not understand the environmental, political, and social repercussions of a system that draws on the natural and human capital of the entire planet, cannot act as moral agents. High-tech products, such as the computer, which are perceived as environmentally benign technologies of advanced science and

167

are eagerly sought after by affluent consumers, have a production history which is hardly benign and is also beyond the scope of individual moral judgment.

> About 700 different materials and chemicals went into manufacturing my computer [weighing about 55 pounds]; half of these were hazardous. Computer plant workers exposed to toxic chemicals have suffered lung diseases, skin rashes, and even increased rates of miscarriage. Electronics manufacturers have bestowed California's Silicon Valley (Santa Clara County) with large areas of contaminated groundwater and the highest concentration of Superfund hazardous waste sites in the United States.[1]

The political capacities of individuals are equally enfeebled by the dominant paradigm system. The commitment of state and especially federal government to advance unlimited growth has created a political/economic power structure at both the state and federal levels which is not accountable to voters in the traditional democratic notion of accountability. The forces that shape the American economy and its integration into a global economy are largely invisible to the American public, particularly since the operations of these agencies and organizations are not open to debate in the state and national election campaigns. The Federal Reserve Board, the U.S. Agency for International Development, the Office of the United States Trade Representative, the International Trade Administration, the Export-Import Bank, the International Monetary Fund, the World Bank, and the World Trade Organization are some of the national and international organizations that shape the American and international economy and significantly affect the lives of American citizens. Yet, comparatively few Americans know of the existence of these entities and fewer yet could explain the specific economic role they play. Moreover, the individuals who serve in these entities are appointed, not elected, and they are as unaccountable to the general public as they are invisible. Citizenship under these circumstances is reduced, for the great majority of Americans, to the act of voting, paying taxes, and obeying the laws. Since a majority of eligible Americans[2] in fact do not vote in state or national elections and do not contact their elected officials about issues that affect them, even this relatively passive form of citizenship is forgone by many. In this political context, the term citizenship loses the meaning it has when knowledgeable citizens directly involve themselves in the issues which significantly affect their social and natural environments.

> . . . [There is] the widespread belief that citizenship requires little or nothing of us. . . . The philosophy of cheap citizenship likewise prevents any serious discussion about paying the full cost of what

we consume, including the costs of biotic impoverishment. . . . Real citizens pay their bills, exercise foresight, assign costs and benefits fairly, work hard at maintaining their communities and are willing to sacrifice when necessary and consider doing so a privilege. All of this is to say that authentic citizenship—political and ecological—is not cheap, but it is, sooner or later, less costly by far than dereliction and counterfeit citizenship.[3]

Active citizenship and robust communities call forth one another and the decline of one leads to the decline of the other. As citizenship erodes, the fabric of community life unravels for community is about common interests shared by individuals who collectively endeavor to protect and promote these interests. If politics, as Aristotle said, is the business of the community, the polis, engaged in by all of its members, then active citizenship makes community possible. Without a common engagement in community affairs, individuals are connected only as consumers through market activities, a connection which offers no basis for the transmarket and transpersonal common interests which characterize community. As both community and citizenship are enervated by the dominant institutions of the techno-industrial society, individuals are further distanced from the ongoing operations of the system and its consequences for humans and the natural environment. Out of sight and out of range of political and moral judgment becomes the norm for most individuals. The capacity for political and moral agency, expressed publicly through active citizenship, needs to be exercised if it and the elements of character that enable it are not to atrophy. As Paul W. Taylor has pointed out, the capacity for moral agency rests on traits of character essential for moral strength and moral concern. Among these are conscientiousness, integrity, patience, self-control, benevolence, compassion, courage, and perseverance.[4]

As the opportunities and occasions for moral judgment on issues of substance are diminished, the character traits of moral agency are also diminished. The result is the trivialization of moral judgment and the marginalization of its associated character traits.[5] Similarly diminished is the human capacity for altering existing social institutions when these are no longer producing desired social outcomes. The end result of the decline of both active citizenship and moral agency is the enculturation of a moral and political flaccidity manifested in the widespread acquiescence to the supposed inevitability of centralized economic and political power, of the unrestricted introduction into the social and natural environments of ever new technologies via the market, and of unlimited economic growth on a global scale. To accept these dominant paradigm propositions is to relinquish any notion of individual and collective freedom to shape social institutions so that they serve public purposes as these are articulated in public discourse. It is possible that an informed public discourse on social goals conducted through the media, political parties, professional organizations, institutions of higher education, and other forms of public communication, could result in a mandate by a majority of citizens to continue with business as usual. Such a decision by a majority in democracy would have to be respected even if it sanctioned the continued devastation of the natural environment with its associated destructive impacts on human communities. Such a mandate, however, has not been provided and given the attenuated nature of citizenship and moral agency in a techno-industrial society, it is unlikely that it will ever be on the political agenda. The dominant paradigm system seems likely to stay on course immune from any effective public scrutiny and accountable de facto only to economic and political elites. In this sense, the system has emasculated the political and moral capacities of the great majority of citizens. The consumer, unaware of the social and environmental consequences of the system that produces the items purchased and ever more distanced from the centers of power, has by and large replaced the democratic citizen.[6]

The aesthetic and religious/spiritual capacities of individuals in the techno-industrial society have also been substantially diminished. Direct contact with the natural environment is progressively less possible as urbanization proceeds apace and denatured human environments replace natural environments. The one-dimensionality of techno-industrial society as described by Herbert Marcuse is evident in the life-styles of individuals and in the made environments in which they work, travel and live.[7] With the exception of natural environments located in areas where extreme temperatures preclude significant human presence, natural environments everywhere else are exposed to some form of human visitation, if not for development at the moment then for recreation and tourism. Most natural environments under federal control in the United States are subject to the Multiple Use-Sustained Yield Act of 1960 which requires that wildlife refuges also "provide grazing, hunting, and . . . mining opportunities to private interests" and that the Forest Service "assist state and private forest owners in obtaining access to federal forests."[8] The growth of the United States population and the incessant pressures for development are eliminating the natural environments experienced by Henry David Thoreau, John Muir, Henry Beston, Aldo Leopold, Edward Abbey, Rachel Carson, and other American naturalists who transmitted to generations their sense of the beauty and inherent worth of nature. The techno-industrial vision of the natural world and the ultimate destiny of humans is reflected in J. H. Fremlin's estimation of how many humans the earth could accommodate.

> . . . [T]he total human population on Earth could be allowed to reach 60 quadrillion people, about 120 per square meter of the planet's surface area. . . . Everyone would be housed in a two-

thousand story structure that covered the entire surface of the Earth; the bottom half would be living quarters and the top half refrigeration and food-production machinery. Fremlin assumed the complete elimination of land-based wildlife; replacement of all ocean-dwelling wildlife with the most efficient photosynthesizing microorganisms (to increase food yields) . . . [and] direct synthesis of food from recycled wastes and corpses. . . . [According to Fremlin the] extrapolation from the present life of a car-owning, flat-dwelling office worker to such an existence might well be less than from that of the neolithic hunter to that of the aforesaid office worker.[9]

The assumptions of the technocratic mind set of the dominant paradigm are clearly established in Fremlin's future world scenario. Technology can provide housing, food, and presumably breathable air, and potable water for a population larger by several orders of magnitude than that which exists at the start of the twenty-first century. Political, economic, and social institutions can adapt in some unspecified way to a planet with sixty quadrillion people. All natural environments and wild species of animals and plants can be eliminated and climate patterns and other biospheric functions can be replaced by engineered systems. Qualitative indices of human life such as privacy, open space, community relations, and aesthetic and religious interactions with nature can be replaced by such quantitative indices as the largest supportable human population, volume of food produced, and maximum size of a planetary apartment housing the human population. Technology is its own end and what can be done should and will be done. What is ironic about the technocratic mind set is that in treating technology as the sine qua non of the human enterprise it reduces humans, as in the scenario envisioned by Fremlin, to a species whose destiny is to swarm the planet for the purpose of—swarming.

While Fremlin's specific scenario is very unlikely to occur,[10] the technocratic assumptions lodged in the dominant paradigm would, if allowed free reign, move human society toward rather than away from that scenario. What needs to be understood is that Fremlin's and similar technocratic scenarios can be extrapolated as Fremlin himself notes, "from the present life of a car-owning, flat [urban]-dwelling office worker." Present-day consumption activities which seem innocent enough if separated, as they normally are, from unseen social and environmental consequences, necessarily entail, if continued on a global scale, something like the Fremlin scenario. In a world even remotely resembling Fremlin's future world scenario, Beston's statement that "the ancient values of dignity, beauty, and poetry which sustain [human life] are of Nature's inspiration; they are born of the mystery and beauty of the world" would be unintelligible.[11]

In the aggregate, the economics, political economy, ethics, and pedagogy of ecologism are based on assumptions and values very different from those that characterize their counterparts in techno-industrial society, and constitute an alternative American vision. The ecological paradigm calls for economic and political institutions that require an honest accounting of costs and benefits, a transparency of the impacts of human action on social and natural environments, an ethical or other-regarding stance toward nonhumans, a decentralization of economics and politics and focus on place and community to revitalize citizenship and participatory democracy—all of which would lift the curtain that the techno-industrial society places between the individual and the social and ecological consequences of that society. An honest accounting of costs means full-cost pricing or internalizing in the market price structure the cost to humans and the natural environment of economic growth. Understanding that the economy is a subsystem of the planetary environment entails the notion of an appropriate or sustainable scale for the economy. The notion of appropriate scale, in turn, entails a sense of self-limitation and an other-regarding respect for the welfare of present and future generations of humans and nonhumans. Making transparent to individuals the consequences of their actions and that of key social institutions requires the decentralization of these institutions and the empowerment of communities where citizens are brought face-to-face with the visible social and environmental impacts of public policies and private behavior.

A society based on an ecological paradigm resurrects moral agency and active citizenship. It supports a strong democracy and a strong civic culture which restricts the market to its proper subordinate instrumental role in providing the material foundation consonant with the values of that civic culture. It empowers communities appropriately sized to practice participatory democracy and effective moral agency. It encourages a rapprochement with nature and its myriad life forms by affirming an ecological ethics that recognizes the inherent worth of nonhuman life. It seeks a harmony between human societies and nature.

> . . . [H]armony means the preserving of a balance between human values and the well-being of animals and plants in natural ecosystem. It is a condition on Earth in which people are able to pursue their individual interests and the cultural ways of life they have adopted while at the same time allowing many biotic communities in a great variety of natural ecosystems to carry on their existence without interference. . . . The realm of nature is not considered as something to be consumed, exploited, or controlled only for human ends, but is shared with other creatures.[12]

Ecological pedagogy supports these values by replacing both the anthropocentrism that currently permeates education and the implicit agenda of educating for techno-industrial job skills and dominant paradigm values with a curriculum educating for ecological literacy. Understood in its widest sense, ecological literacy means understanding the dependency of economics on the planet's ecological life systems and the role of humans in the Earth's community of life. It means recognizing the importance of character in enabling individuals to avoid the disjunctive egoism prevalent in the techno-industrial society and of educating for effective moral agency and active citizenship. To be ecologically literate is to understand individual events within a larger context, to distinguish social and environmental effects from economic and political causes, and to clearly differentiate between qualitative and quantitative indices of what passes for a good life. Ecological literacy, as David W. Orr has said, has to do with intelligence in contrast to cleverness.

> True intelligence is long range and aims toward wholeness. Cleverness is mostly short range and tends to break reality into bits and pieces. Cleverness is personified by the functionally rational technician armed with know-how and methods but without a clue about the higher ends technique should serve. The goal of [ecological] education should be to connect intelligence with an emphasis on whole systems and the long range with cleverness, which involves being smart about details.[13]

Taken as a whole, the ecological paradigm represents a world view that appears to satisfy the criteria, proposed by Paul W. Taylor,[14] that determine whether or not rational, factually informed, and enlightened individuals could justifiably accept it as such. The ecological paradigm or world view is comprehensive, coherent, free from obscurity, and consistent with known empirical facts. It is comprehensive, because it accounts for and examines all human activity in its relationship to the planetary biosphere. It is coherent, because its economics, political economy, ethics, and pedagogy are logically and integrally related to the ecologistic vision of a humane society in harmony with its natural environment. It is free from obscurity in that its specific social and ecological goals are clearly defined and the institutional means to achieve those goals identified. It is consistent with known empirical facts provided, among others, by climatologists, biologists, sociologists, economists, political scientists, historians, psychologists, and educators who have studied the destabilizing impact of the dominant paradigm on human communities, on other planetary biotic communities, and on the ecological life services which the natural environment provides when not impaired by human activities. The ecological world view meets a fifth criterion not listed by Taylor. It provides answers to troubling questions which cannot even be asked within the framework of a dominant paradigm that does not recognize the legitimacy or relevance of such questions. The ecological paradigm can explain, for example, why there is a moral crisis in education, why genuine human communities are the exception rather than the rule, why addiction and violence are so manifest in all sectors of contemporary society, why so many individuals equate the possession of material goods with self-worth and identity, why active citizenship has eroded, and why political campaigns and elections are increasingly transformed into rituals devoid of substantive content. In responding to such questions, the ecological world view suggests another way for the individual to find purpose and meaning in life, a way that enables the individual to escape the straitjacket of market egoism and enlarge one's image of self. As Arne Naess has stated, the small self of the market society can be transmuted into a larger Self which identifies with other humans and other forms of life and thus expands its experiental field and its set of values.[15]

Thus, the ecological world view directly confronts the dominant techno-industrial paradigm on the issue of what humans are and what they can be. From the ecological perspective, the almost exclusive focus of the dominant paradigm on the economic functions of humans as their defining characteristic is a bizzare misreading of the evolutionary and cultural history of Homo sapiens. It is misreading of the evolutionary history of humans because there is ample evidence that all forms of life represent a genetic continuum in which differences, while significant, are more a matter of degree than of kind, and that, therefore, the total appropriation of nonhuman life forms as economic resources for human use is based on an untenable anthropocentrism. The dominant paradigm justifies its treatment of animals, for example, on the now discredited Cartesian proposition that animals, unlike humans, are unthinking and unfeeling machines, a proposition completely at odds with contemporary animal studies and with the views of Charles Darwin himself.[16]

It a is misreading of the cultural history of humans in that by virtually reducing human capacities to economic production and consumption, the religious/mythic, artistic, philosophical, aesthetic, and other non-market related faculties and activities of humans are subordinated to the operations of the economy. Art, literature, music, and philosophy have not been rendered extinct by the superordinate market culture. However, if mind is shaped by both the natural and cultural landscapes, then as these landscapes are reduced and impoverished by the devastation of nature and the increasing one-dimensionality of techno-industrial culture, art, literature, music, and philosophy will come to occupy a diminishing space in the cultural sector, accessible to a small, educated minority increasingly marginalized within the mainstream culture and its dominant paradigm values. In effect, the dominant paradigm has taken the two-and-a-half-century experience with the Industrial Revolution and its associated cultural and characterological features as the prototypical human situation.

While the ecological world view offers a comprehensive, coherent, clear, and factually grounded alternative to the dominant techno-industrial paradigm, an alternative that rational, factually informed and reality-aware individuals could justifiably accept, such qualifications do not carry much weight outside a small circle of academicians and scientists. Within the mainstream society shaped as it is by the values and institutions of the dominant paradigm, the ecological world view faces various significant and perhaps insurmountable obstacles to its challenge of the dominant paradigm. These obstacles have been discussed in previous chapters and need only be briefly listed here. In economics, the reigning unlimited growth dogma has powerful allies, including most working people whose livelihood is linked presently to an expanding economy. In politics, the commitment of both major parties to an expanding economy based on corporate leadership and globalization of the techno-industrial market means continued political and economic centralization with its further distancing of individuals as citizens, workers, and consumers from the centers of political and economic power. In ethics, the prevalent anthropocentrism of the dominant paradigm is the major obstacle to any kind of thoroughgoing ecological ethics that would condemn as morally reprehensible the reduction of nonhuman life forms to mere instrumentalities for human purposes as in the current uses of animals in commercial farming and various forms of experimentation.

> There should be no illusion about how hard it will be for many people to change their values, their beliefs, their whole way of living if they are sincerely to adopt the attitude of respect for nature and act accordingly. Psychologically, this may require a profound moral reorientation.[17]

Reinforcing the prevalent cultural anthropocentrism are linguistic usages which reflect the assumed inferiority of animals, the twentieth-century scientific emphasis on physics and chemistry rather than zoology and the consequent focus on molecular rather than organismic structures, and the still dominant Western religious view of humans as created in the image of God and authorized to exercise dominion over all the creatures of the Earth. In education, the values of the dominant paradigm are embedded in both the explicit and implicit curricula which serve to provide specific skills deemed valuable by a techno-industrial society and to inculcate in students the taken-for-granted assumptions that constitute the dominant paradigm world view.

Among these taken-for-granted assumptions are the self-evidency of unlimited economic growth, of an anthropocentric attitude toward nonhuman life forms, of centralized political and economic institutions, and of the role of the economy in providing the major purpose and direction in the life of individuals. Education with very few exceptions thus serves the interests of the dominant paradigm, each year graduating hundreds of thousands of young people who will find a niche in the techno-industrial society and never look back at the choices they have made. For those who can afford a four-year college, particularly a private liberal arts college, the ever rising costs mandate that colleges justify higher education by persuading students that the costs should be seen as investments that will result in higher-income employment. Such investments, therefore, represent a vote of confidence in the techno-industrial society and bind students to the system even more tightly than is probably the case with blue-collar workers who are more likely to experience the system's dark side.

Such are the major impediments to the ascension of the ecological paradigm and its alternative American vision for the twenty-first century. Combined with the momentum that the dominant system has acquired over the more than two centuries of its existence, they constitute a powerful force against any challenge to the dominant paradigm. However, the ecological paradigm and the diverse literature in which it is reflected would not now exist if it did not respond to the needs, beliefs, and values of certain sectors of American society. Specific themes of the ecological paradigm do resonate with some traditional and contemporary values in American culture. The call for the decentralization of political and economic institutions and the strengthening of communities and active citizenship echoes the Jeffersonian tradition with its persistent distrust of large and distant centers of political power. The defense of free market mechanisms given policies to ensure appropriate scale, efficiency, and fair distribution, and the support for a broader ownership of capital resources, especially at the community level, represent an ecologically adjusted version of familiar American populist themes. The call for the moral accountability of the individual for the consequences of his or her actions is frequently sounded in American churches and among various conservative groups. The demand for full-cost pricing which accounts for the true costs of business is consonant with the classical market theory of Adam Smith. Policies which urge conservation and the frugal use of scarce resources reflect the common sense practices of earlier American generations who had learned "waste not, want not." The extension of moral considerability to nonhumans is part of the widening circle of compassion which historically has been expanded by the efforts of abolitionists, suffragettes, and animal rights organizations and advocates. The conceptualization of the economy as a subsystem of the planetary environment is supported by ongoing scientific research on the life-support services provided by the biosphere and evidence of the utter dependence of any stable economy on well-functioning ecosystems. The notion that there is an optimal limit to human productive, consumptive, and reproductive activities which can be determined by weighing the benefits of additional such activities against the associated social and environmental costs is implicit in standard marginal economic cost-benefit analysis. The ecological paradigm vision of human life enriched by the values of community and a nonanthropocentric relationship with the natural environment speaks to all those who sense that their full human capacities are suppressed in a system that reduces their humanity to the one dimension of economics.

These elements in the contemporary American culture that support the ecological paradigm must be acknowledged, but their influence in the mainstream culture must not be overstated. For example, candidates for political office frequently run against big government, stressing the need to bring power back to the people. More often than not, this theme is sounded by Republicans whose party, at least on the national level, solidly supports the globalization of the techno-industrial market and thus further strengthens those very forces that are presently eroding regional or local control of economic and political policies. Moreover, calling for devolution of power from the central government to state and local governments may result in benefiting regional political and economic vested interests rather than strengthening grassroots participatory democracy. Without policies designed to encourage a greater degree of local economic self-reliance which decreases vulnerability to the operations of national and global markets, demands to return power to the people constitute mere campaign rhetoric. The fact that the ecological paradigm has an increasing scientific warrant for its views on the appropriate human relationships with the natural environment does not provide it with any kind of cultural cachet. Scientific data can be disputed, revised, and reinterpreted. Science and scientists can be politicized, particularly when they become enmeshed in social, political, and economic issues in which powerful and organized groups have vested interests. Such issues are not resolved by marshaling sufficient scientific data to convince all rational protagonists that there is only one correct position on an issue.

As regards a popular base for the ecological paradigm, there are presently some seven million Americans who are members of environmental organizations, with the great majority of these enrolled in the so-called Group of Ten which includes the National Audubon Society, the Environmental Defense Fund, the Natural Resources Defense Council, the Wilderness Society, the Sierra Club, the National Wildlife Federation, and Friends of the Earth.[18] More than half of the total membership of these organizations, some 4,400,000, is in the National Wildlife Federation. Seven million environmentally oriented individuals would appear to be an impressive support base for an ecological paradigm. However, the mainline organizations, most of whom supported NAFTA despite its less than impressive environmental protection provisions, are more interested in conservation, wildlife, and antipollution issues than in challenging the political and economic institutions of the techno-industrial society. Most of these organizations accept corporate support and have corporate officers on their boards. The multimillion member National Wildlife Federation focuses on issues that attract the sports-minded individual rather than the critic of unlimited economic growth. While there are radical environmental groups that "espouse a fundamental cultural transformation that rejects the dominant political and economic institutions of most advanced societies as incompatible with global ecological vitality,"[19] these organizations, such as Earth First!, are small and frequently splinter as dissident groups leave to create their own, supposedly more principled, organizations. The engagement of such organizations as Greenpeace and the Sea Shepherd Society in direct action to protect dolphins or whales may result in worldwide media attention but also associates these organizations with violence and thus indirectly lessens, for many, the credibility of challenges to the dominant paradigm. The organizations that represent the American environmental movement are clearly not of one mind on the environmental agenda, and most would not enlist under the banner of the ecological paradigm. Considering that Ralph Nader received some 2.7 million votes in the 2000 presidential election, the majority of the seven million members of environmental organizations apparently voted for the two parties that despite their tactical differences support the policies of the dominant techno-industrial paradigm.

Robert Paehlke ties the future of environmentalism to an alliance with progressive elements in American society and support for such issues as restoration and enhancement of urban cores and urban transportation systems, deficit reduction, improvement and enforcement of occupational health standards, strengthening of environmental protection policies, and ending subsidies to corporations.[20] These are common issues on which environmentalists, labor unions, and various social justice groups can unite, as they did in Seattle to protest the policies of the World Trade Organization.[21] These common issues, however, are thoroughly anthropocentric and are mainly contested within the framework of the dominant paradigm. An environmental/progressive/populist program, as preferable as it may be to the political status quo, does not represent the substance of the ecological paradigm. All in all, the elements in American society that constitute the ground for a new social paradigm currently represent minority traditions, values, and groups; and unless there are some major social transformations this minority status will not change in the foreseeable future.

Contemporary writers have speculated about the future of the ecological paradigm and the transformative events that would make it a potent influence in the American society. William Ophuls has argued that under conditions of ecological scarcity a society that permits individuals to pursue their material self-interest unrestrained by a public authority that upholds the common interest invites a common environmental disaster.[22] It may be expected, therefore, that faced by undeniable signs of environmental collapse brought on by the political and economic institutions of the dominant techno-industrial society, a new structure of incentives and disincentives will be designed to achieve the common interest of avoiding environmental disaster.

> Under conditions of ecological scarcity the individual, possessing an inalienable rights to pursue happiness as he defines it and exercising his liberty in a basically laissez-faire system, will inevitably produce the ruin of the commons. Accordingly, the individualistic basis of society, the concept of inalienable rights, the purely self-defined pursuit of happiness, liberty as maximum freedom of action, and laissez-faire itself all become problematic, requiring major modifications or perhaps even abandonment if we wish to avert inexorable environmental degradation and eventual extinction as a civilization. Certainly, democracy as we know it cannot conceivably survive.[23]

Alluding to Edmund Burke's famous dictum that men of intemperate minds can never be free because their passions forge their chains, Ophuls concludes that the only alternatives to the mutual self-restraint required to avoid environmental disaster are the coercion of nature or the coercion of "an iron regime that will compel our consent to living life with less."[24] Such necessary mutual self-restraint will accompany an emerging new world view that recognizes the realities of the ecological predicament and accepts the limitations that ecological systems place on human behavior. Such an emerging new world view constitutes for Ophuls a metanoia or a profound transformation of mind and character likened to a spiritual conversion which radically alters the way in which humans view themselves, their relationships with others, and their relationships with nature. Without metanoia, the psychological conditions and the political will to reshape the institutions and values that threaten ecological disaster will be absent.

Other writers also recognize that there must be a transformation of the cultural psyche, of the very psychology of individuals, if the ecological paradigm is to supplant the environmentally destructive dominant techno-industrial paradigm. The political, economic, ethical, and pedagogical features of an ecologically viable society are clear in general outline if not in all detail. The consequences of further temporization in regard to the dominant paradigm can also be foreseen. Contemporary generations stand, as it were, before a door that needs to be opened to afford access to a new vista but remains closed out of cultural lethargy and habit reinforced by the social institutions of the dominant paradigm. In concluding *Respect for Nature*, Taylor states:

> A world of harmony between human civilization and nature . . . is a distinct empirical possibility. . . . [I]t should be evident from my discussion of the biocentric outlook and the attitude of repect for nature than an *inner* change in our moral beliefs and commitments is the first, indispensable step. And this inner change is itself a psychological possibility. Some people have actually made such a change, exercising their autonomy in the decision to adopt new moral principles regarding their treatment of the natural environment and its living inhabitants.[25]

For Taylor, this inner change can be accomplished by moral agents exercising their powers of autonomy and rationality. For Ophuls, this inner change can be triggered by a series of social and ecological calamities that can no longer be rationalized by dominant paradigm arguments. For Maguire, the inner change is occasioned by an experience of the sacred in the Earth context, accepting "earth as our home and the plants and animals of earth as our kindred."[26] For Beston, the inner change is really the reawakening of the ties that bind humans to nature: "Whatever attitude to human existence you fashion for yourself, know that it is valid only if it be the shadow of an attitude to Nature."[27] Rather remarkably in a book that is primarily about the need to redirect economic theory and practice toward community, the environment and a sustainable future, Herman E. Daly and John B. Cobb, Jr. locate the source of the moral energy for this redirection, the needed inner change, in what they describe as prophetic theism.

> But whatever else God is, God is also the inclusive whole. The diversity of the interconnected parts of the biosphere gives richness to the whole that is the divine life. The extinction of species and simplification of the ecosystem impoverishes God even when it does not threaten the capacity of the biosphere to sustain ongoing human life. . . . We affirm . . . that this prophetic theism can lead beyond some of the costly conflicts among those seeking to break out of the anthropocentric heritage which continues to bind the culture.[28]

For Thomas Berry the inner change corresponds to the realization that humans, however intrinsically valuable, exist for the integrity of the universe and that "the sacred community is primarily the universe community, not the human community."[29] Given the frequency of such references to metanoia, inner change and spiritual insight in ecological literature, it is difficult not to conclude that underlying the ecological paradigm is a pervasive religious dimension which energizes those who challenge the dominant paradigm in all its manifestations. This religious dimension is neither denominational nor even always theistic,[30] but it is a major source of the moral fervor that so often characterizes the opposition to techno-industrial society.

There is a saying that an old paradigm does not die until its last believer dies. But long before the last believer passes on, efforts to salvage a dominant pradigm under stress will be made. Such efforts by true believers include exhortations not to abandon the old paradigm or charges that the old paradigm is not being applied vigorously enough. From this perspective the problems stressing the old paradigm are seen as the result of a failure to utilize the actual or latent strengths of the old paradigm. In the case of the still dominant paradigm of unlimited economic growth, chronic environmental and social problems are addressed according to the norms of the paradigm. Essentially more of the same is recommended to address the problems caused by previous applications of the same. There are those who do not even acknowledge that the economic and political forces that operate under the unlimited growth paradigm are creating serious problems. For this group the social and environmental degradation that accompanies the workings of this paradigm is simply an acceptable price that one pays for "progress." That the human impact on the environment increases by an order of magnitude through the instrumentalities of the techno-industrial system and that this impact has reached global proportions, is no reason for true believers to question the dominant paradigm. Given the dependency of most Americans on the economic system and the commitment of government to an expanding economy it is not likely that the dominant paradigm will be abandoned in the near future. What is more likely is that the techno-industrial system will accommodate such green strategies as recycling, energy conservation, a slow transition to nonfossil fuels, subsidies for non-car transportation modes, and international agreements on CO_2 and other greenhouse gas emissions.[31] Such accommodations will not, however, compromise the dynamics of an ever-expanding economy or the appropriation of the global natural environment for economic purposes. If, in fact, the ascendance of the ecological paradigm will have to wait for further transformative and probably deeply traumatic events then it is entirely possible that under conditions of profoundly disturbed social and natural environments, the democratic, communitarian, moral, and aesthetic vision of that paradigm will fall far short of fulfillment. Those who are impelled by the moral, intellectual, and spiritual urgency of moving toward that vision while there is still time to fulfill its promise, will feel the poignancy of a concluding observation by Daly and Cobb.

The recognition of possibilities gone forever inspires us with a
sense of urgency. Delay is costly to us and even more to our
descendants and to the other species with which we share the
planet. It is already very late. It is hard to avoid bitterness about
what might have been done and about the additional missed opportunities each day.[32]

At this juncture Plato's allegory of the cave comes to mind.[33] One
pictures the prisoners with their backs to a fire, facing a wall on which flicker
shadows of objects carried by other residents of the cave who pass between
the prisoners and the fire. The prisoners can never see the fire or the objects
which cast the shadows unless liberated and can never see the sun unless they
make the steep ascent out of the cave into the world above. One is tempted
to believe that what is at stake as the battle is joined between the dominant
techno-industrial paradigm and the developing ecological paradigm is the
release of the prisoners and their ascent out of the shadows into the real
world, the community of life on Earth powered by the sun.

Plato's allegory signifies both a dominant paradigm which distorts the
way humans perceive the world and themselves and the painful and pro-
longed process of overcoming a dominant paradigm, however false and pernicious in its effects it may be. The taken-for-granted assumptions of the
contemporary techno-industrial paradigm are deeply rooted in the behavior
and psyche of most Americans and the transition to an ecological paradigm
will take several generations, if it occurs at all. It is possible in the short term
for individuals and societies to function within social and physical environments which are being progressively destabilized by their actions; and it is
psychologically comfortable for most individuals to live as if there is only the
short term to take into account. In the longer term, however, the consequences
of misguided human actions and policies will prove to be far more painful
than the ascent out of the cave of the dominant paradigm and into the light
of the developing ecological paradigm.[34]

Notes

Introduction

1. Aldo Leopold, *A Sand County Almanac* (1949, reprint, New York, NY: Ballantine, 1966), p. 197.

2. Documentation of environmental degradation is prolific. Sources include *Worldwatch*, EPA data, ecology journals, and standard environmental science textbooks such as Daniel B. Botkin and Edward A. Keller, *Environmental Science* (New York, NY: John Wiley and Sons, Inc., 2000).

3. Documentation of crime rates, divorce, drug and alcohol addiction, and homelessness is obtainable from government agencies and private research groups. The deterioration of democracy, apart from data on Americans who do not register or do not vote, requires verification based on such factors as economic dependence, two-party domination of political discourse, media marginalization of substantive public issues, and the negative impact of a materialistic consumer culture on political values. Much less concern is expressed about the condition of democracy than about crime, violence, and drug addiction.

4. Russell Jacoby, *Social Amnesia* (Boston, MA: Beacon Press, 1975). From the Marxist perspective, a dominant social paradigm represents the beliefs and values of an elite. Social practices and institutions embody these elite beliefs and values without revealing to the masses their elite origins. For deconstructionists, a dominant social paradigm is to be understood by examining the philosophic, social, or political implications of the language employed in the paradigm rather than by examining any extratextual reality the paradigm ostensibly refers to. What are usually ignored in both these perspectives are the psychological processes by which the dominant paradigm values are internalized in the individual and the social institutions, including the family, that assist in this internalization. Russell Jacoby has stressed the importance

183

of understanding the dialectical relationship between the dominant social institutions and individual psychology and behavior.

5. Sanford Lakoff, *Democracy: History, Theory, Practice* (Boulder, CO: Westview Press, 1996), Chap. 10. The dominant social paradigm allows for a simplistic statement of the relationship of economic growth to democracy: the greater the economic growth, the stronger the democracy. In fact, as Sandford Lakoff and others points out, economic growth which results in capital accumulation rather than in the improvement of general living standards and promotion of literacy, education, and widespread well-being, exacerbates inequality and undermines the public sense of security without which a flourishing democracy cannot exist.

6. Thomas Berry, *The Dream of the Earth* (San Francisco, CA: Sierra Club Books, 1988), pp. 123–124. For an earlier challenge to the dominant paradigm in the social sciences see "Ecology and the Social Sciences: An Emerging Paradigm," ed., Riley E. Dunlap in *American Behavioral Scientist*, 24, no. 1 (Sept./Oct, 1980).

7. C. A. Bowers, *The Culture of Denial* (Albany, NY: State University of New York Press, 1997), p. 4.

8. Berry, *Dream of the Earth*, p. 184.

9. Bowers, *Culture of Denial*, p. 5.

10. Unlike the dominant techno-industrial paradigm, the ecological paradigm makes no universalistic claims and does not preempt other cultural forms and indigenous knowledge systems which allow for sustainable human interaction with the natural environment. The ecological paradigm is offered as a better story for Americans, taking into account their history and present stage of economic and social development. For a comprehensive case study of an indigenous knowledge system in Kenya see chapter 13. Philip Porter and Eric S. Sheppard, "The Management of Tropical and Subtropical Ecosystems," in *A World of Difference* (New York, NY: The Guilford Press, 1998) p. 260–303. Porter and Sheppard view the globalization project, that is, the attempt to globalize the dominant techno-industrial paradigm values and institutions, as unsustainable in the long run. They conclude: "To live harmoniously with nature and humankind, to negotiate a tricky 'sustainability transition,' will necessitate reshaping human consciousness and mentality. . . . A radical—that is, literally, rooted-rethinking of *everyone's* lifestyle, and a re-visioning of our future, are in order." Ibid., p. 555. [Italics in original.]

11. *Bowers, Culture of Denial*, pp. 4–5. Bowers lists as elements of an ecologically centered culture a metaphorical language and mythopoetic narrative that together represent human and nonhuman forms of life as equal participants in a sacred moral universe; a sense of time that understands how the past and future influence present decisions; forms of community and transgenerational communication which ensure that economic production and exchange do not become the dominant influences in everyday life; and technologies that are integrated with natural systems and the culture's symbolic world of moral and spiritual connectedness. All of these elements are evident in the writings discussed in the following chapters.

12. The egocentricity and solipsism of contemporary American culture are starkly revealed by the popular view that terrorist attacks on America are aimed at the "American way of life." Since this way of life is regarded as self-evidently the highest expression of human development, such attacks are incomprehensible. Why would

anyone stand in the way, let alone wish to destroy, a way of life that by all rational standards should be globalized as the norm for all existing societies?

13. See Ralph Nader, *The Case Against "Free Trade"* (San Francisco, CA: Earth Island Press, 1993), especially chap. 1; Ralph Nader, "Introduction: Free Trade and the Decline of Democracy," and chap. 3, Lori Wallach, "Hidden Dangers of GATT and NAFTA."

14. A key reference is Robert Costanza, John H. Cumberland, Herman E. Daly, Robert Goodland, Richard B. Norgaard, *An Introduction to Ecological Economics* (Boca Raton, FL: St. Lucie Press, 1997).

15. A key reference is Roy Morrison, *Ecological Democracy* (Boston, MA: South End Press, 1995).

16. A key reference is Paul W. Taylor, *Respect for Nature* (Princeton, NJ: Princeton University Press, 1986).

17. A key reference is David W. Orr, *Earth in Mind: On Education, Environment and the Human Prospect* (Washington, DC: Island Press, 1994).

18. Andrew Dobson, *Green Political Thought*, 2d ed. (New York, NY: Routledge and Kegan Paul, 1955), p. 1. While there are some semantic difficulties in substituting "ecologism" for "environmentalism" (e.g., if an advocate of environmentalism is an environmentalist, is an advocate of ecologism an ecologist?), "ecologism" better designates the body of thought discussed here than "environmentalism."

19. See Brian Swimme and Thomas Berry, *The Universe Story* (San Francisco, CA: Harper, 1992); Daniel C. Maguire and Larry L. Rasmussen, *Ethics for a Small Planet* (Albany, NY: State University Press, 1998); and Thomas Berry, *The Great Work* (New York, NY: Bell Tower, 1999). There is also an ecologistic literature that deals with a cosmology that offers a scientifically grounded account of the origins of the Earth and its place in the galaxy. This cosmology suggests a shift from salvation-focused religion to creation-focused religion.

20. The 2000 national election demonstrated that the Green Party has more claim to ecologistic programs and goals than any other political party, major or minor.

21. Kirkpatrick Sale, *The Conquest of Paradise* (New York, NY: Penguin Books, 1991).

22. Berry, *The Great Work* pp. 33–47.

23. Such federal and state protective policies came about largely through the influence of individuals such as John Muir and Theodore Roosevelt and organizations like the Sierra Club, rather than by widespread public demand.

24. This faith in education was earlier expressed by Thomas Jefferson when he made public education one of the primary functions of the wards or townships. His personal contribution to the establishment of the University of Virginia further expresses his belief in the primacy of education in a free society.

25. Orr, *Earth in Mind*, p. 5.

26. Since ecological economics accepts the principle of cost/benefit accounting, albeit an accounting that significantly broadens the scope of costs and benefits, the assigning of infinite value (inherent worth) to nonhuman organic life, as is the case in a biocentric ethics, becomes quite problematic.

27. Social ecology as represented by such writers as Murray Bookchin emphasizes the social and historic roots of the ecological crisis, views the evolutionary

development of increasing subjectivity and intentionality or self-consciousness of life forms as immanent in nature itself, and anticipates that humans (second nature) will bring their "consciousness to the service of first nature by . . . promoting the thrust of natural evolution toward diversity and ending needless suffering. . . ." Michael E. Zimmerman, ed. *Environmental Philosophy* (Englewood Cliffs, NJ: Prentice Hall, 1993), p. 387. Deep ecology as represented by such writers as George Sessions and Bill Devall has been criticized for its lack of a comprehensive social critique and a naive romanticism toward a "nature" which some social ecologists argue is more a conceptual construction than a thing-in-itself. Kirkpatrick Sale responded to the critics of deep ecology in the May 1989 issue of *The Nation*. A later publication *Defending the Earth: A Dialogue between Murray Bookchin and Dave Foreman* (Boston, MA: South End Press, 1991) represents an attempt by proponents of social and deep ecology to bridge differences. Although these debates may clarify the positions and conceptual usages of the protagonists, the debates as such are not very helpful in the construction of the overall ecological paradigm presented here.

1. Ecological Economics

1. Aldo Leopold, *A Sand County Almanac and Sketches Here and There* (New York, NY: Oxford University Press, 1969), p. 223.

2. Ibid., pp. 224–225.

3. Herman E. Daly, *Steady-State Economics* (San Francisco, CA: W. H. Freeman and Company, 1977).

4. Nicholas Georgescu-Roegen, *The Entropy Law and the Economic Process* (Cambridge, MA: Harvard University Press, 1971).

5. Adam Smith assumed limits to worker's wages; Thomas Robert Malthus assumed limits to human population; David Ricardo assumed limits to the availability of prime agricultural land.

6. Flow here refers to the volume of energy and matter that is available from a source.

7. Healthy in terms of being assured a renewable supply of resources and sufficient sinks in which to deposit wastes which have been reduced to a minimum.

8. Herman E. Daly, *Steady-State Economics*, 2d ed. (Washington, DC: Island Press, 1991), p. xi.

9. Mary Clifford, *Environmental Crime* (Gaithersburg, MD: Aspen Publishers, Inc., 1998), p. 236. While major federal environmental legislation provides civil and criminal penalties for violations "most federal prosecutions of organizations for environmental crimes involve small, closely held corporations. Only about 40 percent of these companies are large enough to be listed in the Standard and Poor's Register which requires annual sales of $1 million and 50 employees."

The tension between enforcing environmental law and encouraging economic growth is expressed thusly: "So, while society has an important interest in reducing pollution and deterring illegal environmental activities, society also has an interest in ensuring that the requirements for complying and the penalties for not complying are not so severe that firms are inhibited from engaging in socially beneficial activities, *such as the production of automobiles.*" Ibid., p. 232. [Italics added.]

10. A comprehensive account of the current economic status of Americans is provided by Donald L. Barlett and James B. Steele, *America: Who Stole the Dream?* (Kansas City, KS: Andrews and McMeel, 1996).

11. Discounting which is discussed more fully later refers to valuing the future in terms of present investment; thus, a dollar twenty years from now is worth only eleven cents today, assuming a 10 percent interest rate, compounded annually.

12. Goods produced with cheap overseas labor but with a price tag reflecting transportation, energy, advertising, status symbols, and profit.

13. See Allan Schnaiberg, *The Environment from Surplus to Scarcity* (Oxford, Eng., New York, NY: Oxford University Press, 1980), pp. 205–247, for an early and insightful analysis of the treadmill of production.

14. Robert L. Heilbroner, *An Inquiry into the Human Prospect* (New York, NY: W.W. Norton, 1980), pp. 77–111.

15. Limits of renewable resources depend on whether or not extraction exceeds reproductive rates; limits of nonrenewable sources are defined by rates of extraction.

16. Thresholds of ecological services (waste absorption, soil creation, ozone layer, oxygen supply) are exceeded when the ecosystem elements (trees, aquifers, stratospheric ozone molecules) essential to ecosystem services are destroyed or impaired.

17. Growth refers to quantitative expansion (more cars); development refers to qualitative improvement (more energy-efficient cars). The Brundtland Report, however, also called for economic growth five to ten times higher in the future so that developing nations could experience a significant increase in per capita income.

18. Herman E. Daly, *Beyond Growth* (Boston, MA: Beacon Press, 1996), p. 3.

19. Natural capital is any stock of natural resources, e.g. trees, that provides a flow or periodic yield of goods, for example, timber, or services, for example, erosion control and wildlife habitat. Thomas Prugh, Robert Costanza, John H. Cumberland, Herman E. Daly, Robert Goodland, Richard B. Norgaard, *Natural Capital and Human Economic Survival* (Solomons, MD: ISSE Press, 1995), pp. 51–69.

20. Herman E. Daly, *Ecological Economics and the Ecology of Economics* (Northampton, MA: Edward Elgar, 1999), pp. 77–88. See the discussion by Daly of the Solow-Stiglitz variant of the Cobb-Douglas function which demonstrates mathematically that as long as man-made capital increases, natural capital may be reduced to almost zero.

21. Costanza, *Introduction to Ecological Economics.*

22. J. R. Hicks, *Value and Capital*, 2d ed., (Oxford, Eng.: Oxford University Press, 1946).

23. NK refers to natural capital; MMK to man-made capital.

24. Costanza, *Introduction to Ecological Economics*, pp. 123–125.

25. Ibid., p. 173.

26. John Gowdy and Sabine O'Hara, *Economic Theory for Environmentalists* (Delray Beach, FL: St. Lucie Press, 1995), p. 6. A concept central to neoclassical economic theory is Pareto optimality in both consumption and production which is

achieved by unhindered economic exchange (the free market). "Pareto optimality is the end result of a successful trading process of goods and services as well as inputs. This condition is what neoclassical economics means by efficiency."

27. Methods for assigning monetary values to environmental goods and services are discussed later.

28. Herman E. Daly and John B. Cobb Jr., *For the Common Good* (Boston, MA: Beacon Press, 1994), pp. 25–43.

29. Gowdy and O'Hara, *Economic Theory for Environmentalists*, pp. 22–27.

30. Garrett Hardin, "The Tragedy of the Commons," *Science* 162, (December 13, 1968): 1243–1248. Hardin's use of the term "commons" has been replaced by "open access" to differentiate between commons property which historically was regulated by the community of users and open access property where no such regulation, legal, or traditional, exists.

31. For a comprehensive summary of the limitations of the market see Daly and Cobb Jr., *For the Common Good*, pp. 44–61.

32. Failure to provide wages high enough to meet the health costs incurred by the nature of the production process in which the worker is involved or failure to provide health insurance represents an externalization of the costs of production by imposing the costs on workers or the public who through taxes pay for government programs addressing work-related health problems, for example, black lung disease, asbestos-caused lung cancer.

33. This discussion of ecological economic efficiency and the notations used are based on Daly, *Beyond Growth*, pp. 84–85.

34. Daly and Cobb Jr., *For the Common Good*, pp. 443–507.

35. Ibid., pp. 462–463.

36. Daly, *Beyond Growth,* p. 105. The impossibility theorem rejects the notion that current United States per capita consumption of resources can be generalized throughout the world. In the following identity, M represents the factor by which world resource flows would have to expand to make possible a global per capita resource consumption equal to that of the United States, and R represents current world resource extraction:

$$\frac{M \cdot R}{5.9 \times 10^9} = \frac{\dfrac{R}{3}}{2.6 \times 10^8}$$

Solving for R (the denominators represent on the left the world population and on the right United States population) provides a value of approximately eight which means that world resource extraction (excluding the U.S.) would have to increase eightfold, not including the production of needed physical capital to extract and process resources which in itself would necessarily require additional extraction of resources.

37. For a discussion of Manfred Max-Neef's matrix of human needs see Costanza, *Introduction to Ecological Economics*, pp. 135–138.

38. Daly, *Steady-State Economics*, 2d ed., p. 19.

39. See Herbert Marcuse, *One-Dimensional Man* (Boston, MA: Beacon Press, 1968), pp. 84–120 for a discussion of one-dimensional society based on neo-Freudian

and neo-Marxian analysis which reaches similar conclusions about the cultural consequences of an economics of unlimited growth.

40. Robert Costanza, "The Value of the World's Ecosystem Services and Natural Capital," *Nature* 387, (1997): 253–260.

41. Marino Gatto and Giulio A. De Leo, "Pricing Biodiversity and Ecosystem Services: The Never-Ending Story," *BioScience*, 50, no. 4, (April 2000): 347–354. " . . . [T]he pricing approach is inadequate—if not misleading and obsolete—because it implies erroneously that complex decisions with important environmental impacts can be based on a single scale of values." See also Michael Jacobs, *The Green Economy* (Concord, MA: Pluto Press, 1971), pp.197–198, and pp. 204–221 for a discussion of the use of contingent valuation for option, bequest, and existence values (nonuse values) and problems associated generally with monetary valuation of the environment.

42. All of which would indicate that strict economic efficiency may be overruled by other considerations.

43. Prugh, *Natural Capital*, pp. 91–92.

44. Gatto and De Leo, "Pricing Biodiversity," p. 354.

45. Ibid. The monetization of environmental stocks and services requires the utilization of the system of market prices. Since existing prices are the monetary reflection of dominant social paradigm practices and institutions, cost benefit analysis that relies exclusively on existing market prices implicitly prejudices the case for environmental protection.

46. These recommendations are discussed in Costanza, *Introduction to Ecological Economics,* pp. 206–242.

47. Given the current corporate claims based on chapter 11 of the North American Free Trade Agreement now pending before NAFTA tribunals, it is very unlikely that such ecological tariffs would be allowed to stand. The insertion of NAFTA chapter 11 provisions into other global free trade agreements would similarly jeopardize the major policies of ecological economics.

48. This idea was first proposed by Kenneth Boulding. Besides the juridical problem of enabling legislation passing constitutional muster, there is the larger problem of reversing the strong pronatalist trend in contemporary American culture that makes any such legislation highly improbable. Apparently, no one causal factor can explain why Americans have children. A sociobiological theory holds that people are "hardwired" or driven by their biology to have children. Another theory based on the psychology of alienation maintains that people have children in order to assert control over a micro part of their lives, thus compensating for their lack of control over the events that shape the macro society in which they participate. "A 1997 article by Robert Schoen, *et. al*, titled 'Why do Americans Want Children?' examined the professional lliterature on the subject and noted gloomily that 'there is no explanation why Americans still want children.' " Christopher Clausen, "Children in Toyland," *The American Scholar*, 71, no. 1 (Winter 2002): 111–121. See Paul Kennedy, *Preparing for the Twenty-First Century* (New York, NY: Vintage Books, 1994), p. 339 for an analysis of the escalating environmental and social impact of an exponentially increasing human population. To bring global birthrates to replacement levels he emphasizes the "three key elements in any *general* effort to prepare global society for the twenty-first century: the

role of education, the place of women, and the need for political leadership." These elements, however, become significant only in societies that have experienced a demographic transition which, according to mainstream thinking, requires the economic systems which are characteristic of highly industrialized societies. Thus, more economic growth which itself is problematic is required to address the population problem. [Italics in the original.]

49. Costanza, *Introduction to Ecological Economics*, pp. 217–219 and Prugh, *Natural Capital*, pp. 133–135.

50. Costanza, *Introduction to Ecological Economics*, pp. 222–228.

51. Ibid., pp. 231–234.

52. John C. Ryan and Alan T. Durning, *Stuff*, (Seattle, WA: Northwest Environment Watch, 1997), pp. 43–52. The manufacture of a fifty-five-pound computer generates 139 pounds of waste, uses 7,300 gallons of water and 2,300 kilowatt-hours of energy. The parts and elements to make the parts come from all over the world.

53. Costanza, *Introduction to Ecological Economics*, p. 81. "Allocative efficiency does not guarantee sustainability. . . . It is clear that scale should not be determined by prices but by a social decision reflecting ecological limits. Distribution should not be determined by prices, but by a social decision reflecting a just distribution of assets. Subject to these social decisions, individualistic trading in the market is then able to allocate the scarce rights efficiently."

54. "Valuable" in ways not always or ever measured in monetary terms.

55. Costanza, *Introduction to Ecological Economics*, p. 240.

56. Ibid., p. 241.

57. Ibid., p. 177.

2. Ecological Political Economy

1. The term ecological rather than environmental is used here to distinguish between a politics based on the acceptance of limits to economic growth (ecological) and what is essentially the politics of environmental regulation (environmental). The former focuses on the decentralization of politics and economics and emphasizes empowerment of citizens through local economies and self-government. The latter accepts the existing economic system and views environmental groups as one interest contending with other interests for the attention and support of government. This distinction is emphasized in a later section.

2. Aristotle, *The Politics* (Chicago, IL: University of Chicago Press, 1984). See especially book 5: 147–181.

3. Adam Smith quoted in Drew A. McCoy, *The Elusive Republic: Political Economy in Jeffersonian America* (Chapel Hill, NC: University of North Carolina Press, 1980), p. 38.

4. For an exposition of Jefferson's political and civic principles see Richard K. Matthews, *The Radical Politics of Thomas Jefferson* (Lawrence, KS: University Press of Kansas, 1984), especially pp. 31–52, and pp. 77–95.

5. The wards would provide public funding for grade school. The best students would merit suppport to receive further education, including admission to the Unniversity of Virginia, founded by Jefferson.

6. Jefferson foresaw an America populated within a century by one hundred million people.

7. Matthews, *The Radical Politics,* p. 115 and McCoy, *Elusive Republic,* p. 133.

8. See McCoy, *Elusive Republic,* pp. 25–27 for Mandeville's position on the positive impact of private vice on social welfare. For Smith's similar view see Adam Smith, *The Wealth of Nations,* ed. Bruce Mazlish (New York, NY: Bobbs-Merrill Co., 1961), pp. 14–15.

9. McCoy, *Elusive Republic,* p. 37.

10. For Aristotle, a moderate oligarchy allowed for a larger minority of the people to meet the property qualifications required to engage in politics and thus direct the course of events in the society.

11. McCoy, *Elusive Republic,* p. 249. In later years, Jefferson identified a republican political economy with the southern and western states. He believed the north's industrial and commercial economy was following the corrupt influence of the English model.

12. "Hard money" is money contributed to candidates and is limited by law. "Soft money" is money ostensibly contributed to parties for organizational programs and registration drives, is only recently limited by law, and has been used, in fact, by the parties to finance campaigns and candidates.

13. William E. Hudson, *American Democracy in Peril,* 3rd ed. (New York, NY: Chatham House Publishers, 2001). The other three challenges to democracy are separation of powers, radical individualism, and inequaliity. Two of the three can also be linked to the ideology of endless growth, namely, inequality and radical individualism.

14. The refusal to allow Ralph Nader and Buchanan to participate in the 2000 presidential debates meant that issues such as the World Trade Organization and the World Bank, capital punishment, corporate lobbying and campaign contributions, sustainable energy policy and single-payer national health coverage would not be discussed. Instead, Social Security, Medicare, and prescription drug payments were focal issues, not unimportant in themselves but debated outside a larger context of issues which will shape the American future.

15. Hudson, *American Democracy,* p. 268. Hudson comes closer to an ecologic political perspective himself when he describes the emergence of grassroots citizen organizations in various cities as "one of the most heartening developments in contemporary American politics." The examples he cites of such grassroots emergences, however, are citizen associations created to put pressure on city governments to be more responsive to the needs of neighborhoods. None of these associations represents an alternative to the corporate-dominated forms of production and governance, which must be replaced to make possible a sustainable and democratic future.

16. Roy Morrison, *Ecological Democracy* (Boston, MA: South End Press, 1995).

17. Ibid., p. 137. [Italics added.]

18. Ibid., p. 138.

19. Ibid., p. 142.

20. Ibid., p. 147

21. Ibid., p. 148.

22. Morrison, *Ecological Democracy.*

23. Ibid.

24. Ibid., p. 149.

25. Ibid.

26. Ibid., p. 48.

27. Ibid., p. 153.

28. Morrison, *Ecological Democracy*, p. 154.

29. Ibid., p. 156.

30. Ibid., p. 159.

31. Ibid., pp. 164–165. [Italics added.]

32. Ibid., p. 166.

33. Morrison, *Ecological Democracy*, p. 179. Morrison lists the following principles to guide the governance of a commons: clear demarcation of commons boundaries, congruence between use of the commons and local conditions, collective choice, sanctions, conflict resolution procedures, right to organize of people using the commons, nested enterprises for commons that are part of a larger system. The principles are summarized from Elenor Ostrom, *Governing the Commons: The Evolution of Institution for Collective Action* (New York, NY: Cambridge University Press, 1990).

34. Morrison, *Ecological Democracy*, p. 172.

35. Ibid, p. 177.

36. Ibid., p. 205.

37. Peter C. Reynolds, "Organics at the Crossroads," *Acres U.S.A.* 30, no. 9 (September 2000): 1.

38. Ibid., p. 8.

39. Ibid.

40. Ibid., p. 10.

41. See Brian Halweil, "Where Have all the Farmers Gone?," *World Watch*, B, no. 5 (September/October 2000): 20. See also William Greider, "The Last Farm Crisis," *The Nation*, 271, no. 16 (November 20, 2000): 11–18.

42. Halweil, "Where Have all the Farmers Gone?" p. 17.

43. Reynolds, "Organics at the Crossroads," p. 8.

44. James Robertson, "The Economics of Local Recovery," *Society and Nature*, 1, no. 1 (May, 1992): 145–174. Robertson is cofounder of the New Economic Foundation and of The Other Economic Summit (TOES).

45. Ibid., pp. 148–149.

46. Ibid., p. 149.

47. Ibid.

48. Ibid., p. 151. [Italics added.] Robertson's emphasis throughout the article is on the creation of local economies vital enough to sustain themselves against the vicissitudes of national and, increasingly, international markets. See Max H. Kirsch, *In the Wake of the Giant* (Albany, NY: State University Press, 1998), for a similar focus on the vulnerability of local economies dependent on multinational corporations.

49. Robertson, "The Economics of Local Recovery," p. 157.

50. Ibid., pp. 165–169.

51. Ibid., p. 168.

52. Ibid., p. 164.

53. Ibid.

54. Ibid.

55. Murray Bookchin, *Remaking Society* (Cheektowaga, NY: Black Rose Books, 1990). For a critical and constructive discussion of Bookchin's social ecology, see Andrew Light, ed., *Social Ecology after Bookchin* (New York, NY: Guilford Press, 1998). Social ecology is presented as a holistic conception of self, society, and nature, an approach which has "enormous importance for ethics and politics." See John Clark, "What is Social Ecology?" *Society and Nature* 1, no. 1 (May–August, 1992): 85 and 88.

56. Bookchin, *Remaking Society*, p. 44. [Italics in the original.]

57. Ibid., p. 32.

58. Ibid., p. 46. How we experience reality is shaped by the dominant paradigm form of discourse. For a discussion of how, for example, the language used by animal experimenters obfuscates the moral issues in which they are involved, see Joan Dunayer, "In the Name of Science," *Organization and Environment*, 13, no. 4, (December 2000): 432–452.

59. Bookchin relies on the work of Paul Radin for descriptions of the cultural features of early preindustrial societies. Paul Radin, *The World of Primate Man* (New York, NY: Grove Press, 1960).

60. Formal equality refers to equality before the law; substantive equality refers to the possession of the means of existence by all members of a community.

61. The individual referred to is the individual in the community, not the "free-floating, isolated and atomized" individual of the free-market society.

62. Usufruct involves the personal use of a property but without the exclusion of others from its use and with an obligation not to degrade the property while using it.

63. Bookchin, *Remaking Society*, p. 53.

64. Ibid.

65. Ibid., p. 57.

66. Ibid.

67. The parable of the tribes refers to a dispersed system of communities in which the emergence of even a single aggressive actor can transform the whole system. Because of the system's fragmentation "no one is free to choose peace, but *any one* can impose upon all the necessity for power." See Andrew B. Schmookler, *The Parable of the Tribes: The Problem of Power in Social Evolution* (Berkley, CA: University of California Press, 1984), p. 21. [Italics in the original.]

68. Ibid., p. 67.

69. Statecraft is defined as the administration of armies, bureaucracies, the judicial system, and police and is distinguished sharply from politics.

70. Bookchin, *Remaking Society*, p. 69. Politics is defined, in the Aristotelian sense, as the direct participation of citizens in the decisions that affect the life of the community. For Bookchin, politics was invented by the Athenians since it was in Athens that there existed the "direct administration of public affairs by a community as a whole."

71. Ibid., pp. 70–71.

72. Ibid., pp. 83–84.

73. Ibid., p. 84.

74. Yeoman refers to one who owns and cultivates his own land and may pass it on through inheritance.

75. Bookchin, *Remaking Society,* pp. 92–93.

76. Bookchin views evolution as tending toward development from the simple organism to the complex organism, such as man, endowed with consciousness, a sense of self, and the ability to alter itself and the nature in which it exists.

77. Bookchin, *Remaking Society,* p. 94.

78. Ibid., p. 136. This criticism, however, ignores Marx's *Economic and Philosophic Manuscripts of 1844* in which he defines a rich human being in distinctly non-economic terms. Karl Marx, *Economic and Philosophic Manuscripts of 1844* (Moscow, USSR: Progress Publishers, 1982), especially pp. 94–101.

79. Classic Marxism is represented by the works of Marx and Engels, particularly Marx's *Capital*. Karl Marx, *Capital: A Critique of Political Economy* (New York, NY: Vintage Books, 1977).

80. The New Left represents a melange of philosophic ideas, including those of such earlier utopian writers as Charles Fourier. Perhaps the strongest single influence in the New Left was represented by Herbert Marcuse whose works drew on certain themes in the young Marx and Sigmund Freud. In his *Eros and Civilization*, Marcuse advocates a liberation of man from the repressive performance (work) principle of contemporary capitalism. Herbert Marcuse, *Eros and Civilization* (New York, NY: Vintage Books, 1962).

81. Bookchin, *Remaking Society,* p. 143. The similarity to Marcuse's notion of a liberating new sensuousness is obvious.

82. Ibid.

83. Ibid., p. 55.

84. The term applies to political, social, and economic principles embedded in municipal structures as countervailing forces to the prevailing state power.

85. Ibid., p. 174. [Italics in the original.]

86. Ibid., p. 175. Once again, Bookchin sounds a Rousseauean theme.

87. Ibid.

88. Ibid., p. 181.

89. Ibid., p. 184.

90. Ibid., p. 187.

91. Ibid., p. 195.

92. Ibid., p. 197.

93. Murray Bookchin, "Libertarian Municipalism: An Overview," *Society and Nature*, 1, no. 1 (May 1992): 93–94. Bookchin's description of American politics is confirmed by the 2000 election.

94. Kirkpatrick Sale, *Dwellers in the Land* (Philadelphia, PA: New Society Publishers, 1991).

95. Ibid., p. 54. [Italics in the original.]

96. Ibid., p. 64.

97. Ibid., p. 65.

98. Ibid., p. 48. [Italics in the original.]

99. Sale uses the term "self-sufficiency" rather than "self-reliance," but the former functions more as a synonym for the latter since Sale makes it quite clear that bioregions will interact with one another, learning from and drawing on the material and cultural resources of each other.

100. Sale calculates that 132 workers would be needed in a community of 10,000 to provide the industrial work force for textile products; 56 for apparel; 29 for lumber and wood products; 50 for furniture and fixtures; 104 for paper and allied products; 43 for soap cleansers and toilet goods; 39 for stone, clay, and glass products; 163 for primary metal processes; 50 for fabricated metal products; 45 for machinery (excluding electric); 135 for electrical and electronic equipment; 81 for motorcycles, bicycles, and parts; 75 for instruments and related products; a total industrial force of 1,002.

101. In the South American bioregions mesquite is used as a parquet floor tile. The Austin group also explored the possibility of using mesquite sawdust to make an insulating building block as well as converting mesquite scrap material into high energy, clean burning fuel.

102. Sale, *Dwellers in the Land*, p. 79. [Italics in the original.]

103. Ibid., p. 84. [Italics in the original.]

104. Ibid., p. 110.

105. Ibid., pp. 103–104.

106. For Lewis Mumford's contribution to regionalism see Mark Luccarelli, *Lewis Mumford and the Ecological Region* (New York, NY: The Guilford Press, 1995).

107. Sale, *Dwellers in the Land*, p. 168. Sale states that concern for the environment also characterizes these ostensibly opposed groups. Given the role of the NRA in the 2000 presidential election it seems that Second Amendment issues rather than the natural environment are at the forefront of NRA members' concern.

108. Ibid., p. 175. Sale goes on to say that in the future the Greens could establish a national party and elect a president committed to a program of bioregional empowerment provided Green bioregional bases were well established. Sale's emphasis on the need to create viable local or regional bases for a Green national party is seconded in Sifry's book on third party politics in America. Micah L. Sifry, *Spoiling For a Fight* (New York, NY: Routledge and Kegan Paul, 2002), especially pp. 223–309.

109. WWW.votenader.com. For Nader's own post-election analysis of his presidential campaign, see Ralph Nader, *Crashing the Party* (New York, NY: Thomas Dunne Books, St. Martin's Press, 2002). The Green Party platform is an expression of ecologistic principles. Nader's book is a retrospective examination of his electioneering tactics and the overall campaign strategy to achieve 5 percent of the total presidential vote and thus qualify for public funding for the Green Party in the 2004 national elections.

110. Alternative economic structures apparently refers to local currency arrangements such as LETS in Canada and SHARE in Massachusetts which are discussed in the section on James Robertson.

111. Family farms could also be strengthened through arrangements such as CSA or subscription which are discussed in the article by Peter C. Reynolds.

112. Walter A. Rosenbaum, *Environmental Politics and Policy*, 4th ed., (Washington, DC: Congressional Quarterly Press, 1998).

113. Interest-group liberalism is offered as the only realistic way to understand how American democracy actually operates. The term "liberalism" refers to the self-interested motivation of interest groups as well as to the openness of government in responding to interest groups. David Truman's 1951 book, *The Governmental Process* was one of the earliest to focus on the role of interest groups in the political process. David Truman, *The Governmental Process* (New York, NY: Alfred A. Knopf, Inc., 1951).

114. Rosenbaum, *Environmental Politics,* p. 57.

115. Ibid., pp. 72–73 and pp. 74–75.

116. Matthew A. Cahn, *Environmental Deceptions* (Albany, NY: State University of New York Press, 1995).

117. Ibid., p. 28.

118. Ibid., p. 24.

119. Rosenbaum. *Environmental Politics,* p. 83.

120. Ibid., pp. 11–12.

121. Ibid., p. 191. "Improved air quality, like other environmental gains in recent decades, is fragile, highly vulnerable to technological change, economic cycles, and other social impacts."

122. William C. Ford Jr., chairman of Ford Motors board of directors maintains that the company's three obligations are to "provide superior returns to . . . shareholders; to give customers exactly what they are working for; and to do it in a way that has the least impact—or most benefit—for the environment and for society in general." Ford Motors will continue to produce the SUVs that customers want but the SUVs will be almost totally recyclable, approximate zero emission and be substantially more durable. That SUVs are not energy efficient and that their drivers go off-road with often destructive impact on fragile environments is not to the point. One can conclude that the greening of Ford Motors involves sustaining mass consumption of automobiles, trucks, and SUVs while lessening the environmental costs of mass production. Timothy W. Luke, "SUVs and the Greening of Ford," *Organization and Environment*, 14, no. 3 (September 2001): 311–335.

123. Rosenbaum, *Environmental Politics,* p. 362.

124. Confederal arrangements resemble contemporay American party caucuses in which at the precinct level party members directly elect delegates to a county convention which directly elects delegates to a district convention which directly elects delegates to a state convention. A confederal arrangement thus ensures that local democracy can be extended by direct voting to larger regions.

125. The quadrennial calls from both major parties for a devolution of power from "big government" to states and localities represent only empty rhetoric without the specific measures of individual and community empowerment proposed by Morrison, Robertson, Bookchin, Sale, and the Green Party Platform 2000.

3. Ecological Ethics

1. An empty-world scenario as understood by ecological economics refers to a preindustrial time when the human population was much smaller than now and its economic activities had a minimal impact on the global environment.

2. Animism refers to the belief that all life forms are endowed with a soul, a metaphysical position that is antithetical to the materialist treatment of nature in the industrial economy.

3. The Industrial Revolution was preceded by an intellectual revolution that disenchanted nature by purging it of all animistic elements and reducing it to physical properties that could be understood and controlled through scientific inquiry. Francis Bacon and Réne Descartes are representative of this intellectual revolution which legitimated the valuation of the natural environment as an economic resource only.

4. The full-world scenario as understood by ecological economics refers to the present time when a large and continuously increasing human population along with the globalization of industrial economics threatens to disrupt the Earth's natural environment.

5. The entropy law is reflected in the thermal pollution caused by the use of any form of energy and the rising energy costs as the most accessible petroleum deposits, for example, are exhausted and the extraction of remaining deposits becomes more energy intensive.

6. Leopold, *A Sand County Almanac*, p. 203.

7. Ibid., p. 220.

8. Ibid., p. 223. [Italics added.]

9. To recognize the intrinsic value of a nonhuman life form implies that there are objective characteristics of that life form which are valuable to its possessor. Whether these characteristics connect with the aesthetic, religious, and philosophic sensibilities of humans depends to a large extent on personal experiences in nature. The degradation of the natural environment progressively diminishes the possibility of such experiences.

10. Quite often individuals who in adult life are committed to ecological values recall a deeply felt childhood experience that in retrospect constituted a defining moment in their lives. One example among many is E. O. Wilson's boyhood adventures in woods and swamps in the pursuit of snakes.

11. Significant human others are adults who introduce children to an experience with some aspect of nature, for example, the adult who teaches a young child to recognize edible wild mushrooms. A significant nonhuman other can be a domestic or farm or wild animal with whom a child establishes an emotional bond.

12. While family and personal relationships, for example, typically have a non-econnomic basis, the industrial/corporate economy, particularly as it globalizes itself, treats individuals as workers or managers or owners or consumers, all of which are economic roles shaped by the profit motive.

13. Christopher Stone, *Should Trees Have Standing?* (Los Altos, CA: William Kaufmann, Inc. 1974), p. 6. Thus, Christopher Stone proposes "that we give legal

rights to forests, oceans, rivers and other so-called 'natural objects' in the environment—indeed, to the natural environment as a whole."

14. The term "speciesism" was introduced by Peter Singer in his book *Animal Liberation*, 2d ed. (New York, NY: New York Review of Books Press, 1990).

15. The term "pet" carries with it, even if not intended so, an implicit connotation of a commodity owned by a human, to be used at the discretion of the owner, and is inappropriate within the linguistic usages of an ecological ethics.

16. The Physicians Committee for Responsible Medicine with some four thousand member physicians and one hundred thousand lay members is working to reduce experimentations with live animals. The Committee publishes a list of charities that do not fund animal experiments. Organizations like People for the Ethical Treatment of Animals and In Defense of Animals also focus on reducing experimentation with live animals.

17. Berry, *The Great Work* p. 74.

18. E. O. Wilson, *Biophilia* (Cambridge, MA: Harvard University Press, 1984).

19. The Frankfurt School whose other members included Max Horkheimer, Theodore Adorno, Franz Neumann, Walter Benjamin, and Erich Fromm, transmuted an earlier Marxist critique of capitalist society with its emphasis on the proletarian revolution which would liberate industrial technology from the restriction of capitalist property relations, into a critique of the psychology of repression and the denaturing of man in techno-industrial society. Timothy W. Luke in his chapter "Marcuse and the Politics of Radical Ecology" underlines Marcuse's contribution to ecological thought: ". . . Marcuse is a theoretical force to be reckoned with. Much of today's debate within deep ecology, ecofeminism, social ecology, and bioregionalism merely revisits . . . issues that Marcuse first raised. . . . " Timothy W. Luke, *Ecocritique* (Minneapolis, MN: University of Minnesota Press, 1997), p. 152. I have chosen here to focus on Marcuse's notion of nature as a subject in its own right, a notion central to an ecological ethics.

20. Marcuse, *Eros and Civilization*.

21. Marcuse, *One-Dimensional Man*.

22. Herbert Marcuse, *An Essay on Liberation* (Boston, MA: Beacon Press, 1969).

23. It is not argued that the Industrial Revolution did not in time considerably raise the material standard of living for a large majority of the population in the industrialized nations. What it did not accomplish was the emancipation of man from the realm of necessity, as defined by Marcuse, because of its commitment to never-ending production and consumption. No sooner are existing needs satisfied through production and consumption then new needs appear, needs created by the same system that then satisfies them.

24. Herbert Marcuse, *Counter-Revolution and Revolt* (Boston, MA: Beacon Press, 1972), pp. 71–72. "Thus, the existing society is *reproduced* not only in the mind, the consciousness of men, but also *in their senses*; and no persuasion, no theory, no reasoning can break this prison, unless the fixed, petrified *sensibility* of the individuals is *"dissolved,"* *opened* to a *new dimension of history*, until the oppressive familiarity with the given object world is broken. . . . " [Italics in original.] The "prison" that Marcuse refers to is the dominant techno-industrial paradigm.

25. When human survival is at stake, work is a social necessity and the repression of human tendencies to flee hard work represents necessary repression. In a society where technological capacities exist to reduce significantly both the nature and length of work, the failure to reduce the amount of work demanded by the economic system represents the infliction of unnecessary or surplus repression.

26. Marcuse, *Essay on Liberation*, p. 11.

27. Ibid., p. 27.

28. Marcuse, *Counter-Revolution and Revolt*, p. 60–61. [Italics in original.]

29. Ibid., pp. 66–67.

30. Ibid., p. 60. [Italics in original.]

31. Ibid., p. 63. [Italics in original.]

32. Perhaps only historically irreducible in that what are necessary forms of human violence visited on nature in one historical period may become unnecessary in another period. Currently, a good deal of experimentation with animals, once thought indispensable to research, is being replaced by computer modeling and other methodological alternatives.

33. Marcuse, *Counter-Revolution and Revolt*, p. 68.

34. Henry Beston, *The Outermost House* (New York, NY: Henry Holt and Co., 1992).

35. Ibid., p. xxv.

36. Ibid., p. 215.

37. Ibid., p. 43.

38. Ibid., p. 65.

39. Ibid., p. 143.

40. Beston, *The Outermost House,* pp. 187–188.

41. Ibid., pp. 165–166.

42. Ibid., pp. 24–25. [Italics added.]

43. Thomas Berry states that the members of the earth community would have rights consonant with their mode of being. "Trees would have tree rights, birds would have bird rights, insects would have insect rights." Such rights are related to habitat and other conditions necessary for the full expression of the particular modes of being represented by different life forms. Thomas Berry, "The University," (paper presented at a conference in Washington, DC., 1995), p. 6. Reprinted with changes in *The Great Work.*

44. Beston, *The Outermost House,* pp. 9–10.

45. Ibid., p. xxxv.

46. Ibid., pp. 216–217. [First italics in original; second italics added.]

47. Ibid., p. 218.

48. Maguire and Rasmussen, *Ethics for a Small Planet.*

49. Ibid., pp. 22–23.

50. Ibid., p. 26. [Italics in original.] "Creation-theology" as used here is a synonym for "theism."

51. Ibid., p. 29.

52. Ibid., p. 32.

53. Ibid., pp. 37–38.

54. Ibid., p. 45. [Italics in original.]

55. If Earth is destiny and not a prolegomenon to an afterlife, then humans will have to make their own way on Earth. Their failures will not be redeemed by a creator, any more than will the failures of other species on Earth. The traditional theistic doctrine offers more emotional support to believers but it is increasingly at odds with the science of ecology and principles of ecological ethics.

56. Maguire and Rasmussen, *Ethics for a Small Planet*, p. 41. For a defense of theism in this context see Herman E. Daly and John B. Cobb Jr., *For the Common Good*, pp. 401–404.

57. Berry, "The University," p. 3.

58. Ibid.

59. Ibid., p. 6.

60. Ibid., p. 7.

61. Ibid., p. 2.

62. Ibid., p. 7.

63. See Swimme and Berry, *The Universe Story*, pp. 1–79. Space travel for commercial purposes such as the mining of moon minerals or satellite stations for instant communication required by a global economy are technologies considered important by the techno-industrial economy but such technologies serve the purposes of the economy and do not contribute to what Berry and others call the emerging new universe story.

64. Berry, "The University," p. 5.

65. Ibid., p. 1.

66. Singer, *Animal Liberation*, 2d ed.

67. Tom Regan, *The Case for Animal Rights* (Berkeley, CA: University of California Press, 1990).

68. Singer, *Animal Liberation*, pp. 16–17.

69. Bentham developed this "calculus" to measure the several dimensions of pleasure and pain, including the certainty or uncertainty of experiencing pleasure or pain, the duration of each sensation and its fecundity or capacity to elicit similar sensations. The measurement problems here are obvious.

70. Tom Regan, "The Case for Animal Rights," in *In Defense of Animals*, ed. Peter Singer (Oxford, Eng.: Basil Blackwell, 1985), p. 13. [Italics in original.]

71. Ibid., pp. 77–78.

72. Kenneth Goodpaster, "On Being Morally Considerable," *Journal of Philosophy* 75 (1978): 308–325.

73. Paul W. Taylor, *Respect for Nature* (Princeton, NJ: Princeton University Press, 1986).

74. Although the subtitle of *Respect for Nature* is *A Theory of Environmental Ethics*, the system Taylor constructs is so removed from the anthropocentric assumptions of the dominant paradigm that the adjective "environmental" is misleading and should be replaced by the adjective "ecological."

75. Taylor, *Respect for Nature*, p. 9. Taylor maintains that biological knowledge about organisms and their relationships is categorically different from decisions about how humans are to fit into nature. Biological facts do not, ipso facto, translate into ethical choices.

76. Taylor concludes that the proper ethical approach to the bioculture is to practice vegetarianism. First, eating animals means inflicting pain on sentient beings. Second, vegetarian diets require much less cultivated land for protein production than meat diets and are therefore less destructive of natural habitats. For an anthology of writings on ethical vegetarianism (as distinquished from dietary vegetarianism) from antiquity to the contemporary period see Kerry S. Walters and Lisa Portmess, eds., *Ethical Vegetarianism* (Albany, NY: State University of New York Press, 1999).

77. Taylor, *Respect for Nature,* p. 126.

78. Ibid., p. 127.

79. Ibid., p. 128.

80. Ibid., pp. 135–139.

81. Ibid., p. 142.

82. Ibid., pp. 143–147.

83. Ibid., pp. 147–152.

84. The *ceteris paribus* disappears, however, when humans discover new needs for new commodities. The economy of the techno–industrial society does not permit things to remain the same. Taylor's priority principle of minimum wrong discussed later is an admission of a cultural and economic imperative that brushes aside considerations of nonhuman welfare.

85. Taylor, *Respect for Nature,* pp. 158–161.

86. Hunting if it is for sport and recreation violates the rule of nonmaleficence.

87. Taylor, *Respect for Nature,* p. 177. [Italics in original.]

88. Ibid., p. 197.

89. Why only humans can be said to have moral rights is discussed in a later section.

90. Taylor, *Respect for Nature,* p. 274.

91. Ibid., p. 276. It is true that projects such as the building of a hospital are not inherently deadly to wild life as is sport hunting. But the proliferation of projects powered by a culture that recognizes no limits to human pursuits drives species to extinction without any one project being specifically aimed at the destruction of wild life.

92. Urban human residences cannot be integrated with nature since there is no natural environment left. Suburban residences could permit some degree of coexistence but only with a limited number of species. Even deer while not dangerous to humans stress the limited habitat available. Bears and wolves are out of the question for the spaces represented by suburban development. Farm and ranch residences obviously provide more latitude for coexistence with wild life but these are not where most Americans reside.

93. The principles of minimum wrong and distributive justice give priority to humans with the condition that moral agents will provide proper restitution for harm done. The assumption is that moral agents have the means to provide whatever degree of reparation is required. The moral imperative to compensate for harm done might be better shared with the larger society by way of legally sanctioned reparation.

94. Taylor, *Respect for Nature,* p. 305. Taylor's recommendation that the maintenance of the health of the entire ecosystem is the most effective way to compensate for harm to the individual organism undercuts the criticism of biocentrism as being indifferent to the integrity of ecosystems.

95. Ibid., pp. 223–224.

96. Rationalist because it is based on reasoned and logical propositions and deontological because it stresses the duty of moral agents, who are rational and therefore understand reasoned and logical ethical propositions, to treat nonhuman life with respect and moral consideration.

97. Taylor, *Respect for Nature*, pp. 212–218.

98. David W. Orr, *Earth in Mind*, pp. 61–62. "Modern societies are increasingly operated by and for that subsystem known as the economy, the same economy that, as Lewis Mumford once observed, converted the seven deadly sins of pride, envy, anger, sloth, avarice, gluttony, and lust into virtues after a fashion and the seven virtues of faith, charity, hope, prudence, religion, fortitude, and temperance into sins against gross national product."

99. Ibid., pp. 308–309. [Italics added.]

100. Ibid., p. 313.

101. Berry, *The Great Work*, p. 105.

102. Holmes Rolston, III, "Challenges in Environmental Ethics," *Environmental Philosophy*, ed. Michael E. Zimmerman (Englewood Cliffs, NJ: Prentice Hall, 1993), p. 149. [Italics added.]

103. Since the decision to maintain the integrity, stability, and beauty of ecosystems represents a choice by humans to respect these ecosystem characteristics, one can argue that an ecological ethics derived from ecosystem considerations has clearly anthropogenic but not anthropocentric roots. The distinction is important in its impact on the behavior of moral agents but it does not disconnect an ecocentric ethics from any association with human values.

104. "From the biosocial evolutionary analysis of ethics upon which Leopold builds the [ecocentric] land ethic, it . . . neither replaces nor overrides [ethical] accretions. Prior moral sensibilities and obligations . . . remain operative and preemptive." Callicott, "The Conceptual Foundations of the Land Ethic," in *Environmental Philosophy*, ed. Michael E. Zimmerman, p. 126.

105. Berry, *The Great Work*, p. 74.

106. Taylor, *Respect for Nature*, pp. 201–202.

4. Ecological Pedagogy

1. C. A. Bowers, *The Culture of Denial*, pp. 7–9; C. A. Bowers, *Education, Cultural Myths, and the Ecological Crisis* (Albany, NY: State University of New York Press, 1993), pp. 117–122; Gregory A. Smith, *Education and the Environment* (Albany, NY: State University of New York Press, 1992), pp. 1–17.

2. Bowers, *The Culture of Denial*, pp. 55–60, and *Educating for an Ecologically Sustainable Culture* (Albany, NY: State University of New York Press, 1995), pp. 75–91.

3. Orr, *Earth in Mind*, and David W. Orr, *Ecological Literacy* (Albany, NY: State University of New York Press, 1992).

4. Orr, *Earth in Mind*, p. 5.

5. Lewis Mumford, *Interpretations and Forecasts: 1922–1972* (New York, NY: Harcourt Brace Jovanovich, Inc, 1973), p. 457. "Paideia is education looked upon as a lifelong transformation of the human personality, in which every aspect of life plays a part. . . . Paideia is not merely a learning; it is a making and a shaping; and [humans themselves are] the work of art that paideia seeks to form."

6. Orr, *Earth in Mind*, p. 13.

7. Bowers, *The Culture of Denial*, p. 120.

8. Orr, *Earth in Mind*, p. 13.

9. Ibid.

10. Ibid.

11. Ibid., p. 14. The faculty and administrators who act as role models of integrity and care are described by Bowers as "elders" who can facilitate a transgeneration communication with the young and share with them the "wisdom of how to live symbolically meaningful lives without destroying the environment." Bowers, *Educating for an Ecologically Sustainable Culture*, p. 170.

12. Peter Singer, *Writings on an Ethical Life* (New York, NY: The Ecco Press, 2000).

13. Orr, *Earth in Mind*, p. 14.

14. "Indeed, there are many for whom the advance of their discipline is the major source of meaning, the organizational center of their lives, their deepest commitment. The discipline becomes their God." We call this "disciplinolatry." Daly and Cobb Jr., *For the Common Good*, pp. 33–34.

15. Page Smith, *Killing the Spirit* (New York, NY: Penquin Books, 1990), p. 7.

16. Ibid., pp. 199–222.

17. Ibid., p. 213.

18. To the extent that a discipline like psychology treats culture-specific psychological traits as innate in Homo sapiens, it accepts the taken-for-granted assumptions of the dominant paradigm about human nature.

19. Orr, *Earth in Mind*, pp. 100–101.

20. Bowers, *The Culture of Denial*, p. 73. As Bowers states, the scholarly efforts of academicians in many cases are "quite separate from their own desire to attain the standard forms of institutional recognition and reward (including promotion and tenure), and to live the bourgeois life-style of the university professor."

21. Orr, *Earth in Mind*, p. 14.

22. Leopold, *A Sand County Almanac*, p. 18.

23. Orr, *Earth in Mind*, p. 14.

24. Smith, *Killing the Spirit*, p. 20.

25. Ibid.

26. Orr, *Earth in Mind*, pp. 17, and 72–73. For elements of what Orr calls "design intelligence" see *Earth in Mind*, p. 105, and *Ecological Literacy*, pp. 33, and 62.

27. Orr, *Earth in Mind*, p. 50.

28. The emphasis on character is typical of ecologistic literature and distinguishes it from dominant paradigm literature where "character" is transmuted into "skill" and "technique."

29. Orr, *Earth in Mind*, p. 51.

30. Ibid., p. 43.

31. Ibid., p. 46.

32. Ibid., p. 22.

33. Those whose formal education ends with graduation from high school are also "counseled" but more by cultural expectations for high school graduates than by paid high school counselors.

34. Orr, *Earth in Mind*, p. 5.

35. One hundred thousand dollars for four years at a private, liberal arts college is now at or below the median cost for such schools.

36. Orr, *Earth in Mind*, p. 90.

37. Ibid.

38. Ibid., p. 91.

39. Ibid., p. 92.

40. Ibid., p. 97.

41. Ibid., p. 102.

42. Courses that deal with the rudimentary elements of a discipline such as a foreign language or with the rudimentary principles and methodologies of mathematics and the sciences provide a necessary technical service within the curriculum.

43. Orr, *Earth in Mind*, p. 52.

44. Such questions which are typically asked screen for candidates who will fit into the current academic orthodoxy which favors peer-reviewed publication and evidence of scholarship in a recognized discipline or specialization. These criteria offer no assurance whatsoever that the person hired will advance the ecological literacy of students.

45. Rarely, if ever, are members of departments evaluated in terms of how their courses contribute to the educational aim of the department. In many cases, the educational aim of the department consists of offering the courses listed in the catalogue, nothing more. This latter situation is less likely in science departments where a strict schedule of prerequisites is followed.

46. Smith, *Killing the Spirit*, p. 5. Academic fundamentalism is defined as "the stubborn refusal of the academy to acknowledge any truth that does not conform to professorial dogmas."

47. Orr, *Earth in Mind*, p. 103.

48. A moral imperative exists when an overarching moral principle "commands" action on its behalf. Moral agents in a situation where harm will occur to moral subjects are enjoined to take action to prevent the harm—thus, the moral imperative.

49. Quoted in recent newspaper accounts of the report. The report is available at the IPCC web site.

50. Jonathan Collett and Stephen Karakashian, eds., *Greening the College Curriculum* (Washington, DC: Island Press, 1966), p. 236. The book discusses specific ways in which departments in liberal arts colleges can contribute to environmental education. [Italics added.]

51. Orr, *Earth in Mind*, p. 95.

52. Bruce Willshire, *The Moral Collapse of the University* (Albany, NY: State University of New York Press, 1990), p. 40.

53. In *Ecological Literacy*, Orr provides a comprehensive syllabus for ecological literacy (pp. 109–124) and the kind of environmental focus appropriate for various disciplines (pp. 135–136).

54. Berry, "The University," p. 3.

55. Bowers, *Culture of Denial*.

56. Ibid., p. 39.

57. Ibid., pp. 56–59.

58. Orr, *Earth in Mind*, p. 52. This individually-centered way of understanding intelligence is amplified by the computer and constitutes what Orr refers to as cleverness, rather than intelligence.

59. Bowers, *Culture of Denial*, pp. 4–5. See pp. 8–9 in the introduction for a discussion of how ecologism views the knowledge of indigenous cultures. Literacy-based thought and communication are the foundation of the Western techno-industrial form of knowledge and their absence in what are referred to as indigenous or native cultures supposedly means that these cultures possess no knowledge worth saving. Bowers stresses that indigenous cultures have developed a metaphorical language and thought process rooted in the natural world which enables them to exist sustainably in the environment. Such cultures, therefore, have something of value to offer to a techno-industrial society that is on an unsustainable course.

60. Ibid., pp. 135–136.

61. Ibid., pp. 108–113.

62. Ibid., pp. 113–126.

63. Ibid., pp. 105–108.

64. Ibid., p. 106.

65. Ibid., p. 148.

66. Ibid., pp. 148–149. See Gregory Bateson, *Steps to an Ecology of Mind* (New York, NY: Ballantine Books, 1972), pp. 478–487 for a discussion of the minimal characteristics of an ecological epistemology.

67. For discussion of the coevolution of ecological and economic systems see Costanza, *Introduction to Ecological Economics*, pp. 64–69, and Prugh, *Natural Capital*, pp. 21–24.

68. Costanza, *Introduction to Ecological Economics*, p. 66.

69. Ibid., p. 68.

70. Bowers, *Culture of Denial*, p. 151.

71. Ibid., and endnote # 59.

72. Bowers, *Culture of Denial* p. 262.

73. Gregory A. Smith, *Education and the Environment*.

74. Ibid., p. 50. "Universalism is thus tied to another primary rule of the marketplace, which insists that individuals set aside in-group loyalties and obligations to protect civil peace and to maintain unimpeded trade."

75. Ibid., p. 63.

76. Ibid., p. 94.

77. The reference is to the extended families typical of many nonwhite ethnic groups where the individual's welfare is linked to still existing patterns of obligation and mutual aid.

78. Smith, *Education and the Environment*, p. 113. See Bowers, *Educating for an Ecologically Sustainable Culture*, pp. 183–213, for an examination of several other pedagogic models for community and environmental renewal.

79. Smith, *Education and the Environment*, pp. 124–128.

80. Ibid., p. 106.

81. Berry, *The Great Work,* p. 73.

82. Ibid., p. 80.

83. Berry, *The Dream of the Earth,* p. 98.

84. Ibid., p. 97.

85. Ibid., p. 100.

86. Ibid., p. 101.

87. Ibid., p. 102.

88. Ibid., p. 105.

89. Ibid., p. 106.

90. Ibid., p. 108.

91. Ibid., p. 107.

92. The text of the Declaration can be found in *Priorities,* no. 14 (Spring 2000): 15.

93. Recent editions have dealt with such topics as "Religions of the World and Ecology" and "A Revitalized Production Ethic for Agriculture."

94. Christopher Uhl and Amy Anderson, "Green Destiny: Universities Leading the Way to a Sustainable Future," *BioScience,* 51, no. 1 (January 2001): 36–42.

95. Ibid., p. 37.

96. Schools mentioned are SUNY Buffalo, Carleton University, California State University, Hendrix College, Connecticut College, Cornell University, Oberlin College, Northland College, Florida Gulf Coast University, George Washington University, and University of Kansas. Schools listed in other surveys include Tufts University, Middlebury College, University of Maryland, Michigan Technological University, Clemson University joined with University of South Carolina and Medical College of South Carolina, Lehman College of the City University of New York, University of Virginia, University of Texas, and Pacific University. The annual Campus Environmental Yearbook published by the National Wildlife Federation updates the list of environmental projects in higher education.

97. Berry, *Dream of the Earth,* p. 108.

5. Conclusion

1. Ryan and Durning, *Stuff,* p. 47.

2. Includes American citizens who meet voting requirements but have not registered in their voting district.

3. Orr, *Earth in Mind,* p. 124.

4. Taylor, *Respect for Nature,* pp. 212–213.

5. The atrophy of moral agency contributes to the paradoxical perception that while the physical environment is endlessly susceptible to human control through science and technology, social institutions are givens to which individuals must accomodate. Such a perception undermines the possibility of substantive democracy.

6. A democratic citizen is one who participates actively in a political environment that allows citizens to shape the policies that affect them. Voting regularly in elections for candidates who occupy offices in distant centers of power does not make one a democratic citizen.

7. Marcuse, *One-Dimensional Man,* especially pp. 1–120.

8. Rosenbaum, *Environmental Politics and Policy,* pp. 305–306.

9. Prugh, *Natural Capital,* p. 30.

10. Long before the global population reached sixty quadrillion, the fabric of human society would have unraveled. Twenty-five billion people at current rates of per capita resource use would result in overshoot and die-back of the human population.

11. Beston, *The Outermost House,* p. 218.

12. Taylor, *Respect for Nature,* pp. 309–310.

13. Orr, *Earth in Mind,* p. 11.

14. Taylor, *Respect for Nature,* p. 165.

15. Arne Naess, *Ecology, Community and Lifestyle* (Cambridge, Eng.: Cambridge University Press, 1989), pp. 85–86.

16. David W. Orr, "A Literature of Redemption," *Conservation Biology* 6: no. 2 (April 2000): 306.

17. Taylor, *Respect for Nature,* pp. 312–313.

18. Rosenbaum, *Environmental Politics,* p. 35.

19. Ibid., p. 33.

20. Robert C. Paehlke, *Environmentalism and the Future of Progressive Politics* (New Haven, CT: Yale University Press,1989), pp. 243–283.

21. John McMurty has identified fifteen principles of what he calls the "meta-program for global corporate rule" which shapes the policies and regulations of "servant governments." Among these principles are: the ultimate sovereign ruler of the world is the transnational corporation operating by extra-parliamentary and transnational fiat; individual transnational corporations are the moving parts of the global corporate system and represent nonliving aggregates of dominant private stockholders who as individuals are legally immune from any liability for corporate harm to societies and environments; all treaties and agreements obligating compliance with transnational corporate rights are negotiated and finalized behind closed doors even though the exercise of such rights may require that national governments pay fines and trade penalties for environmental protection laws deemed to damage such rights; there is no requirement to recognize any life need of an individual or society as an issue of choice within the global system.

These principles are readily identifiable as integral elements of the dominant techno-industrial paradigm extrapolated to a global scale with transnational corporations replacing national governments as the sources of policy decisions. In this global context all the pernicious effects of the dominant techno-industrial paradigm on humans and natural environments are significantly magnified. John McMurty, "The FTAA and the WTO: 15 Principles of the Meta-Program for Global Corporate Rule," *Capitalism, Nature, Socialism,* 12 (3), issue 47 (September 2001): 37–43. For a summary of the social and environmental effects of World Bank and IMF policies see "Bearing the Burden of IMF and World Bank Policies." *Multinational Monitor,* 22, no. 9 (September 2001): 7–32.

22. William Ophuls, *Ecology and the Politics of Scarcity* (San Francisco, CA: W. H. Freeman and Co. 1977).

23. Ibid., p. 152.

24. Ibid., p. 156.

25. Taylor, *Respect for Nature,* p. 312. [Italics in original.]

26. Maguire and Rasmussen, *Ethics for a Small Planet,* p. 44.

27. Beston, *The Outmost House,* p. 218.

28. Daly and Cobb Jr., *For the Common Good,* p. 393.

29. Berry, *The Great Work,* p. 77.

30. Maguire and Rasmussen, *Ethics for a Small Planet,* pp. 38–42.

31. The announcement by the Bush administration early in 2001 that it would not join international efforts to reduce CO_2 emissions is an indication that there will be resistance even to accommodations within the context of the dominant paradigm.

32. Daly and Cobb Jr., *For the Common Good,* pp. 405–406.

33. Plato, B. Jowett, trans., *The Republic* (New York, NY: The Modern Library), pp. 253–257.

34. Gregory Bateson who stressed that the roots of the ecological crisis were located in a "pathological" epistemology and paradigm understood full well the difficulty inherent in effecting a transition from a non-ecological to an ecological epistemology and paradigm: "Nobody knows how long we have, under the present system, before some disaster strikes us, more serious than the destruction of any group of nations. The most important task, today is, perhaps, to learn to think in the new way. Let me say that *I* don't know how to think that way. Intellectually, I can stand here and I can give you a reasoned exposition of the matter; but if I am cutting down a tree I still think 'Gregory Bateson' is cutting down a tree. *I* am cutting down the tree. 'Myself' is to me still an excessively concrete object, different from the rest of what I have been calling 'mind.' " Gregory Bateson, *Steps to an Ecology of Mind,* p. 462. [Italics in original.] If a paradigm can be designated as "pathological," that is, inducing social policies and practices that have pathological consequences for both human and natural environments, then Theodore Adorno's dictum—that in a mad world the patient who adapts to that world becomes truly ill—can be read to mean that conversion to a pathological social paradigm results in a related derangement of individual behavior. That some elements of the currently dominant social paradigm might be retained with the new ecological paradigm does not obviate the conclusion that the transition from the former to the latter will be extremely difficult to effect.

Bibliography

Aristotle. *The Politics*. Chicago, IL: University of Chicago Press, 1984.

Aquinas, Thomas. *Summa Theologica*. New York, NY: Benzinger Brothers, 1946.

Barlett, Donald L., and James B. Steele. *America: Who Stole the Dream?* Kansas City, KS: Andrews and McMeel, 1996.

Bateson, Gregory. *Steps to an Ecology of Mind*. New York, NY: Ballantine Books, 1972.

Bateson, Gregory, and Rodney E. Donaldson, ed. *A Sacred Unity*. New York, NY: A. Cornelia and Michael Bessie Book, Harper Collins, 1991.

Berry, Thomas. *The Great Work*. New York, NY: Bell Tower, 1999.

———. "The University." Paper presented at a conference in Washington, DC in 1995.

———. *The Dream of the Earth*. San Francisco, CA: Sierra Club Books, 1988.

Beston, Henry. *The Outermost House*. New York, NY: Henry Holt and Co., 1992.

Bookchin, Murray. "Libertarian Municipalism: An Overview." *Society and Nature*, 1, No. 1 (May 1992).

———. *Remaking Society*. Cheektowaga, NY: Black Rose Books, 1990.

Botkin, Daniel B., and Edward A. Keller. *Environmental Science*. New York, NY: John Wiley and Sons, Inc., 2000.

Bowers, C. A. *The Culture of Denial*. Albany, NY: State University of New York Press, 1997.

———. *Educating for an Ecologically Sustainable Culture*. Albany, NY: State University of New York Press, 1995.

———. *Education, Cultural Myths, and the Ecological Crisis*. Albany, NY: State University of New York Press, 1993.

Cahn, Matthew A. *Environmental Deceptions*. Albany, NY: State University of New York Press, 1995.

Callicott, J. Baird. "The Conceptual Foundations of the Land Ethic." In *Environmental Philosophy*. Edited by Michael E. Zimmerman, Englewood Cliffs, NJ: Prentice Hall, 1973.

Chase, Steve, ed. *Defending the Earth: A Dialogue Between Murray Bookchin and Dave Foreman*. Boston, MA: South End Press, 1991.

Clark, John. "What is Social Ecology?" *Society and Nature*, 1, No. 1 (May 1992).

Clausen, Christopher. "Children in Toyland." *The American Scholar* 71, No. 1 (Winter 2002): 111–121.

Clifford, Mary. *Environmental Crime*. Gaithersburg, MD: Aspen Publishers, Inc., 1998.

Collett, Jonathan, and Stephen Karakashian, eds. *Greening the College Curriculum*. Washington, DC: Island Press, 1966.

Costanza, Robert, John H. Cumberland, Herman E. Daly, Robert Goodland, and Richard B. Norgaard. *An Introduction to Ecological Economics*. Boca Raton, FL: St. Lucie Press, 1997.

———. "The Value of the World's Ecosystem Services and Natural Capital," *Nature* 387, 1997.

Daly, Herman E. *Ecological Economics and the Ecology of Economics*. Northampton, MA: Edward Elgar, 1999.

———. *Beyond Growth*. Boston, MA: Beacon Press, 1996.

———. *Steady-State Economics*. 2d ed. Washington, DC: Island Press, 1991.

———. *Steady-State Economics*. San Francisco, CA: W. H. Freeman and Company, 1977.

Daly, Herman E., and John B. Cobb, Jr. *For the Common Good*. Boston, MA: Beacon Press, 1994.

Devall, Bill, and George Sessions. *Deep Ecology*. Salt Lake City, UT: Peregrine Smith Books, 1985.

Dobson, Andrew. *Green Political Thought*. 2d ed. New York, NY: Routledge and Kegan Paul, 1995.

Dunayer, Joan. "In the Name of Science," *Organization and Environment*, 13, No. 4 (December 2000).

Dunlap, Riley E., ed. "Ecology and the Social Sciences: An Emerging Paradigm." *American Behavioral Scientist* 24, No. 1 (Sep./Oct, 1980).

Durning, Alan. *How Much is Enough?* New York, NY: W. W. Norton and Co., 1992.

Eckersley, Robyn. *Environmentalism and Political Theory*. Albany, NY: State University of New York Press, 1992.

Fremlin, J. H. "How Many People Can the World Support?" *New Scientist* (October 1964): 285–287.

Gatto, Marino, and Giulio A. DeLeo. "Pricing Biodiversity and Ecosystem Services: The Never-Ending Story." *BioScience* 50, No. 4 (April 2000): 347–354.

Georgescu-Roegen, Nicholas. *The Entropy Law and the Economic Process*. Cambridge, MA: Harvard University Press, 1971.

Goodpaster, Kenneth. "On Being Morally Considerable." *Journey of Philosophy* 75 (1978).

Gould, Stephen J. "Enchanted Evening." *Natural History* (September 1991): 14.

Gowdy, John, and Sabine O'Hara. *Economic Theory for Environmentalists*. Delray Beach, FL: St. Lucie Press, 1995.

Greider, William. "The Last Farm Crisis." *The Nation* (November 20, 2000).

Halweil, Brian. "Where Have all the Farmers Gone?" *World Watch* (September/October, 2000).

Hardin, Garrett. "The Tragedy of the Commons." *Science* 162 (December 13, 1968).
Heilbroner, Robert L. *An Inquiry into the Human Prospect.* New York, NY: W. W. Norton, 1980.
Hicks, J. R. *Value and Capital.* 2d ed. Oxford, Eng.: Oxford University Press, 1946.
Hudson, William E. *American Democracy in Peril.* 3rd ed. New York, NY: Chatham House Publishers, 2001.
Jacobs, Michael. *The Green Economy.* Concord, MA: Pluto Press, 1971.
Jacoby, Russell. *Social Amnesia.* Boston, MA: Beacon Press, 1975.
Kassiola, Joel J. *The Death of Industrial Civilization.* Albany NY: State University of New York Press, 1990.
Kennedy, Paul. *Preparing for the Twenty-First Century.* New York, NY: Vintage Books, 1994.
Kirsch, Max H. *In the Wake of the Giant.* Albany, NY: State University of New York Press, 1998.
Korten, David C. *When Corporations Rule the World.* West Hartford, CT: Kumarian Press, Inc. 1995.
Lakoff, Sanford. *Democracy: History, Theory, Practice.* Boulder, CO: Westview Press, 1996.
Leopold, Aldo. *A Sand County Almanac and Sketches Here and There.* New York, NY: Oxford University Press, 1969.
Light, Andrew, ed. *Social Ecology after Bookchin.* New York, NY: Guilford Press, 1998.
Lloyd, Vincent, Robert Weissman, Sara Grusky, Charlie Cray. "Bearing the Burden of IMF and World Bank Policies." *Multinational Monitor* 22, No. 9 (September 2001).
Luccarelli, Mark. *Lewis Mumford and the Ecological Region.* New York, NY: The Guilford Press, 1995.
Luke, Timothy W. *Ecocritique.* Minneapolis, MN: University of Minnesota Press, 1997.
———. "SUVs and the Greening of Ford." *Organization and Environment* 14, No. 3 (September 2001).
Maguire, Daniel C., and Larry L. Rasmussen. *Ethics for a Small Planet.* Albany, NY: State University of New York Press, 1998.
Marcuse, Herbert. *Counter-Revolution and Revolt.* Boston, MA: Beacon Press, 1972.
———. *An Essay on Liberation.* Boston, MA: Beacon Press, 1969.
———. *One-Dimensional Man.* Boston, MA: Beacon Press, 1968.
———. *Eros and Civilization.* New York, NY: Vintage Books, 1962.
Marx, Karl. *Economic and Philosophic Manuscripts of 1844.* Moscow, USSR: Progress Publishers, 1982.
———. *Capital: A Critique of Political Economy.* New York, NY: Vintage Books, 1977.
Matthews, Richard K. *The Radical Politics of Thomas Jefferson.* Lawrence, KS: University Press of Kansas, 1984.
McCoy, Drew A. *The Elusive Republic: Political Economy in Jeffersonian America.* Chapel Hill, NC: University of North Carolina Press, 1980.
McMurty, John. "The FTAA and the WTO: 15 Principles of the Metaprogram for Corporate Rule." *Capitalism, Nature, Socialism* 12 (3), Issue 47 (September 2001).

Merchant, Carolyn. *The Death of Nature.* San Francisco, CA: Harper and Row, 1989.

Milbrath, Lester W. *Envisioning a Sustainable Society.* Albany, NY: State University of New York Press, 1989.

Morrison, Roy. *Ecological Democracy.* Boston, MA: South End Press, 1995.

Mumford, Lewis. *Interpretations and Forecasts: 1922–1972.* New York, NY: Harcourt Brace Jovanovich, Inc. 1973.

———. *The Pentagon of Power.* New York, NY: Harcourt Brace Jovanovich, Inc., 1970.

Nader, Ralph. *Crashing the Party.* New York, NY: Thomas Dunne Books, St. Martin's Press, 2002.

———. "Free Trade and the Decline of Democracy." *The Case Against "Free Trade."* San Francisco, CA: Earth Island Press, 1993.

Naess, Arne. *Ecology, Community and Lifestyle.* Cambridge, Eng.: Cambridge University Press, 1989.

Noddings, Nel. *Caring: A Feminist Approach to Ethics and Moral Education.* Berkeley, CA: University of California Press, 1984.

Ophuls, William. *Ecology and the Politics of Scarcity.* San Francisco, CA: W. H. Freeman and Co., 1977.

Orr, David W. "A Literature of Redemption." *Conservation Biology* 15, No. 2 (April 2000).

———. *Earth in Mind: On Education, Environment, and the Human Prospect.* Washington, DC: Island Press, 1994.

———. *Ecological Literacy.* Albany, NY: State University of New York Press, 1992.

Ostrom, Elenor. *Governing the Commons: the Evolution of Institution for Collective Action.* New York, NY: Cambridge University Press, 1990.

Paehlke, Robert C. *Environmentalism and the Future of Progressive Politics.* New Haven, CT: Yale University Press, 1989.

Porter, Philip W., and Eric S. Sheppard. *A World of Difference.* New York, NY: The Guilford Press, 1998.

Prugh, Thomas, Robert Costanza, John H. Cumberland, Herman E. Daly, Robert Goodland, Richard B. Norgaard. *Natural Capital and Human Economic Survival.* Solomons, MD: ISSE Press, 1995.

Radin, Paul. *The World of Primate Man.* New York, NY: Grove Press, 1960.

Regan, Tom. *The Case for Animal Rights.* Berkeley, CA: University of California Press, 1990.

Reynolds, Peter C. "Organics at the Crossroads." *Acres U.S.A.* 30, No. 9 (September 2000).

Robertson, James. "The Economics of Local Recovery." *Society and Nature* 1, No. 1 (May, 1992).

Rolston, Holmes III. "Challenges in Environmental Ethics." In *Environmental Philosophy.* Edited by Michael E. Zimmerman. Englewood Cliffs, NJ: Prentice Hall, 1993.

Rosenbaum, Walter A. *Environmental Politics and Policy*, 4th ed. Washington, DC: Congressional Quarterly Press, 1998.

Ryan, John C., and Allan T. Durning. *Stuff.* Seattle, WA: Northwest Environmental Watch, 1997.

Sale, Kirkpatrick. *The Conquest of Paradise*. New York, NY. Penguin Books, 1991.

———. *Dwellers in the Land*. Philadelphia, PA: New Society Publishers, 1991.

———. "Deep Ecology and its Critics." *The Nation* (May 14, 1988).

Schmookler, Andrew B. *The Parable of the Tribes: The Problem of Power in Social Evolution*. Berkley, CA: University of California Press, 1984.

Schnaiberg, Allan. *The Environment from Surplus to Scarcity*. Oxford, Eng.: Oxford University Press, 1980.

Schumacher, E. F. *Small is Beautiful*. New York, NY: Harper and Row 1975.

Sifry, Micah L. *Spoiling for a Fight*. New York, NY: Routledge and Kegan Paul, 2002.

Singer, Peter. *Writings on an Ethical Life*. New York, NY: The Ecco Press, 2000.

———. *Animal Liberation*. 2d. ed. New York, NY: New York Review of Books Press, 1990.

———. *In Defense of Animals*, ed. Oxford, Eng.: Basil Blackwell, 1985.

Smith, Adam. *The Wealth of Nations*. Edited by Bruce Mazlish. New York, NY: Bobbs-Merrill Co., 1961.

Smith, Page. *Killing the Spirit*. New York, NY: Penguin Books, 1990.

Smith, Gregory A. *Education and the Environment*. Albany, NY: State University of New York Press, 1992.

Stone, Christopher. *Should Trees Have Standing?* Los Altos, CA: William Kaufmann, Inc., 1974.

Swimme, Brian, and Thomas Berry. *The Universe Story*. San Francisco, CA: Harper, 1992.

Talloires Declaration of the Association of University Leaders for a Sustainable Future, *Priorities* No. 14 (Spring 2000).

Taylor, Bob P. *Our Limits Transgressed*. Laurence, KS: University Press of Kansas, 1992.

Taylor, Paul W. *Respect for Nature: A Theory of Environmental Ethics*. Princeton, NJ: Princeton University Press, 1986.

Truman, David. *The Governmental Process*. New York, NY: Alfred Knopf, Inc., 1951.

Uhl, Christopher and Amy Anderson. "Green Destiny: Universities Leading the way to a Sustainable Future." *BioScience* 51, No. 1 (January 2001).

Walters, Kerry S., and Lisa Portmess. *Ethical Vegetarianism*. Albany, NY: State University of New York Press, 1999.

Wilshire, Bruce. *The Moral Collapse of the University*. Albany, NY: State University of New York Press, 1990.

Wilson, E. O. *Biophilia*. Cambridge, MA: Harvard University Press, 1984.

Zimmerman, Michael, ed. *Environmental Philosophy*. Englewood Cliffs, NJ: Prentice Hall, 1993.

Index

A
anthropocentric/economic valuation,
    94
anthropocentric valuation, 92–93
anthropogenic valuation, 93

B
Bateson, Gregory
    immanent mind, 155
    pathological epistemology, 167
    transition to an ecological epistemol-
        ogy, 208 n. 34
Berry, Thomas
    core courses for an ecological
        pedagogy, 163–64
    distorted dream experience of the
        modern world, 1
    ecological imperative, 125
    failure of the university, 162
    need for a new explanatory narrative,
        5, 6
    primary revelatory experience, 109
    salvation-oriented and creation-
        oriented religion, 108–9
    United States Constitution, 95, 127
    universe community, 108–9
    universe story, 162

Beston, Henry
    ecological aesthetics, 102–5
    ongoing creation in nature, 105
    wiser concept of animals, 104
Bookchin, Murray
    appearance of state, 68
    capitalism, 69–70
    direction of evolution, 70, 194 n. 76
    domination of nature, 66–67
    hierarchy, 67–68
    libertarian municipalism, 71–73
    Marxism, 70–71
    New Left, 71
    social ecology, 193 n. 55
Bowers, C. A.
    coevolution, 155–57
    computer as communication icon,
        153
    cultural/bio-conservatism, 154
    high-status knowledge, 152–53
    pedagogic liberalism, 154
    taken-for-granted pedagogical and
        cultural assumptions, 153–54,
        158
    traditional and indigenous knowledge,
        6, 154–55, 205 n. 59
Brundtland Report, 24

215

C
Cahn, Matthew A.
  symbolic politics, 84
Costanza, Robert, et al.
  complementarity of natural and man-
    made capital, 25
  ecological meaning of efficiency, 32–
    34. *See also* Herman E. Daly,
    ecological cost/benefit ratio
  ecological tariffs, 43
  economic welfare, 34. *See also*
    Herman E. Daly, index of sustain-
    able economic welfare
  graded ecozoning, 45
  Hicksian income, 26
  impossibility theorem, 36, 188 n. 36
  local land use planning criteria, 45–
    46
  major goals of ecological economics,
    29–30
  monetizing environmental stocks and
    services, 39–42
  natural capital, 25–26
  natural capital depletion tax, 42
  precautionary polluter pays principle,
    42
  scale of the economy to the environ-
    ment, 30, 47
  uses and limitations of the market,
    29–30, 31–32
  weak and strong sustainability, 26
culture of unlimited growth, 21–22

D
Daly, Herman E.
  birth licenses, 44
  cap on maximum income, 43
  ecological cost/benefit ratio, 33. *See
    also* Robert Costanza et al.,
    ecological meaning of efficiency
  economics and the entropy law, 18
  economics and ultimate means and
    ends, 36–37
  fallacy of misplaced concreteness, 27
  Homo economicus, 28

index of sustainable economic wel-
    fare, 34. *See also* Robert Costanza
    et al., economic welfare
  questioning the optimal scale of the
    economy, 17
  sustainable development, 25
  theism, 180
dominant social paradigm defined, 4–5
  and techno-industrial paradigm, 4

E
ecocentric ecological ethics, 125–27.
    See also Holmes Rolston, III
ecological paradigm defined, 5
  as a Western paradigm, 6
ecologism contrasted to environmental-
    ism, 8–10
economic dependency in contemporary
    America, 2, 10–11, 20, 54
economic development, 24–25
economic growth, 18–21, 24, 187 n. 17
empty world scenario, 24
Endangered Species Act of 1973, 123
environmental organizations and green
    politics, 177–78
environmental politics and policy, 82–
    86
Environmental Protection Agency, 20

F
Fremlin, J. H.
  technocratic vision of the future,
    170–71
full world scenario, 24

G
Goodpaster, Kenneth
  criteria for moral considerability,
    113–14
government promotion of unlimited
    growth, 19–21
Green Party Platform 2000, 79–82

H
Hamilton's political economy, 53–54

I
interest-group liberalism, 83, 196 n. 113

J
Jefferson's political economy, 52–53

L
Leopold, Aldo
    economic system as an impediment
        to a land ethic, 17
    land ethic, 91–92
    penalties of an ecological education, 1

M
Maguire, Daniel C.
    contemporary Western religion and
        the ecological movement, 105, 107
    earth as destiny, 106–7
    generic religion and reverence for
        creation, 106
    God as adjective, 106
    nontheism and ecological values, 107
Marcuse, Herbert
    Frankfurt School, 198 n. 19
    historical a priori of science and
        technology, 97
    instrumental reason, 97
    liberation of nature, 99–100
    nature as subject, 100
    new sensibility, 99–101
    one-dimensional society, 98
    reality principle, 98
    regulative idea of reason, 102
    second human nature, 98, 99
market concentration in agribusiness,
    62
metanoia, 175, 179
monetary value of global natural capi-
    tal, 39
moral extensionism, 112. *See also* Tom
    Regan and Peter Singer
Morrison, Roy
    associative democracy, 57–63
    community centered economics and
        politics, 51

community-supported agriculture,
    61–63
economic cooperatives, 59–60

N
nature in the dominant techno-industrial
    paradigm, 11–12, 21, 90, 92–94,
    111, 127, 170–71
nature in the ecological paradigm, 79–
    80, 89, 91–92, 96, 100–1, 105,
    115, 123, 172
neutrality and objectivity in academia,
    149–50

O
obstacles in the way of the ecological
    paradigm, 10–13, 175–76
Ophuls, William
    politics of ecological scarcity, 179
Orr, David W.
    authentic citizenship, 168–69
    ecological intelligence, 140–41, 173
    ecological literacy, 140
    ecologically informed knowing, 134–
        35
    principles of ecological education,
        131–40
    ranking institutions of higher learn-
        ing, 143–45
    recruitment of new faculty, 146–49

P
Paehlke, Robert C.
    environmentalism and progressive
        politics, 178

R
Regan, Tom
    inherent value and moral subjects,
        112–13. *See also* moral
        extensionism
Robertson, James
    economics of local recovery, 63–66
    local employment initiatives, 63–65

Robertson, James *(continued)*
  Local Employment and Trade
    System, 65
  Self-Help Association for a Regional
    Economy, 65
Rolston, Holmes, III
  ecosystems and moral duty, 126. *See
    also* ecocentric ecological ethics
Rosenbaum, Walter A.
  environmentalism as enlightened
    stewardship, 85
  overloading of EPA, 84

S
Sale, Kirkpatrick
  bioregion defined, 74
  bioregional economics, 75–76
  bioregional politics, 76–79
  community land trust, 76
  green politics, 79
  hetarchy, 77
  self-sufficiency, 76
Singer, Peter
  sentience and moral subjects, 112.
    See also moral extensionism
Smith, Gregory A.
  educating for interdependence, 160
  norms of mainstream education, 158–
    59
  schools for at-risk youth, 161
Smith, Page
  research in the modern university,
    137
social ecology, 15, 67, 71, 185 n. 27,
  193 n. 55

social paradigm defined, 3
specialization in higher education, 149,
  151

T
Tailloires Declaration of University
  Leaders for a Sustainable Future,
  164, 165
Taylor, Paul W.
  attitude of respect for nature, 115–16
  biocentrism, 115
  bioculture, 115
  denial of human superiority, 118–19
  harmony between humans and na-
    ture, 172, 180
  moral agent, 114
  moral character traits, 116, 123–24,
    169
  moral rights of nonhumans, 122–23
  moral subject, 114
  objectivity and wholeness of vision,
    117–18
  rules to guide moral agents, 119–22
  wild nature and ecological ethics,
    115

U
Uhl, Christopher and Amy Anderson
  programs for ecological literacy in
    colleges and universities, 165,
    206 n. 96

W
Wilson, E. O.
  biophilia, 96